False Choice

The Bipartisan Attack on the Working Class, the Poor and Communities of Color

By David Samuels

Dedication

Mary L. Sanders for your hard work and dedication to the Community Party. John Hollis for joining me in the fight against workplace bullying and State Representative Matt Ritter for supporting CP initiatives when others would not. R.I.P Trayvon Martin, Meagan Hockaday (your sister Misha Charlton is fighting for you), Mike Brown, Eric Garner, Freddie Gray, Sandra Bland and all victims of extrajudicial killings, and last but not least, Ena Mae Sterling. Peace to Rosa Parks, Fannie Lou Hamer, Dorothy Height, Betty Shabazz, Coretta Scott King, Malcolm X, Martin Luther King, the Black Panthers, and all the other racial justice soldiers, famous and anonymous. Hands off Assata Shakur! She is innocent! Shout out to my Facebook family: Donna Jones, Debbie Duncan-Cook, and Janet Frazao-Conaci. Thanks to Andy Hart of the Hartford News for giving me a platform every week, Ken Rose of So-Metro Radio and Kelly Wick for supporting Community Party Radio. Special Thanks to Yolanda Lawrence.

Part 1

Americans have always been suckers for sequels. On March 24, 1975, then unknown actor Sylvester Stallone went to a Los Angeles movie theater and watched the closed circuit telecast of a heavyweight title fight between champion Muhammad Ali and challenger Chuck Wepner, which took place at the Richfield Coliseum in Cleveland, Ohio. Ali was a global icon, "The Greatest." Wepner was a journeyman fighter known as "The Bayonne Bleeder." No one gave Wepner a chance, but he managed to last until the 15th and final round, losing by a technical knockout. After watching the fight, Stallone went straight home and spent the next three days writing the script for Rocky, a film about an obscure club fighter named Rocky Balboa, who gets a once in a lifetime opportunity to fight for the heavyweight title. Rocky doesn't win, but he achieves his goal of lasting 15 rounds with the champ. Rocky was released nationally on December 3, 1976 and catapulted Stallone to stardom, spawning five sequels. Stallone then denied that Wepner's fight against Ali was the basis for Rocky, despite the obvious similarities. After years of getting the run around from Stallone, Wepner sued in 2003. Stallone settled with Wepner for an undisclosed amount.

November 2010

The 2014 gubernatorial election in Connecticut (CT) presented the possibility of a sequel. In 2010 Democrat Dan Malloy, a former prosecutor and mayor of Stamford battled Republican businessman and George W. Bush administration hatchet man Tom Foley in a race that was about as close as the fictional championship fight between Rocky and Apollo Creed. Foley received more Republican votes than Malloy got on the Democratic ballot line, but the 25,000 votes Malloy garnered on the Working Families Party (WFP) ballot gave him the win by the thin margin of 6,404 votes. Malloy arguably owed his victory to votes from public employees, as WFP enjoys strong support from this voter block.

2011

Malloy promptly showed his appreciation by introducing an education bill that blogger and former legislator Jonathan Pelto described this way, "Malloy's 'education reform' legislation has earned him the title of the most anti-teacher, anti-public education, pro-charter school Democratic governor in the nation." Malloy's initial budget plan hinged on concessions that he demanded from state workers. In 2011, Malloy put employees on notice. "We will begin the process of laying off people on a large scale, for which I will not feel responsible, having done everything in our power to reach agreements with the negotiating team representing my fellow state employees," Malloy said. These workers, who had already agreed to concessions in 2009 during the M. Jodi Rell administration, responded by voting down a concessions deal reached by the State Employees Bargaining Agent Coalition (SEBAC) and Malloy's budget chief, Benjamin Barnes. Malloy's reaction was swift; he warned that 7500 layoffs were soon to come.

The Democratic Party controlled Senate responded by passing a bill which would place limits on state workers' wages and benefits. Panicked union leaders quickly rewrote the SEBAC bylaws and arranged a second vote. House Speaker Chris Donovan, a Democrat who was viewed as a champion of organized labor, warned state employees that the House would vote on the bill if the concessions deal were rejected again. Malloy followed Donovan's threat by issuing 4500 layoff notices. In July terrified workers voted to ratify a deal they had rejected weeks before.

Pelto, a strategist for the Democrats who was excluded from a position in the Malloy administration and in effect cast out of the party, would become a key figure in the months leading up to the 2014 election. Malloy's abuse of public employees would create a golden political opportunity for the exiled party insider. The coming months would reveal an inconvenient truth, which is that the Democrats and Republicans are a duopoly, representing two wings of the same corporate-controlled party.

Liberals across the country mourned the May 5, 2011 victory of union busting Republican Governor Scott Walker over Democratic challenger Tom Barrett in the Wisconsin recall election. There were plenty of Facebook posts over the previous sixteen months by Connecticut liberal Democrats railing against Walker, who implemented a budget plan, which severely curbs nearly all collective bargaining rights for state employees. The same individuals who were typing in capital letters as they cursed Walker were silent later that year as Malloy and the Democrats bullied state employees into overwhelmingly ratifying the same concessions deal that they had voted down weeks before. Democratic Party supporters on Facebook used Wisconsin solidarity photos as their profile pictures, while they pretended not to notice that Malloy and the Senate were pushing a bill, which curbed state employee collective bargaining rights in their own backyard.

The silence of liberals in response to the Democrats' union busting tactics in Connecticut and elsewhere in the country directly contributed to the outcome in Wisconsin. The truth is that anti-labor legislation similar to Walker's has been passed by Democrats in Massachusetts, New York, Rhode Island and California. The socialistworker.org article, "Why are the Democrats Behind in Wisconsin?" detailed the calculated strategy by Barrett and Senate Democrats to distance themselves from the massive labor movement which drew international attention, as hundreds of thousands of people from in and outside of Wisconsin converged on the state capitol in Madison and refused to budge. A historic workers rights movement was co-opted by the Democrats and their obedient union lackeys and transformed into just another election campaign. The Senate recall candidates dropped any mention of the restoration of collective bargaining and union rights (the issue that sparked the uprising against Walker) from their campaign speeches. Barrett proclaimed that he would not tax the rich and corporations, while rolling out a budget plan that was actually similar to Walker's. Barrett's plan also proposed cuts to state employee benefits and pensions. While Walker's plan exempted the police and firefighters from his provisions, Barrett's did not.

More people signed the recall petition than actually voted in the recall election, which clearly shows that folks were turned off by what they heard during the campaign from Barrett and the Democrats. Bruce Dixon of the *Black Agenda Report* pointed out in his commentary, "Wisconsin: What Happens When Movements Turn into Campaigns" that the poor and communities of color were ignored as usual during the Democrats' campaign (Wisconsin has the highest Black imprisonment rate in the nation). The result was Walker winning by a wider margin than when he was first elected. If liberals around the country had pressured the Democrats to live up to their claim of being a friend of labor, Barrett and the Senate recall candidates in Wisconsin would have had to represent the interests of the public employees who started the revolt in their state. Because Democratic Party supporters did not speak up about their own party's attacks on workers' rights, Wisconsin voters were left with the choice of two candidates who made it clear that they didn't give a crap about the labor movement. The nationwide attack on public employees will have a ripple effect on workers in the private sector, as the decreased benefits and pensions of state workers will eventually lower the threshold for already underpaid and overworked nonunion employees across the country.

Walker's victory had national repercussions, as the Republicans have employed their "all in" Wisconsin strategy of massive ad campaigns and intensive grassroots organizing in other states. The Democrats faced the prospect of being steamrolled in the 2012 elections because they chose to continue their traditional mode of operation, which is to constantly move to the right in an effort to keep up with the Republicans. Presidential candidate Barack Obama vowed in 2007 to walk the picket lines with workers who were denied their right to organize. Obama made a point of staying out of Wisconsin during the recall campaign and limited his "support" to a shout out to Barrett on Twitter. While liberals continued to delude themselves about the Democrats, Mitt Romney and the Republicans made their move to reclaim the keys to the empire. The events in Wisconsin again underscored similarities between the Democrats and Republicans. Neither party represented the interests of oppressed people of any color.

July 27

On July 27, 2011, Jeanine Molloff of OpEdNews.com reported on a press conference by the House of Representatives Out of Poverty Caucus where Rep. Conyers revealed that Obama was the one who demanded Social Security cuts as part of the budget deal. If you're wondering, why you never heard about this before, it's because the corporate media didn't cover the press conference. Conyers said, "My response to him [President Obama] is TO AMASS THOUSANDS OF PEOPLE IN FRONT OF THE WHITE HOUSE TO PROTEST THIS." Conyers added, "We want full employment as a matter of government policy, which was passed in 1978 when I stood with Hubert Humphrey. We passed the first bill that allowed the government—in areas of high unemployment—to directly intervene and create jobs. Well, we've got the bill in here again and I'VE HEARD NOTHING FROM THE WHITE HOUSE." Conyers, who was the first member of Congress to endorse Obama, concluded his direct challenge to the President by saying, "We want him to know from this day forward that we've had it. We want him to come out on our side, not to watch and wait. WE'RE SUFFERING. What Obama hasn't said to us is 'make me do it,' BUT WE HAVE TO MAKE HIM DO IT. THIS IS ONE OF

THE MOST IMPORTANT ISSUES WE'RE FACED WITH." Again, where were the liberals who are currently so outraged at Romney's comments? Conyers and the Out of Poverty Caucus could have used their support to put pressure on the Obama administration. Obviously, liberals only get upset when a Republican disses people who have no voice.

January 2012

On January 20, Gov. Dannel P. Malloy's administration announced that because the state budget surplus had dwindled to $1.4 million, the consensus was that Malloy would most likely implement unilateral budget cuts without legislative approval by the end of the month. We all knew what that meant—already underfunded social services would be targeted for downsizing and elimination by a governor who pledged not to shred the safety net. Malloy had gone out of his way to portray himself as a tough, no nonsense guy who gets his way. A recent newspaper series on Malloy's first year in office, documented a bruising politician who verbally slapped around union "leaders" during labor negotiations. He effectively used pink slips to frighten disobedient, ingrate state workers into overwhelmingly ratifying a concessions deal that they had previously voted down (for the record, I'm a state employee), and got legislators in his party to fall in line and pass his "shared sacrifice" budget. Malloy's influence had also been apparent in the recent Hartford municipal elections and the subsequent back-room shenanigans at City Hall.

Malloy's rough and tumble attitude quickly evaporated when it came to dealing with the wealthy and corporations, who he coddled and stroked like a newborn puppy. One of Malloy's top campaign contributors was Goldman Sachs, who of course is the proud co-sponsor of the financial meltdown, which has this country mired in the worst economic crisis since the Great Depression. Malloy had thrown millions of dollars in tax subsidies at companies like Cigna, NBC Sports and ESPN. A report by Connecticut Voices for Children found that corporate tax subsidies have a track record of adding to the state deficit and killing jobs. These subsidies are not subject to legislative oversight or any type of subsequent independent review. Connecticut's regressive tax structure results in the middle class and the poor; both are paying more in state taxes than the wealthy. Malloy's economic policies were nothing new, of course. The result is a working class that is being soaked with taxes, while the poor and other vulnerable populations are faced with the prospect of an even more precarious existence due to the aforementioned impending budget cuts.

While this sad saga played out year after year at the State Capitol and the rest of the country, there was one state, which was thriving. North Dakota had a 3.5% unemployment rate, the lowest in the country, and a $1 billion budget surplus. North Dakota is rich in natural resources, but so are other states, which are currently drowning in red ink. The factor that sets North Dakota apart is that it is the home of the only publicly owned bank in the country, the Bank of North Dakota. The Bank of ND was established in 1919 and has empowered the state with economic sovereignty, and insulated it against the Wall Street practices, which have plunged the US into its current economic quagmire. The Bank of ND generates revenue, which goes back into the state's General Fund, as opposed to big banks whose profits go to Wall Street. The money that returns to the state is used for job creation, infrastructure projects, preserving and enhancing vital social services and principled lending for homeowners, small business owners and college students. All of this is done at no cost to taxpayers.

It is painfully obvious that conventional economic policies are killing this country. The movement for publicly owned banks is growing nationally; Massachusetts, Washington State, Virginia, and Arizona are just a few of the states where public bank legislation has been introduced. The Connecticut conservatives who will undoubtedly try to characterize the public bank concept as a far left, socialist plot will have to come up with another angle. The public bank bills in Virginia and Arizona were both introduced by Republicans. This isn't about left or right, it's about common sense solutions that will get states' economies back on track. Hartford and other CT cities and towns would of course benefit from a public bank, as there would be increased funding for municipal aid.

February 2012

The Community Party (CP) hosted a Community Conversation on racial profiling Saturday, February 18 in New London. The event was a success and included some interesting plot twists. The incident that I'm about to discuss involved CP member Mary L. Sanders, and a white New London police officer and me. Being the conscientious activists that we are, Mary and I shook off the emotional pain of getting up early on a Saturday morning and arrived at the Public Library of New London, the site of the meeting, prior to the library opening. As we waited in the library parking lot, the aforementioned patrol officer approached my car. He walked over to the passenger side and asked Mary, a white woman, "Is everything alright?" Mary's polite attempt to respond was drowned out by yours truly. I loudly said, "Yes, we're here to host a meeting on racial profiling." The cop made a hasty retreat, as he appeared to have a vision of the East Haven police scandal flash before his eyes.

Our meeting was well-attended and included lively discussions about police misconduct and the general issue of racism. We left the meeting inspired by our new allies, who promised to attend the upcoming public hearing on the state's racial profiling bill and testify in support of CP's proposed amendments. The word that we received from legislators was that the hearing would probably be scheduled for the first week in March. We would need all of the support that we could get, as groups who claimed to oppose racial profiling in the State of Connecticut were attempting to remove a key component of our bill language. CP was calling for all motorists who are subjected to a traffic stop to receive a copy of the traffic stop demographic form that patrol

8

officers must fill out after they pull someone over. We wanted the copy to include the officer's identifying information, the date, time, and reason for the stop, and contact information that the driver can use if he/she believes that they have been stopped based on their race/religion. Andrew Crumbie, a former state trooper who is now an attorney and law enforcement expert, told us during a 2010 meeting that a traffic stop where the driver does not receive a ticket is the most blatant form of racial profiling. The purpose of our traffic stop receipt concept is to provide an individual with evidence of the traffic stop should he/she decide to pursue a racial profiling complaint.

The previous week, a legislator informed me that groups on both sides of the racial profiling issue were touting a report, which found that individuals would be less likely to file a racial profiling complaint if they are given a record of the traffic stop. Apparently, the report found that citizens said they would feel "awkward" about receiving the record. Yes, you read that correctly—groups who were both supporting and opposing strengthening the state racial profiling law had found some common ground. These people wanted the public to believe that a person, especially a person from a low-income community of color, would be more likely to take on the police by filing a racial profiling complaint if they had no evidence that the traffic stop took place. The fact that opponents of strengthening *the Penn Act* were in agreement with some groups on the other side who produced this report is telling. I'm the most report/fact oriented person that you'll ever meet, but there are times in life when we must put the political crap to the side and use the common sense that God gave us.

While the conclusions of this report defy common sense, you must remember that we are talking about the wonderful world of politics. Our group was informed that we had to produce people at the public hearing who would testify in support of our language.

The problem with the racial profiling issue is that it has become just another political football, especially since the federal indictment of four East Haven police officers for racially profiling Latinos and Taco-gate, starring East Haven Mayor Joseph Maturo, made national headlines. When a New York reporter asked Maturo what he planned to do to reach out to the Latino community, Maturo said that he would probably have tacos for dinner. There are groups who are involved in this issue who are more interested in making the racial profiling bill palatable to the police and legislators so it has a better chance of passing, than in passing the strongest bill possible. Our adversaries would certainly cry foul at that statement and accuse me of engaging in "personal attacks", but you're hearing this from someone who works inside the sausage factory. I started CP because I saw a proposed local ordinance watered down by so-called activists, so they could ensure that it would pass a city council vote. This is the problem with the funded community-organizing model. Nonprofits must constantly present proof of "victories" to funders in order to secure grant money. This includes passing bills. They then present these fake "victories" to the people in order to maintain community support. Then there's the problem of personal political ambitions by people in this work, coupled with good old-fashioned egos.

American Civil Liberties Union (ACLU)-CT Legal Director Sandra Staub continued to make the fatally flawed argument that if *the Penn Act* had been properly funded since it was enacted in 1999; the East Haven police scandal would have been averted. The Yale Law School and the Department of Justice (DOJ) both found that the East Haven patrol officers who have been indicted were lying on the traffic stop forms, entering Latino drivers as white to cover up their biased policing. The current *Penn Act* data analysis system would have revealed no misconduct. As a matter of fact, I'll share the observation of former West Hartford police chief James Strillacci, a staunch opponent of strengthening *the Penn Act*, who said in an interview last year with Fox CT that *the Penn Act* data reports that have been completed had proven "nothing." The root problem of *the Penn Act* is that the citizen is excluded from the data collection process. The crooked East Haven cops knew that their victims would have no evidence to refute the data that they entered on the traffic stop forms. They also knew that the data was controlled completely by their department, who wouldn't hold them accountable and according to the DOJ report, in fact, supported their criminal behavior.

The goons in East Haven weren't brought down by a sophisticated electronic data collection system such as the one that is now being developed at the State Capitol. The racial profiling and harassment of Latinos by East Haven cops was exposed by one man with a video camera. Father James Manship recorded East Haven Police Department (EHPD) officers David Cari and Dennis Spaulding harassing Latinos in a local store. Cari arrested Father Manship for recording the incident. Cari claimed that he thought the priest was pointing a gun at him, but the video showed Cari asking Father Manship why he was videotaping him.

The publicity over the video led the DOJ to begin their investigation of the East Haven police. Cari and Spaulding were two of the cops who had been indicted. I'm certain that Father Manship felt "awkward" as he pointed his camera at Cari and Spaulding, as he knew that these cops would turn their wrath on him. Holding the police accountable is "awkward," scary, and necessary.

None of us would have ever heard the name Rodney King if a citizen had not videotaped him being beaten within an inch of his life by LAPD officers in 1991. *The Penn Act* was passed to great fanfare in 1999. Legislators claimed that this law would end the scourge of racial profiling in Connecticut. Fast forward to 2012—the East Haven police scandal is a national story and elected officials were making the same promises that were made thirteen years ago. If community residents were again frozen out of the data collection process, dirty cops would once again figure out a way to circumvent *the Penn Act* and another East Haven would emerge sometime in the future. There are other groups who are involved in the racial profiling issue here in Connecticut who don't like CP's traffic stop receipt concept simply because it isn't their idea. *The Penn Act* isn't just a racial profiling bill; it's a referendum on the culture of politics in this state.

March 2012

Spring was approaching, but CP had been placed in the deep freeze at the State Capitol. There was clearly a structured effort by elected officials, their bureaucrat flunkies and so-called activists to marginalize CP as we attempted to enforce the *Alvin W. Penn Act*, the state racial profiling law. Our group was excluded from a December federal briefing on the racial profiling issue at the Capitol, despite the fact that we authored the profiling bill that was debated during the 2011 legislative session. Judiciary Committee co-chair Senator Eric Coleman cancelled a meeting with us last month about an hour before the meet was scheduled to take place. We never received an explanation from Coleman's office. Werner Oyanadel, Acting Executive Director of the Latino Puerto Rican Affairs Commission (LPRAC), invited Mary Sanders, who wrote the bill language for CP's *Penn Act* amendments, to a March 5 press conference on racial profiling at the Capitol. The catch was that she was not billed as representing CP. When she told Oyanadel that she wanted to talk about CP's bill language at the press conference, she was met with what Mary described as "resistance" from Oyanadel. Mary opted instead to accept an invitation that was extended to our group by the New Haven Register for CP to provide live online commentary on the press conference.

I checked out LPRAC's Facebook page later on that night. They posted a "report" on the press conference by CT News Junkie, which they described as "great coverage"—the article again repeated the lie by the CT Police Chiefs Association that our traffic stop receipt concept could require that printers be installed in police cruisers. Our group had clearly communicated to folks at the Capitol including Oyanadel that our language would only require that the traffic stop demographic data form, which cops are already required to fill out be issued in duplicate, with a copy going to the driver. All the state would have to do is spring for some carbon paper.

Our bill included an enforcement provision, which would ban patrol officers from harassing motorists and their passengers about their immigration status. ColorLines.com reporter Seth Wessler reported a few weeks earlier that U.S. Immigration Customs and Enforcement (ICE) was working with the East Haven police to detain and deport immigrants, even after the Department of Justice began their investigation of the EHPD. I shared the ColorLines article with Oyanadel in an email and pointed out the importance of our bill language, which would provide protection to Latinos. He never responded to the email. The question I think that the Latino/Puerto Rican community should consider regarding Oyanadel is why he is not supporting CP's efforts. This is not an isolated incident—Oyanadel was on the panel at the December federal briefing on racial profiling. He did not invite CP to testify at the hearing, despite the fact that he had worked with us on *the Penn Act* in 2011. The collaboration ended poorly, because Oyanadel exhibited a clear lack of support for our bill. ACLU-CT legal director Sandra Staub and Jack McDevitt, director of the Institute on Race and Justice at Northeastern University, were given an exclusive platform to promote a watered down version of our bill, which did not include any enforcement language. During the televised hearing, Oyandel asked McDevitt a leading question about CP's traffic stop receipt (which Oyanadel ominously referred to as a "ticket"). McDevitt, who was at the hearing to promote his own racial profiling bill model, predictably said that a traffic stop receipt would be "no benefit." Because Oyanadel did not invite CP to the hearing, we were unable to issue a rebuttal to McDevitt bashing our idea on statewide TV.

The bad news for CP continued as the Judiciary Committee's raised bill, S.B. No. 364 *An Act Concerning Traffic Stop Information*, was posted on the Connecticut General Assembly website. Much to our chagrin, the bill was stripped of our language except for the traffic stop receipt.

April 2012

The Connecticut House of Representatives passed a minimum wage bill—as usual, this legislation was watered down so that it would be palatable to conservative legislators. The original proposed 75 cent a year increase (which wasn't enough to begin with) was cut to a quarter. Even worse, the provision, which would have increased the minimum wage in proportion to the Consumer Price Index (one of the primary measures of inflation), was removed from the bill. The Democrats and their operatives attempted to convince the community that they would be doing a good deed by throwing the working poor a couple of pennies; that is if the Senate passed the bill. Half of the Senate was undecided as to whether or not they would vote for this legislation. Malloy continued to hem and haw when asked if he would sign the bill, even after it had been gutted. Funny how the Democrats were claiming to have sleepless nights, thinking about whether or not they would pass legislation, which would raise the minimum wage by a lousy 25 cents with no cost of living provision. Yet, they were not at all conflicted about a regressive tax structure in which the poor and working class in Connecticut pay more in taxes than the wealthy. The silly minimum wage debate took place in Hartford, the city with one of the highest poverty rates in the United States at 31.9%. If legislators were being paid minimum wage, the bill wouldn't have sucked.

Meanwhile, President Barack Obama, who became the country's first Black president in 2008 after defeating Republican opponent John McCain, was running for re-election. Obama moved into official campaign mode as he appeared on Jimmy Fallon's late-night talk show on April 24. While Obama yukked it up with Fallon, he slipped in a comment regarding the so-called "War on Drugs." Obama said that he

14

would not be talking about legalizing marijuana "anytime soon." The Global Commission on Drugs reports, "Drug policy and the incarceration of low-level drug offenders is the primary cause of mass incarceration in the United States. 40% of drug arrests are for simple possession of marijuana." This same president refuses to address Black/Latino unemployment, as the jobless rate in communities of color continues to skyrocket. Independent website Voxunion reported on an outrageous remark by Obama Administration Surgeon General, Dr. Regina Benjamin. Dr. Benjamin told *The New York Times* that Black women suffer from obesity because they would rather preserve their hairstyles than exercise.

If a Republican said something like that, Obama supporters would be screaming. Because this comment came from a member of Team Obama, those same people had nothing to say. Voxunion pointed out the obvious intent of Benjamin's remark, which was to trivialize the factors, which contribute to obesity among Black women. These factors include poverty, expensive hormone-free foods, the absence of grocers in communities of color who carry healthy foods, the stress of living in a racist society, the impact of environmental racism, and the link between income disparity and access to good quality health care and safe communities. This was a calculated attempt by a member of the Obama administration to deny the effects of structural racism on Black women.

The upcoming presidential election between Obama and GOP challenger Mitt Romney represented a win-win situation for the Republicans. Barack Obama has basically carried out the entire GOP agenda since he has been in office. The Pew Hispanic Center reports that Obama has deported nearly 400,000 undocumented immigrants since 2009, approximately 30% higher than the annual average during the second term of the George W. Bush administration and about double the annual average during Bush's first term. Obama's approval rating among Latinos has dropped to 49%. Obama signed the National Defense Authorization Act (NDAA) in January. This law allows any individual who is suspected to be an enemy of the state to be detained

15

without being accused of a crime—no evidence or trial is required. NDAA eliminates the rights that are outlined in the 4, 5, 6, 7 and 8th Amendments to the U.S. Constitution.

NDAA strips away our rights against unlawful search and seizure, rights to due process of law, relief from indefinite detention and protection from the military imprisoning US civilians. The NDAA moves the central prosecutorial, investigative, law enforcement, penal and custodial authority from the Department of Justice to the Department of Defense (DOD). The many people in this country who are still delirious from Obamamania should stop and take a look at Obama's actual record. The election in November 2012 was a false choice. Obama and Romney represented two political parties who serve their masters in Wall Street and the military industrial complex.

The Democrats passed the death penalty repeal bill—sort of. True to form, the Dems excluded the 11 current death row inmates. These individuals will likely have their sentences overturned through appeals and receive life sentences. I found myself in the extremely rare position of agreeing with Republican House Minority Leader Larry Cafero, who pointed out the absurdity of passing a death penalty repeal bill, which does not commute the sentences of current death row inmates to life. Ironically, the CT House of Representatives debate on the bill came on the same day as the parole hearing in California for Charles Manson, the most infamous murderer in the history of the United States. Manson was originally sentenced to death for orchestrating the Tate/LaBianca murders in 1969, a crime spree which drew international attention. Manson's sentence was automatically reduced to life imprisonment after the California Supreme Court abolished capital punishment in 1972. The presence of Steven Hayes and Joshua Komisarjevsky, the perpetrators of the Petit family murders, on death row has been cited as the reason for the prospective repeal bill. This factor again underscores the failure of the Democrats to discuss one of the most compelling reasons to abolish capital punishment (along with the exoneration of prisoners as a result of the advent of DNA

16

testing), which is the fact that it is applied in a racist manner. I presented statistics in my previous column, which point out the racial disparities that are prevalent in the application of the death penalty. Assemblyman Gary Holder-Winfield was the only legislator that I heard address race at all in his comments on the House floor. Once again, race was mostly ignored during the House debate on the repeal bill. People of color who support the Democrats should ask themselves why this party refused to use the damning statistics on racism and the death penalty to support their case for repeal.

The Democratic Party claims to be a friend to people of color, yet they act as if the issue of Black/Latino unemployment does not exist. Black unemployment has reached Depression-era levels. Hartford has one of the highest Latino jobless rates in the United States. Hartford has the highest poverty rate in the nation at 31.9%. Blacks and Latinos earn about 60 cents for every dollar that whites make. People of color possess about 10 cents of net wealth for every dollar that whites have. These issues were never discussed by Mayor Pedro Segarra, City Council President Shawn Wooden or the other Democrats on the city council board, or on the Senate or House floor by Democratic Party legislators. Why isn't addressing racial economic disparity a top priority issue for them? The East Haven police scandal became a national story after a federal investigation revealed that East Haven cops were harassing and brutalizing Latinos in that town. S.B. 364; *An Act Concerning Traffic Stop Information*, which excluded all but one of the amendments introduced by CP, sat on the Senate calendar, awaiting a vote. The bill in its present form would do NOTHING to protect people of color and religious minorities from biased policing. Democrat legislators, State of Connecticut Office of Policy and Management Under Secretary Mike Lawlor (who takes his orders from Gov. Dannel Malloy), the African-American Affairs Commission (AAAC) and the Latino Puerto Rican Affairs Commission (LPRAC) were involved in a structured effort to freeze CP out of the racial profiling issue.

I cited numerous examples in my Hartford News columns, which supported my claim, including our group being excluded from a December federal briefing on racial profiling and several press conferences at the State Capitol. Our proposed *Penn Act* amendments, written by CP member Mary Sanders, had been kept out of S.B. 364, with the exception of our traffic stop receipt language (motorists would receive a copy of the traffic stop report that patrol officers fill out). Crucial enforcement provisions, including utilizing an entity which is independent of law enforcement to process and investigate confidential racial profiling complaints and establishing a *Penn Act*/racial profiling oversight committee including at least two community stakeholders, have been kept out of the bill. There was no language to protect state residents against religious profiling and harassment about their immigration status; important provisions that were also proposed by our group. Far-right Republicans such as Rep. Themis Klarides and Sen. John Kissel supported the Judiciary Committee's version of this bill, which tells you all that you need to know about how weak S.B. 364 really was.

The legislative process is rigged. Every year, corporate controlled Democrats and Republicans crank out watered down legislation, which maintains the status quo. Agencies like AAAC and LPRAC, who supposedly are representing the interests of people of color, scheme to keep the Black and Latino communities in line, while sabotaging groups like CP. Gatekeepers who work at funded community organizations step and fetch for their Democrat masters while telling community residents about the "victories" that are being achieved on their behalf. During a March interview on the National Public Radio program, *Where We Live*, Rep. Holder-Winfield stated that Community Party's racial profiling bill was killed by the legislature last year because the police didn't like it. The situation this year is no different—Holder- Winfield and Rep. Matt Ritter are the only legislators who have publicly supported our bill language. People of color need to wake up and realize that they are being kept out of the legislative and judicial process in this country. The U.S. has a long history of Blacks and Latinos being systematically excluded from juries, with the blessing of the U.S. Supreme Court. None of this will change until communities of color realize that they are being lied to every day by the Democrats (including President Obama). We need a far-left third party political movement in order to achieve true racial justice in Connecticut and nationwide.

April 19

The Senate passed S.B. 364 *An Act Concerning Traffic Stop Information* by a 31-3 vote. The House was expected to vote it through and Malloy said that he would sign it. Thanks to community residents' emails to legislators, three out of the CP's five *Penn Act* amendments were added to the racial profiling bill (traffic stop receipt, religious profiling ban and an advisory committee with community stakeholders). We immediately started planning to get our other amendments (third party agency to handle profiling complaints/ban on harassment of individuals regarding their immigration status) in the law in 2013. The bill still did not go far enough to protect people of color and religious minorities, as individuals who want to file a profiling complaint will have to do so through the police. We all know that ain't happening.

CNN's report on the passage of the racial profiling bill included a mention of CP's traffic stop receipt provision; no Connecticut media outlets talked about the receipt at all.

Racial profiling law passes in Connecticut:

• Connecticut's House of Representatives passes an anti-racial profiling law;

• The state Senate earlier passed the bill; the governor says he will sign it;

• It mandates police bar discrimination in who they stop, detain or search;

• Months ago, 4 East Haven police were arrested in a federal racial profiling probe.

(CNN)—A few months after four East Haven police officers were arrested for allegedly targeting and harassing Latinos, Connecticut's state legislature passed a bill Monday to beef up safeguards against racial profiling.

Titled *An Act Concerning Traffic Stop Information*, S.B. 364 mandates that local and state law enforcement agencies adopt their own "written policy that prohibits the stopping, detention or search of any person when such action is solely motivated by considerations of race, color, ethnicity, age, gender or sexual orientation, and the action would constitute a violation of the civil rights of the person."

In addition, the legislation sets up reporting requirements for police whenever they conduct traffic stop, as well as a system for citizen complaints or for state authorities to collect and assess pertinent data from municipal departments.

Initially passed by the state Senate on April 19, the legislation made it through the House of Representatives on Monday and is now expected to be signed by Gov. Dannel Malloy. "I will continue to insist that every effort is taken to protect individual rights in every community and that racial profiling is eliminated," Malloy said Monday in a statement. "This is a real problem that deserves a real solution, and my administration is committed to carrying out the spirit and letter of this law."

If and when the bill goes into effect, those pulled over after January 1, 2013, would get a copy of the "standardized form" filled out by police containing details about the driver and circumstances of their case. Those who feel they were profiled due to their race, color, ethnicity, gender or sexual orientation can file a complaint, which must be reviewed by the local police department and be passed on to a state agency.

The bill doesn't mention any locality or case specifically. But it follows the arrests, in January, of an East Haven police sergeant and three officers following a federal investigation into racial profiling. They all pleaded not guilty. A civil lawsuit has also been filed related to that case.

According to a federal indictment, the four allegedly conspired to "injure, oppress, threaten and intimidate various members of the East Haven community," by profiling Latino residents during traffic stops, performing illegal searches and harassing Latino business owners and their advocates.

The men allegedly threatened and assaulted detainees, made false arrests—including a local clergy member—and later conspired to cover up evidence of their conduct by falsifying reports and blocking an investigation, prosecutors said.

The men also thwarted a police commission inquiry into their alleged misconduct, authorities said, calling on the support of local union leaders to block and intimidate municipal investigators.

"They behaved like bullies with badges," said Janice Fedarcyk, assistant FBI director in New York.

Many Latino residents of East Haven—who make up about 10.3% of the town's roughly 29,000 people—say that, for years, they have had to contend with an overly aggressive police force.

"They always come by and bother us," said Esdras Marin, a manager at La Bamba, a Latino-owned bar and restaurant named in the indictment.

"Police come in two or three times a month and ask everyone in the restaurant for their identification," he said. "And if you don't have it, they threaten us and say they're going to call the immigration office."

The Rev. James Manship of St. Rose of Lima Church, a plaintiff in the civil suit, has accused since retired police Chief Leonard Gallo of fostering "a racist and dishonest police force" in East Haven.

Unfortunately our victory was short lived. A week after the legislation was passed; I noticed that our traffic stop receipt provision had mysteriously disappeared from the bill language that was posted on the Connecticut General Assembly website. Lawmakers tried to reassure us that the deletion meant nothing. My suspicions were confirmed a year later.

May 2012

Politicians spin reality in order to maintain and expand their power. Up is down, down is up and no matter what the facts may say otherwise, they're doing a great job. Gov. Dannel Malloy has the lowest approval rating of any Democratic Party governor in the United States. Knowing this it should be no surprise to anyone that King Dannel ran a victory lap after the Democratic controlled Connecticut General Assembly passed the education reform bill during the final week of the 2012 legislative session. Malloy was popping bottles and playing We Are the Champions by Queen in his office loud enough for everyone to hear, despite the fact that the vast majority of his anti-teacher, union busting provisions were removed by the legislature. "Education reform" was Malloy's priority issue this year. Despite the obvious defeat, the governor was telling compliant media outlets the exact opposite.

Elected officials are able to spread their propaganda because most of the reporters who cover them are willing accomplices. These media lackeys know that in order to maintain access to politicians, they must be obedient and regurgitate to the public whatever lies they are fed. Independent journalist Amy Goodman describes this relationship as the "Access of Evil." Prior to the passage of S.B. 364 *An Act Concerning Traffic Stop Information* on May 7, the Office of Policy and Management under Secretary Mike Lawlor had been conspicuously silent on the racial profiling issue. I counted the number of his Twitter posts over the past three months about the East Haven police scandal (Lawlor represented East Haven as a legislator for years!), the Trayvon Martin murder case and most incredibly, S.B. 364 prior to May 7. There were five tweets about East Haven (including a retweet of a supportive shout out to East Haven cops by Hartford Courant columnist Susan Campbell). None of the tweets dealt specifically with the appalling allegations against the four indicted East Haven officers or the plight of the Latino /Puerto Rican community in that town. There were plenty of posts about sports. An especially repugnant tweet mocked pop icon Whitney Houston on February 11, the day that she died ("Impressive! Whitney Houston makes it to 48."). Lawlor was well aware of the genuine outpouring of grief in the Black community over Houston's death, yet he still posted that remark. Someone should tell Lawlor that there is nothing funny about a person dying from the disease of addiction. There was also an apology for his childish April Fool's Day tweet in which he falsely reported that a legislator had been injured in a car accident. It doesn't get any better after May 7. During the legislative session, I emailed Lawlor the link to the ColorLines.com investigative report on the joint effort between East Haven cops, and U.S. Immigration and Customs Enforcement (ICE) to deport Latinos. This collaboration continued even after the Department of Justice started its investigation of the East Haven police.

I stressed the importance of Lawlor supporting the CP's *Penn Act* Amendment, which calls for patrol officers to be banned from harassing motorists and their passengers about their immigration status. Lawlor never responded and our immigration provision was one of two amendments, which didn't make it into the bill. Since S.B. 364 was passed by the General Assembly, Lawlor suddenly can't shut up about racial profiling. He appeared at a profiling forum in West Hartford and was quoted last week in a CT News Junkie article about the impact of the Federal Secure Communities program on the Latino community in Connecticut. Secure Communities is a domestic deportation initiative, which in effect turns local police officers into immigration agents, giving them an excuse to profile Latinos. Federal law trumps state law, but including CP's immigration and third party complaint agency language in S.B. 364 would have helped to expose cops who use Secure Communities for racial profiling purposes.

Lawlor pretended to be concerned about the valid fears of the Latino/Puerto Rican community as he spoke to the newly established racial profiling advisory board, while at the same time reverting to a talking point about profiling which should be alarming to communities of color. During a December 2011 federal briefing on racial profiling at the State Capitol, Lawlor described profiling as "a problem, whether real or perceived." After members of CP expressed our concerns about this comment in a meeting with East Haven State Representative James Albis (who succeeded Lawlor) and I mentioned the remark in this column, Lawlor was subsequently quoted as referring to racial profiling as "a real problem."

Lawlor again reversed himself in the CT News Junkie article. He referred to a Courant investigative report which found that Black and Latino drivers are more likely to be ticketed for traffic violations than whites by saying, "The perception that this is happening for no apparent reason other than racial profiling is real." Once again, Lawlor was saying that racial profiling is a theory, which must be proven as fact. The DOJ has issued a report, which found that Blacks/ Latinos are three to four times more likely to be searched, arrested and subjected to the use of force during traffic stops than whites. How much more "proof" does Lawlor need?

Lawlor ignored CP because the Malloy administration didn't want a small group of volunteers (especially a far left, politically independent group) being seen as the change agents of the Alvin W. *Penn Act*. The Capitol is a white male dominated institution. The CT News Junkie article featured quotes from two white men, Lawlor and Northeastern University Professor Jack McDevitt. The protocol at the Capitol is that all issues are viewed through a white male lens, with handpicked people of color strategically placed in front of the public to do the required stepping and fetching for their masters. We are the "political pariahs," as my CP colleague Benjamin Reyes eloquently put it. That's our problem and we'll deal with it accordingly. What Blacks/Latinos and religious minorities in Connecticut should really be worried about is that Lawlor and his boss only view the racial profiling issue in terms of how they can benefit from it politically; they are not truly interested in enhancing the public safety of those who are impacted by biased policing. It appears that the U.S. Supreme Court will uphold the racist Arizona anti-immigrant law and Secure Communities is up and running here. Vulnerable populations are in jeopardy because Malloy and his flunkies such as Lawlor are continuing to use *the Penn Act* as a political football.

September 2012

The Republicans and Democrats both threw plenty of mud at their respective conventions in Tampa, Florida and Charlotte, North Carolina. GOP challengers Mitt Romney and Paul Ryan whipped up their base with coded racist language about the Democrats promoting entitlements, while President Barack Obama and Vice President Joe Biden claimed to be on the side of the working class and painted Romney and Ryan as agents of the rich. Liberals went ballistic on Twitter and Facebook about "Lyin' Ryan," while they ignored the history of Democratic Party lies like the whopper that was told by then presidential candidate Obama in 2008, who promised to support single payer health care if he was elected.

Single payer advocates were excluded from the so-called health care summit Obama hosted during his first term.

Days after the conventions liberals flew into a rage when The Nation magazine posted a secret video of Romney telling a roomful of moldy, rich campaign donors at a $50,000-a-plate dinner that 47% of Americans—whom he identified as supporters of President Obama—are a bunch of freeloaders who see themselves as "victims" and "pay no income tax." Romney assured his elitist benefactors that if he's elected he plans to leave "those people" for dead and concentrate on giving the donors a return on their investment. Liberals immediately roasted Romney for telling the truth about how he feels about the poor. These same people have nothing to say regarding facts, which underscore the Democrats' similar disregard for vulnerable populations. The poverty rate in Hartford for families is 36% while the rate for children is 47.9%. Bill Clinton signed the 1996 "welfare reform" law, which has continued the vicious cycle of poverty in this city. Michelle Chen's In These Times August article "Reforming Welfare and Gutting the Poor: A Bipartisan Platform," cited a report by the Center on Budget and Policy Priorities (CBPP). The article found that since the Temporary Assistance for Needy Families (TANF) program was enacted by Clinton in 1996, the TANF caseload has dropped by 60 percent, even though poverty and deep poverty in the United States has increased. Chen said, "This punitive approach to poverty has driven poor mothers of color further to the margins of the economy, making them even more politically invisible." Chen further cited the CBPP report, which states that many of the people who have been kicked off TANF are "disconnected from welfare and work." Where was the outrage from the left?

September 21

September 21, 2012 marked the one-year anniversary of the State of Georgia's lynching of Troy Anthony Davis. Troy was executed by lethal injection for the August 19, 1989 murder of Savannah police officer Mark MacPhail despite overwhelming evidence which pointed to Troy's innocence and implicated Sylvester "Redd" Coles as being the man who shot MacPhail twice: once in the heart and once in the face. There was no physical evidence linking Troy to the murder. Seven of the nine non-police witnesses who testified against Troy have recanted their testimony, claiming that the police intimidated them into fingering Troy as the shooter. Legal experts say that this number of recantations is unprecedented. One of the two remaining witnesses who have not changed their statements is Coles, who has been identified by witnesses as MacPhail's killer. MacPhail was shot as he intervened on the pistol-whipping of a homeless man; the girlfriend of the man told police that Coles is the one who administered the beating and shot MacPhail. Another woman says that shortly after the shooting Coles gave her a 38-caliber pistol to hide; a .38 was the weapon, which was used to shoot MacPhail. Brenda Forrest, who was a juror at Troy's trial, told CNN that if she knew during the trial what she knows now, she would have voted for an acquittal. President Obama could have stopped Troy's execution as the case had a federal precedent, but he did nothing. The liberals who railed against Troy's execution on Facebook did not mention this fact. If liberals held the Democrats accountable with the same gusto that they show against the Republicans, Troy Davis may be alive today.

Did you know that Dr. Jill Stein was the Green Party presidential candidate in 2012? If you live in a community of color, there's a good chance that you didn't. As usual, the Greens ignored Black/Latino neighborhoods in Hartford during Dr. Stein's campaign, a snub that can only be chalked up to good old-fashioned liberal racism. Dissing the urban community is pure stupidity on the part of the Greens, as there are disenchanted voters in these areas and throughout the country who are looking for an alternative to the false choice between President Barack Obama and Republican challenger Mitt Romney. A nationwide USA Today/Suffolk University Poll found that 90 million voters (1 out of 2 eligible voters) planned to sit out the 2012 presidential election. Obama's approval rating among Blacks had dropped to 85% while his rating with Latinos had fallen to 49%. Bill Quigley of the *Black Agenda Report* listed 15 issues that neither Obama nor Romney were discussing during their campaigns; a living wage, raising the minimum wage, creating public jobs and mass incarceration were on the list, all of which are key issues for communities of color. Dr. Stein supported a living wage as the minimum wage, ensuring equal pay for equal work and the implementation of a single payer health care system; all of these positions would certainly be music to the ears of residents who live in low-income urban neighborhoods, a population which is routinely ignored by the Democrats and the GOP. The petition campaign to get Dr. Stein on the ballot in Connecticut came up woefully short. They sure could have gotten some signatures in communities of color if residents had heard the message of Dr. Stein and her running mate, homelessness advocate Cheri Honkala. The Greens' insistence on maintaining their status as an overwhelmingly white political country club is the reason why they will continue to have little to no impact on state and national politics.

Malloy's first term as governor continued to underwhelm state residents; his approval rating was a dismal 31%; among Democrats, it was 49%. Malloy responded by sending out an email kissing up to his "fellow state employees" whom he successfully intimidated into ratifying the concessions deal. Malloy remained one of the most unpopular governors in the United States.

It's not hard to figure out why; another budget crisis loomed as the last fiscal year ended with a $143 million deficit and a projected shortfall in the hundreds of millions of dollars for 2013-14. Malloy did not rule out more tax increases.

The presidential, vice presidential, and congressional candidate debates were the focus of corporate media attention as Election Day 2012 approached. Conservatives claimed victory following the first debate between President Barack Obama and Republican challenger

Mitt Romney. Vice President Joe Biden and Romney's running mate Paul Ryan tangled the previous week, generating discussion among political pundits about Biden's combative style. Massachusetts Senator Scott Brown and Democratic Party challenger Elizabeth Warren traded barbs. The Connecticut Senate debates between Congressman Chris Murphy and former World Wrestling Entertainment CEO Linda McMahon looked more like episodes of Divorce Court. If you were looking for drama, these debates did not disappoint. If you were interested in learning more about the candidates' actual issue positions, you were out of luck.

The debates between the Democrats and Republicans are nothing but a display of dueling talking points. Each candidate is "fighting for the middle class" (how about the poor?). They're all going to create jobs and fix the economy. Of course, they don't want you to think about the fact that the Democrats and the Republicans are both responsible for the current economic crisis. Margaret Kimberley of the *Black Agenda Report* provided a succinct analysis of the first Obama/Romney debate. Kimberley pointed out that Obama, who was characterized as disinterested or detached during the first debate, was actually demonstrating the fact that his policies represent the Democrats' ongoing shift toward the right.

Kimberley cited Obama's response to moderator Jim Lehrer's question as to whether or not Obama saw a difference between himself and Romney regarding Social Security. Obama replied that their positions are actually similar, which is an inconvenient fact for Obama supporters. Kimberley wrote, "Those words may have been shocking but they were true. It is Obama who appointed a deficit reduction commission, which called for cuts to entitlement programs. Only intransigence from Republicans prevented him from further double dealing with the people he is supposed to be working against." Kimberley went on to describe the root problem with the Democrats, which was exposed during the Obama/Romney debate. "As the Democrats have moved ever more to the right and become more dependent on corporate largesse, Obama and other Democrats have gone along with their (the Republicans) program even as they pretend to be their opposition. Obama was caught unprepared and unable to state plainly how he differs from his opponent, mostly because he doesn't differ much." Opaque campaigns were another position that Obama and Romney shared.

October 2012

During the last week of the month, Superstorm Sandy caused catastrophic damage to southeastern Connecticut, the shoreline and areas of New York and New Jersey. Three people died in Connecticut, while 630,000 customers lost power.

Hartford fortunately emerged relatively unscathed. All eyes in the state quickly turned to Connecticut Light and Power and United Illuminating, the two utility companies who were blasted for their inept response to Winter Storm Alfred exactly one year earlier. This natural disaster underscored the issues of racism, classism and climate change.

Livescience.com reported the death toll as of November 1, 2012. "The death toll from Sandy as of Nov. 1 was at least 149. The confirmed deaths include 42 in New York; 12 in New Jersey; nine in Maryland; six in Pennsylvania; five in West Virginia; four in Connecticut; two in Virginia; and one in North Carolina. One person died in Canada, and at least 67 people were killed in the Caribbean, including 54 in Haiti."

The corporate media mostly ignored the impact that Sandy had on the Caribbean as Puerto Rico, the Dominican Republic, Haiti, Jamaica, the Bahamas and Cuba were all caught in the storm's path. The Associated Press reported that while Puerto Rico was spared a direct hit, heavy rains caused major flooding. The Bahamas suffered an estimated $300 million in damage. Nearly 30,000 people were evacuated in the Dominican Republic. Haiti, a country that has been ravaged by Western

30

economic exploitation and is still reeling from a 2010 earthquake, was deluged with 20 inches of rain. Cuba was hit hard as 200,000 homes were damaged, tourist hotels were leveled and vital industries were affected. Salon.com reported that Cuba's Communist Party newspaper Granma "acknowledged 'severe damage to housing, economic activity, fundamental public services, and institutions of education, health and culture.'" Gary Pierre-Pierre, a columnist for *The Guardian* and editor and publisher of the Haitian Times, noted how the Western media's coverage of the Haiti earthquake focused on the aid workers, rescue and mission teams while ignoring the heroic efforts of the Haitian people. "In Haiti, like many other places, locals pulled together and helped each other. The first responders were indeed Haitians. It took the international cavalcade days to reach Haiti and by then most of the death and destruction had already occurred."

Pierre-Pierre added that floods as a result of Sandy have exacerbated Haiti's cholera epidemic. Laurent Lamothe, Haiti's Prime Minister, issued an international plea for aid. The dearth of U.S. media coverage of Sandy's impact on the Caribbean reeks of racism. The story of Glenda Moore is a prime example of the consequences of bigotry. ColorLines.com reported that Glenda left her home in Staten Island, New York during the storm and was driving to a relative's home in Brooklyn when her SUV became submerged under waves of water that crashed into her vehicle. Glenda freed her sons Connor and Brandon, ages 2 and 4, from the backseat but the waves knocked both children out of her arms. The New York Daily News reports that Glenda frantically knocked on the doors of her neighbors seeking help. Glenda's sister says that these neighbors refused to assist her. "They answered the door and said, 'I don't know you, I'm not going to help you,'" Glenda's sister said. British newspaper the Daily Mail reports that Glenda knocked on the door of another neighbor, who refused to answer the door and turned off the lights. The Daily Mail went on to report that Glenda spent the next 12 hours screaming in the street. Neighbors still refused to help.

Police found the bodies of Connor and Brandon only yards from where they disappeared.

While people in areas such as Staten Island, Manhattan's Lower East Side and the Rockaways waited days for aid, Mayor Mike Bloomberg announced that he intended to go forward with plans to host the New York City Marathon. Investigative reporters showed outraged TV audiences trailers filled with apples intended for marathon runners and generators, which had been set up for tents, so the runners could stay warm. Displaced community residents reported being evicted from their hotel rooms so the hotels could make room for people coming to town for the marathon. The hotels had already been inflating their room rates after Sandy decimated New York. Bloomberg finally came to his damn senses and canceled the marathon. Disgusted people nationwide were left with the memory of trailers filled with fruit and humming generators, while people throughout New York waited desperately for food and power restoration.

Superstorm Sandy forced a renewed conversation about climate change. As right wing media outlets such as Fox News continued to deny science by referring to Sandy as "the so-called superstorm," blog sites such as hurricanesandyspeaks.com used facts to point out that the air and seas have become warmer. The blog sites attributed this to the burning of coal, oil and natural gas has released millions of tons of carbon dioxide (CO_2) into the atmosphere. CO_2 keeps the earth warm by trapping some of the heat from the sun. The increased amount of CO_2 has resulted in the climate becoming warmer and large parts of the ocean remaining warmer for longer periods. This combination resulted in the superstorm, a term that has quickly become a household word. Hurricanes need warm water to maintain and increase their strength; Sandy fed on an abundance of warm ocean water.

In Connecticut, WFSB-TV's Chief Meteorologist Bruce DePrest noted that it was highly unusual for a hurricane to form so late in the year. However, he never mentioned climate change as a factor. Activists

32

have warned that there will be bigger and more destructive superstorms to come, unless the U.S. government stops what it's doing to the environment. Superstorm Sandy left death, destruction, and many unresolved issues in her wake.

November 2012

President Barack Obama's election victory over Republican challenger Mitt Romney triggered a racial firestorm in this country. Conservatives immediately portrayed Blacks and Latinos who voted for Obama as freeloaders who wanted welfare checks; they obviously chose to ignore the statistical fact that most welfare recipients are white. Right-wing extremists, who are always yapping about "freedom and liberty," called for an armed insurrection in response to an election outcome that they didn't like. Racist rants by blowhards Rush Limbaugh and Bill O'Reilly angered Obama supporters throughout the country. Third party candidates were in effect shut out of yet another presidential election, as their exclusion from the debates clearly hurt their support at the polls. The Republicans took a beating in Connecticut, as the Democrats swept the congressional races and retained their advantages in the state House and Senate.

State Representative Matt Ritter, who easily defeated GOP candidate Ken Lerman in the 1st District, called for an end to the partisan gridlock, which has dominated the political landscape. "On issues such as the economy, reproductive rights and foreign policy, I think Democrats are more in tune with the majority of voters than Republicans and (the November 6 election results) proved that," Rep. Ritter said. "Having said that, we also have serious issues in this country and state that need to be addressed and the bickering of the past year will not get us any closer to solving those problems. I hope we lose the party affiliation for a while and move back to working together for the common good."

Blogger and activist Adam Hudson believed that the reelection of Obama was a victory for imperialism. "Four more years of drone strikes, targeted killing, indefinite detention (National Defense Authorization Act), permanent war, surveillance, curtailment of other civil liberties, support for Israeli apartheid and colonialism, pro-corporate free trade on steroids (Trans-Pacific Partnership), favors to Wall Street, austerity, cuts to Social Security ('Grand Bargain'), massive underemployment/unemployment, deterioration and oppression of Black communities, and global warming," Hudson said. "Manufactured change you can believe in brought to you by Corporate America, the military-industrial complex and Wall Street."

Obama continued to enjoy tremendous support from the Black community despite the fact that he had not given one speech about poverty or Black unemployment since he's been in office, nor had he implemented any policy initiatives to combat these problems. Black unemployment in some areas of Connecticut is as high as 50%. Obama supporters were heated about Limbaugh's comments, but Limbaugh wasn't the president. Obama rejected a 2009 demand from members of the Congressional Black Caucus (CBC) that he implement targeted job creation in low-income communities of color, where Black unemployment has reached Depression-era levels. Obama's inaction is more harmful to Black America than anything Limbaugh could ever say. Why aren't Obama boosters holding the first Black President accountable for his refusal to respond to this crisis?

Glen Ford of the *Black Agenda Report* opined in 2008 that Obama's ascent had revealed some inconvenient truths regarding Black Democrats, so-called activists and a community that supports a president who has gone out of his way to avoid addressing issues affecting Black America. "We have learned that Black politicians and activist-poseurs have an infinite capacity to celebrate not having engaged in struggle with power, and that the Black masses can be made drunk by the prospect of vicariously (through Obama) coming to power." The last four years have indeed been baffling. Women have demanded that Obama come

34

through on women's rights issues, the gay community has demanded that Obama come through on LGBT issues, supporters of Israel have demanded that Obama do the same. However, Obama apologists have told the Black community not to make any demands of the President because "Obama isn't the president of Black America; he's the president of America." Huh? So why the hell should Black folks have voted for him?

Why aren't Black Democrats following the example of CBC founder Rep. John Conyers?

Conyers was the first member of Congress to endorse then presidential candidate Sen. Obama in 2008, but he has not been shy about putting Obama on blast for demanding Social Security cuts as part of the budget deal and doing nothing to support a jobs bill that Conyers introduced. Ford recently summarized the Obama Effect as he made a blunt assessment of the Black left. "The rulers had at long last, found our Achilles Heel, the weakest spot in African Americans' political armor. Our reflexive racial solidarity (actually an aspect of Black nationalism) which had served us so well, for so long, short-circuited our progressive political instincts. We became fodder for Obama, the slicker-than-Slick-Willie corporate guy with the brown face." The reality that Black Obama supporters refuse to acknowledge is that Obama is a center-right president who has totally ignored Black America, except for when he was asking for our votes. For his next trick, Obama offered up Social Security cuts as a means of resolving the so-called fiscal cliff stalemate between the Democrats and the Republicans. Obama's campaign slogan was "Forward." His policies represented another step backward for the Blacks who supported him.

It doesn't help that Black so-called activists are defending Obama. Their obligatory apology for Obama's refusal to address issues facing Black America is the preposterous claim that Obama is "not allowed" to do so. Obama sycophants portray the First Black President as Martin Luther King, Malcolm X and Fred Hampton all rolled into one, but the big, bad Republicans are stopping this poor brother from getting his political swerve on. During the first two years of Obama's term, the Democrats controlled the House and the Senate. Obama rejected a 2009 demand by members of the Congressional Black Caucus that he implement targeted job creation in low-income urban communities, where Black unemployment has reached Depression-era levels. Who was stopping Obama then? Strom Thurmond's ghost? This stepping and fetching by "Black leaders" is the reason why Democrats such as Malloy refused to tax millionaires, then rolled out a budget plan, which slashed funding to services for the poor, children, the developmentally disabled and the aged in addition to vital substance abuse treatment and mental health services. Where was the outcry from the left? If a Republican governor did this, liberals would be marching in the streets.

The budget deficit in Connecticut for 2012 was $365 million. The projected shortfall for 2013 was $1.1 billion. Pelto, who regularly criticized Malloy's policies in his blog, pointed out that a tax on millionaires would have produced about $350 million in revenue. The nation's only publicly owned bank, the Bank of North Dakota, has generated $300 million in revenue over the past 10 years. If a public bank had been established there could potentially have been another $30 million in the state's coffers. Democrats and Republicans have introduced public banking legislation in 20 states. Despite the growing bipartisan national movement to establish state banks, Malloy and lawmakers in Connecticut continued to recycle the same economic policies, which have failed this country, except for the wealthy.

A state substance abuse services employee said that Malloy's cuts would cause serious harm. "We have just started to grow our substance abuse treatment services in the Eastern Connecticut area," the employee said. "Of course with cuts in substance abuse treatment, we will not have the ability to serve as many clients as need the help. Also with cuts to Medicaid/Husky that may leave our clients that had qualified for insurance uninsured, and with more uninsured clients we can lose

36

money; with Husky we will get paid for sure, many of our uninsured clients cannot even afford five or ten dollars a session and we have to spend money trying to either go after clients for payment, or just take a hit and lose money and that has a great impact."

December 14, 2012

Twenty-year-old Adam Lanza fatally shot twenty children and six adult staff members at the Sandy Hook Elementary School in Newtown, Connecticut. Lanza shot and killed his mother at their Newtown home prior to the school shooting. As police arrived at Sandy Hook, Lanza committed suicide by shooting himself in the head. The crime was the deadliest mass shooting at a high school or grade school in the history of the country and the second-deadliest mass shooting by a single person in U.S. history; the 2007 killing spree at Virginia Tech was the worst.

The two major questions people asked was: why did this happen? And, how do we stop it from happening again? Everybody on Facebook and Twitter had the answer of course; we need to ban guns... No, we need more guns... No, we need prayer in the schools... The all talk and no action types who social media feast on stories of this magnitude. These are the folks who will never get from behind their keyboards and actually become involved in changing the public policies that they complain about every day. Then there are "community leaders" on the left who are either busy sucking up to those in power, maintaining their fiefdoms or both. They're running around to meetings, forums and rallies, basking in the adoration of their respective followers while this country is sinking like the Titanic. Elected officials weighed in with their two cents. Everybody was standing on their soapbox.

The inconvenient fact is that there is no easy answer to what happened in Newtown. Spree killings are a global phenomenon. If someone wants to commit an act like this, there is really nothing that will stop them; minimizing the threat is our best hope. The miracle is that these heinous acts don't occur more often. The most we can hope for is that we, or someone we care about, aren't in the vicinity when a mass murder takes place.

New York Times op-ed columnist David Brooks wrote a piece in July 2012 on the internal motivations of spree killers and the flawed arguments of those who focus on external factors as the causes of these acts of mayhem. "When you investigate the minds of these killers, you find yourself deep in a world of delusion, untreated schizophrenia and ferociously injured pride. George Hennard of Belton, TX, was angry that women kept rejecting him. He drove his car through the window of a restaurant and began firing, killing fourteen women and eight men. Many of the killers had an exaggerated sense of their own significance, which, they felt, was not properly recognized by the rest of the world. Many suffered a grievous blow to their self-esteem—a lost job, a divorce or a school failure—and decided to strike back in some showy way." Brooks, who supports stricter gun control laws, pointed out the obvious hole in the gun control argument. "Gun control laws are probably even less germane in these cases. Rampage killers tend to be meticulous planners. If they can't find an easy way to get a new gun, they'll surely find a way to get one of the 200 million guns that already exist in this country. Or they'll use a bomb or find another way." Brooks noted that mental health treatment, especially for men in their 20's, is the key to addressing spree killings.

The substance abuse services worker who talked about Malloy's budget cuts summed up the Newtown tragedy and the importance of social services perfectly. "I do want everyone to think about the mental health workers and crisis response workers who will now be helping a lot of people get through the tragedy at Sandy Hook. They will have a very difficult job on their hands, and many people will need intensive counseling to get through this awful time in their lives. The crisis response teams where I work are such great people, and have such difficult jobs. They go into homes of dangerous people, suicidal people, and do an excellent job reaching out to them, and saving lives! Let us

38

also focus on the fact that the mental health system in this country is just awful, and added to that so many people do not reach out and get help due to the stigma. I think of so many clients calling and saying, 'I never called before I don't want people thinking I am crazy'—it is NOT crazy to reach out and get help. Mental health services were just slashed in CT. I have written to my legislators and called the governor on this BEFORE the shooting but now I think it's REALLY going to be an issue. A lot of folks mentioned the brave teachers involved and teachers do have a hard job and deserve more pay and praise than they get, but we mental health workers have difficult jobs as well."

Malloy appeared on NBC's *Meet the Press* to talk about the Newtown tragedy. In a classic display of political double-talk, Malloy spoke of the importance of mental health treatment. This is the same guy who refused to tax millionaires, then rolled out a budget plan which included over $80 million in cuts to health and human services. Writer Liza Long wrote about the lack of mental health services for her 13-year-old son in a column entitled, "I Am Adam Lanza's Mother." The piece went viral.

"I don't believe my son belongs in jail. The chaotic environment exacerbates Michael's sensitivity to sensory stimuli and doesn't deal with the underlying pathology. But it seems like the United States is using prison as the solution of choice for mentally ill people. According to Human Rights Watch, the number of mentally ill inmates in U.S. prisons quadrupled from 2000 to 2006, and it continues to rise—in fact, the rate of inmate mental illness is five times greater (56 percent) than in the non-incarcerated population. With state-run treatment centers and hospitals shuttered, prison is now the last resort for the mentally ill—Rikers Island, the LA County Jail and Cook County Jail in Illinois housed the nation's largest treatment centers in 2011."

Michael Williams, a columnist for *The Guardian*, and anti-racism educator Tim Wise talked about how the gun violence which plagues inner cities such as Hartford is ignored until it touches the suburbs. Williams broke it down. "This problem is especially acute in Connecticut, *Where We Live* in a semi-apartheid state of rich suburbs and quiet rural communities around decaying, crime-riddled cities such as Hartford,

Bridgeport, and New Haven. For too long, we in suburban and rural Connecticut, as in many other states, have relegated inner-city violence to background noise on the TV news. No one bats an eye as the newscaster reads off lists of murders and shootings in cities just a few miles down the road: it is surreal and we are foolish to think that these problems do not impact us in the long run. We should use these atrocities to address the systemic problem of gun crime in America, not just isolated mass shootings."

Wise pulled no punches in a 2001 column on school shootings. "I said this after Columbine and no one listened so I'll say it again: white people live in an utter state of self-delusion. We think danger is black, brown and poor, and if we can just move far enough away from "those people" in the cities we'll be safe. If we can just find an 'all-American' town, life will be better, because 'things like this just don't happen here.' In case you hadn't noticed, 'here' is about the only place these kinds of things do happen. Oh sure, there is plenty of violence in urban communities and schools. But mass murder; wholesale slaughter; take-a-gun-and-see-how-many-you can-kill kinda craziness seems made for those safe places: the white suburbs or rural communities. I'll tell you what went wrong and it's not TV, rap music, video games or a lack of prayer in school. What went wrong is that white Americans decided to ignore dysfunction and violence when it only affected other communities, and thereby blinded themselves to the inevitable creeping of chaos which never remains isolated too long. What affects the urban 'ghetto' today will be coming to a Wal-Mart near you tomorrow, and unless you address the emptiness, pain, isolation and lack of hope felt by children of color and the poor, then don't be shocked when the support systems aren't there for your kids either."

Whites should feel grief and outrage about gun violence everywhere, not just in their backyards. State legislative leaders and the Malloy administration reached an agreement on a bipartisan plan to close the current state budget deficit. Social services and education took another hit. Additional services cuts during the 2013 legislative session were on the menu in order to close the projected 2013 $1.2 billion deficit. Malloy's senior adviser Roy Occhiogrosso said, "It's going to be tough stuff. People are going to scream." Folks were already screaming in Newtown.

While the mainstream media promoted the Democratic/Republican Party austerity agenda with their coverage of the so-called fiscal cliff deal, Malloy and the Connecticut General Assembly teamed up for their annual activity of pushing social services off the ledge. On December 19, 2012, legislators passed a deficit mitigation bill, which included an unprecedented $250 million in cuts to funding for health and human services; this is in addition to Malloy's November budget recessions, which slashed over $80 million. This hatchet job was a bipartisan effort; Republican House minority leader Larry Cafero spoke with a straight face about Democratic and GOP lawmakers being brought together by the "spirit of Sandy Hook."

The Newtown school shooting sparked a national conversation about the importance of mental health treatment. Pelto reported in his blog that 29 acute-care hospitals, mental health and community services and Medicaid recipients were all hit hard by the legislature's budget plan.

"In addition to hospitals, significant cuts were made to a wide variety of community-based health, mental health and social service programs including autism services, mental health housing programs, re-entry programs for ex-offenders, after school programs and many of the state's arts and culture grants. In addition to the actual cuts, by reducing state funding for Medicaid programs, Connecticut will lose about $60 million in funding from the Federal government, since Washington reimburses Connecticut 50 cents for every dollar the state spends on those programs."

Education funding was another casualty of Malloy's recessions and the lawmakers' budget plan. Malloy's recessions included $10 million in cuts to the University of Connecticut, while state universities and community colleges saw their funding reduced by $14 million. Lower income students who were supposed to receive financial aid in January were denied this assistance, thanks to Malloy. Surprisingly, it was

Republicans such as outgoing Sen. Len Suzio who spoke against the deficit mitigation bill. Suzio raised an important point about the January 2012 non- partisan Office of Fiscal Analysis (OFA) report, which found that the Malloy administration's projection of $4.8 billion in savings from the 2011 state employee benefit concession package was bogus.

OFA's memo to Cafero in response to his questions about the package stated that the administration's numbers were inflated by their estimating each pension change separately. Connecticut Mirror reporter Keith Phaneuf summed up OFA's observations in a January 27, 2012 article. "The Office of Fiscal Analysis also reported that it thinks the pension fund will gain about $3.6 billion over the next two decades— which still falls 25 percent short of the administration's estimate. Yet only about $1.7 billion of that gain is due to the concessions, with the rest produced by a rebounding stock market. 'Investment returns are a significant factor,' OFA analysts wrote in memos Friday to the top Republicans in the House and Senate, Lawrence F. Cafero Jr. of Norwalk and John P. McKinney of Fairfield."

Meanwhile, Malloy still refused to impose a progressive tax on millionaires and no legislators were talking about taxing the rich, either.

While the minutiae of budget talk tends to be confusing, the economic plan of Malloy and the legislature is quite simple; protect the wealthy while balancing the budget through yearly social services cuts and various gimmicks. During the 2012 legislative session, the Democrats voted to change the date of the annual report on the state budget from October to November 15, AFTER Election Day. It's obvious now why this was done. Pelto made an interesting discovery among the cuts in the lawmakers' budget plan. Following a January 2010 school bus accident in Hartford that killed a Rocky Hill student, legislators passed a law which created a Connecticut School Bus Seat Belt Account. $4.7 million was raised for the account through an increase in the fee to restore suspended drivers licenses. Remember Cafero's comment about Sandy Hook? Well, the deficit mitigation bill includes a provision, which transfers the money from the seat belt account to the state's General Fund to close the budget deficit. These people have no shame. Malloy was expected to announce more social services cuts in February 2013 when he rolled out his budget plan for the next fiscal year. The projected deficit was $1.2 billion.

January 2013

Congress passed the so-called fiscal cliff bill on New Year's Day, laying the groundwork for the Grand Bargain, which will include the first step toward dismantling Social Security. This is the ultimate goal of President Barack Obama. Of course, the Republicans have been trying to kill Social Security for years; they now have a willing accomplice in Obama, who can accomplish right-wing objectives as a Black Democrat that George W. Bush could not. Not all Democrats were in lockstep with Obama's scheme to use the manufactured fiscal cliff hysteria to push austerity measures on the people.

Democratic Rep. Raul Grijalva, co-chair of the Congressional Progressive Caucus, appeared on the *Democracy Now!* news program to denounce the fact that Obama was proposing more cuts to Social Security ($130 billion) than the military ($100 billion). "What the Progressive Caucus has said over and over again, Social Security, Medicare and Medicaid, those programs deserve to be strengthened and improved. There should be a discreet discussion about improvement and strengthening. And there should be other things on the table... Other things like a transition tax for corporations and for Wall Street transfers of a million dollars in the stock market. There should be some cuts in the subsidies for corporations. There should be some regulations and oversight to make sure that we don't get in the catastrophe that we got into. This amnesia that we don't know how we got here is possibly the most bothersome, to me, that we will repeat, and use this opportunity and use the debt ceiling as an opportunity to further push the agenda, which has been the hard right's agenda, which is to begin to dismantle systematically the support system that's out there for the American people. And that support system is what the federal government does with programs like Social Security and education."

The Raw Story reported on Democratic Rep. Keith Ellison's comments during his appearance on *The Young Turks* news and political commentary program. "'If Republicans want to have a conversation about cuts, we should have a conversation about cuts'," Ellison, a member of the Congressional Progressive Caucus, told host Cenk Uygur. "'Let's start with Medicare Part D and say, 'If you want to save money, you want to cut the deficit, let's let there be competitive bidding for Medicare Part D prescription drugs.' That would save about $150 billion'." He added that eliminating oil, gas and coal tax breaks and subsidies would leave 'another $100 billion' in government coffers. Ellison also suggested that America's nuclear arsenal could be trimmed down to save even more money. "'My point is, if Republicans want to do cuts, we should do cuts, but we're not going to hurt America's working class and poor to do it'." It's a damn shame that Grijalva and Ellison represent the minority opinion in the Democratic Party. Why weren't Democrats at the State Capitol in Connecticut talking like Grijalva and Ellison in response to Gov. Dannel Malloy's budget plan, which slashed funding for mental health treatment (right after the Newtown school shooting) and other vital social services?

Malloy and the Connecticut General Assembly refuse to impose a progressive income tax on millionaires. According to research by Connecticut Voices for Children, Connecticut's top 1% of income earners will only pay about 5.5% of their income in state and local taxes, while the state's low and middle-class families will pay between 9.6% and 11.4%! This regressive tax system places most of the burden on the people who are least able to pay. A 2009 Connecticut Voices for Children report found that a progressive tax system, which included a marginal 8% tax rate on individuals earning $1 million or more would

44

still leave this state with a more favorable tax rate on the rich than New York or New Jersey.

Malloy's November 2012 budget recessions and the deficit mitigation bill, which was passed in December slashed $80 million and $250 million respectively from already underfunded health and human services. A tax on millionaires would have produced $350 million in revenue, eliminating most of the state's $415 million deficit. Ending corporate tax loopholes and subsidies would bring additional dollars to the state, as would alternative economic development concepts such as a publicly owned bank. The Bank of North Dakota, the nation's only state owned bank, has generated $300 million in revenue during the past ten years AT NO COST TO TAXPAYERS!

January 21 was Martin Luther King Day. Dr. King's Poor People's Campaign was an economic justice initiative aimed at eradicating poverty. He would definitely be disgusted by the attitude of Malloy regarding the poor. The 2013 legislative session in Connecticut began on January 9. Malloy's State of the State address was the focal point of the opening day festivities. The man with the lowest approval rating of any Democratic Party governor in the nation gave his usual "all is well" spiel, despite the fact that he just teamed up with legislators to close a $415 million budget deficit with unprecedented cuts to social services. The state faced a looming $1.2 billion deficit in the next fiscal year. *The Connecticut Mirror*'s Phaneuf reported that the new Earned Income Tax Credit (EITC) for working poor families might also be cut. James Horan, executive director of the Connecticut Association for Human Services, told Phaneuf that cutting EITC would cause tremendous harm to one of the state's vulnerable populations. "Connecticut has taken a giant step forward with the state's EITC," Horan said. "If we go backwards and take money out of the pockets of hardworking families, we are taking money away from the communities where they spend money, and we are jeopardizing our fragile economic recovery."

This writer met Malloy once, when he visited the Connecticut Valley Hospital cafeteria in 2010 during his gubernatorial campaign. A union delegate who worked for Malloy's campaign told workers that good ol' Dan would be hanging out with us during lunchtime and answering questions. I asked Malloy if he would make racial economic disparity a priority issue if he was elected. I cited the 2010 United for a Fair Economy report, which found that Blacks earn 62 cents and Latinos 68 cents for every dollar that whites make. Blacks possess 10 cents of net wealth for every dollar that whites have while Latinos possess 12 cents. I also mentioned that Hartford's poverty rate is consistently one of the highest in the nation, averaging over 30 percent.

Malloy's jovial demeanor changed quickly as he immediately tried to show my co-workers that he was smarter than me. "Look, I went to college; I know about all of that stuff," Malloy said dismissively. "What we need to do with Hartford is clean it up. We've got to make the neighborhoods attractive to people who are looking to buy homes." The unemployment rate for Black males in some areas of Hartford is as high as 50 percent. It was obvious that Malloy was not talking about people who already live in the community; he was talking about gentrification. Seeing that my fellow employees were eagerly awaiting their chance to question Malloy, I thanked him for his time and excused myself. Malloy's reply was not surprising at all. Poverty has not been a priority issue for the Democrats since the Lyndon Johnson administration.

In 2013, the Congressional Progressive Caucus (CPC) submitted H.R. 505 *Balancing Act of 2013*, an alternative to the so-called sequestration cuts. Unfortunately, the CPC, led by Co- Chairs Rep. Keith Ellison (D-Min) and Rep. Raul Grijalva (D-AZ), faced an uphill battle against their own party. *Black Agenda Report* commentator Glen Ford reminded everyone that sequestration, the latest manufactured crisis designed to get the people to accept austerity measures (the government shutdown would follow), was President Barack Obama's idea.

"It was Obama who swallowed whole the corporate argument, previously championed by Republicans, that the national debt was Crisis Number One and that entitlement programs were the root cause. From the moment in January of 2009 when Obama served notice that Social Security and all other entitlements would be put on the chopping block, he became the chief mover and shaker for so-called entitlement reform. He created the model for austerity, through his Simpson-Bowles deficit reduction commission. Simpson-Bowles provided the basis for the massive cuts offered by President Obama in 2011. When the Republicans balked at even a modest tax increase for the rich, it was the White House National Economic Council Director, the corporate dealmaker Gene Sperling, who came up with the sequestration scheme, which was timed to explode right after the 2012 elections. The idea was to make every popular constituency in the country scream-and accept the inevitability of massive entitlement cuts."

A lack of job opportunities is one of the root causes of urban violence in this country. On January 29, fifteen-year-old honors student Hadiya Pendleton was fatally wounded in a gang related shooting one mile from President Barack Obama's Chicago home; Hadiya had performed at Obama's inauguration a week earlier. Local nonprofit The Black Youth Project (BYP) circulated an online petition (close to 50,000 people signed) which resulted in Obama returning to his hometown to talk about gun violence in communities of color. BYP pushed Obama to partner with community groups and state/local officials in Illinois to address the socioeconomic factors which contribute to urban violence. BYP founder Cathy Cohen addressed these factors in a recent op-ed.

"We urge President Obama to make a substantive speech that addresses the underlying factors that perpetuate violence in Black and Latino urban communities across the nation. Issues such as the illegal distribution and loose regulation of arms, the lack of living wage jobs, the varied failures of public schools, the disproportionate rate of incarceration for youth of color, the trauma experienced by young people who live in under-resourced and violent communities, and yes, the misguided choices young people sometimes make."

We need a similarly holistic approach here in Hartford in order to change the economic conditions in the North End and other poverty-stricken areas throughout the city and state.

April 2013

The Connecticut General Assembly passed the hotly debated gun control bill without a public hearing; the bill was immediately signed into law by Gov. Dannel Malloy. During the House of Representatives debate on the legislation Democratic Party lawmaker Doug McCrory, who represents the 7th Assembly District, made a passionate speech (ignored by most of the mainstream media) about how the bill ignored the root causes of gun violence in low-income communities of color, such as a lack of opportunities for young Black/Latino males. McCrory reiterated this point on the WFSB TV *Face the State* political show. Council President Shawn Wooden acted as an apologist for the legislation on the Fox 61 Capitol Report program; Wooden said that the bill didn't go far enough but was "a step in the right direction."

President Obama did not talk about urban gun violence or its connection to poverty during his visit to the University of Hartford, as he continued his effort to pass federal gun control legislation. Obama gave his speech right next door to Hartford, where 300 gun deaths had occurred in the last 10 years, yet grieving families from Hartford, New Haven and Bridgeport were not invited to join families from Newtown at the Obama rally. After the event, the Newtown families left with Obama on Air Force One to assist him in his battle with Congress. Black Obama supporters in Connecticut should ask themselves why no families from urban communities in this state were on the plane.

As our State Capitol source predicted to the Community Party a couple of weeks earlier, *the Penn Act* advisory board's police friendly racial profiling bill, S.B. 1143 *An Act Concerning Traffic Stop Information* was passed by the Judiciary Committee. The advisory board bill repealed the CP's traffic stop receipt provision. The excuse from the advisory board was that the traffic stop data collection process would now be electronic. Motorists would continue to be excluded from the process, as the control of data would remain exclusively with the police. During an April 18 Capitol meeting on CP's *Penn Act* enforcement provisions, Judiciary

Vice Chair Matt Ritter spoke in favor of CP's traffic stop receipt concept, which was scheduled to go in effect July 1. Spanish Speaking Center Executive Director Mary Sanders, who wrote CP's bill language, spoke in support of the receipt along with our provisions, which would ban patrol officers from harassing motorists and their passengers about their immigration status and allow individuals to file racial profiling complaints through the Commission on Human Rights and Opportunities (CHRO)   .

Advisory board member Bill Dyson ducked a direct question from Mary, who asked Dyson if he thought it was fair that passengers in vehicles who were not observed engaging in criminal behavior had to deal with being grilled by a cop about their immigration status. No other urban lawmakers appeared to publicly support our bill, despite our appeal to the Black and Puerto Rican Caucus to support our legislation. The caucus continues to demonstrate a total disregard for communities of color as they serve their masters at the Capitol; I'll examine this problem.

Racial profiling is of course, directly linked to police violence. The Malcolm X Grassroots Movement (MXGM) has issued a follow up to their *Every Thirty-six Hours* report on the extrajudicial killings of 313 Black people, which was published in 2012. This report found that a Black person was killed every thirty-six hours by "police and security guards or self-appointed law enforcers." The new report, *Operation Ghetto Storm*, found that Blacks are now executed on the streets every twenty-eight hours.

Every 28 hours in 2012 someone employed or protected by the US government killed a Black man, woman, or child! This startling fact is revealed in Operation Ghetto Storm: 2012 Annual Report on the Extrajudicial Killings of 313 Black people by police, security guards, and vigilantes.

"When we started this investigation in early 2012, we knew a serious human rights crisis was confronting the Black community", says Kali Akuno, an organizer with the Malcolm X Grassroots Movement (MXGM). "However, we did not have a clear sense of its true depth until we compiled and examined the annual figures. We have uncovered outrageous rates of extrajudicial killings–rates, that when they are found in countries like Mexico or Brazil, are universally condemned. The same outrage inside the U.S. also demands immediate action."[1]

While the MXGM report found that Blacks are being killed by police, security guards and self-appointed vigilantes like George Zimmerman and Michael Dunn, and that racial profiling is a tactic used in police containment of low-income communities of color, the Democrats pimped Trayvon Martin in an effort to get votes while perpetuating a growing police state. I talked about the lynching of Trayvon Martin and the Democrats' exploitation of the case in commentaries that were published in April 2012 and August 2013 in *the Hartford News* following the acquittal of Zimmerman. See Part 2.

WNPR *Where We Live* host John Dankosky clearly demonstrated that he is a part of the Access of Evil, a term coined by *Democracy Now!* Host Amy Goodman to describe so-called journalists who trade truth for access to those who are in positions of power. I presented Dankosky with the MXGM report on the extrajudicial killing of Blacks by the police. Dankosky had been patting himself on the back on his Twitter page for his willingness to have "hard conversations about race." I also told Dankosky about how the so-called Connecticut Racial Profiling Prohibition Project (CRP3) was protecting the police in this state by working to kill CP's *Trayvon Martin Act* enforcement language. Apparently, Dankosky's willingness for "hard conversations" ends when confronted with information about the police killing Black people every 28 hours in this country. I never heard from Dankosky after he ever so sweetly promised to read the MXGM report and discuss its contents with me, along with my fact-based criticism of CRP3.

Smiling, polite, condescending liberals like Dankosky earn their pay by feeding misinformation to the people. They serve the ruling class by giving the illusion of journalism, while they push the agenda of their

---

[1]   https://mxgm.org/operation-ghetto-storm-2012-annual-report-on-the-extrajudicial-killing-of-313-black-people/

50

masters. Dankosky will host vacuous discussions on racial profiling with members of CRP3 and law enforcement shills, allowing racists to call in and defend biased policing without challenging them at all.

Dankosky would never do a show on the MXGM *Operation Ghetto Storm* report, because he knows that would piss off the police. He won't talk about CRP3 killing CP's *Trayvon Martin Act* traffic stop receipt language; because he knows that the advisory board is made up of Gov. Dannel Malloy's flunkies. Dankosky wants to continue having Malloy as a guest on his show. If you're a Connecticut resident who wants real news and information about social justice issues, you should stop listening to *Where We Live*.

The Black and Puerto Rican caucus had never publicly supported CP's bill during the three years it has been debated at the Capitol. In my opinion, this is due to political and personal reasons, which are unrelated to the bill itself. Gov. Dannel Malloy and Office of Policy and Management Undersecretary Mike Lawlor wanted to be viewed as the change agents of *the Penn Act*. Last year Lawlor refused to meet with CP to discuss our immigration language. The Malloy administration publicly took credit for the advisory board, however this concept was submitted to the Connecticut General Assembly by CP before Malloy was even elected. My refusal to support former legislator Ken Green in his 2010 re-election bid has resulted in a cold shoulder from urban lawmakers ever since. Green was a terrible legislator who tried to bully me when I first started in community organizing. My constant public criticism of Malloy and the Democratic Party has obviously been the icing on the cake. We felt an increased sense of urgency for our immigration provision to be added; politicians nationwide were already using the Boston terror attack to argue against immigration reform. Undocumented immigrants certainly would feel the backlash along with the Muslim community.

The Boston bombing was a heinous attack on innocent citizens. Unfortunately, Islamophobia and racism spiked again as a result. CNN's

John King aired what turned out to be a false report about a "dark skinned male" being arrested for the bombing. ColorLines.com reported that in Medford, Massachusetts, a Palestinian woman was assaulted by a white man who blamed Muslims for the Boston attack and a Bangladeshi man was attacked by Latino men in the Bronx. Comcast SportsNet New England refused to allow me on the air during the CSNNE Baseball Show call-in program last Saturday. CSNNE had been covering the Boston bombing and I wanted to talk about the Medford attack and the need for Boston media and athletes to denounce Islamophobia. I was told by the screener that no "negative" calls would be allowed! CSNNE obviously wanted to censor the conversation.

I had an exchange later in the day on Twitter with game show host Chuck Woolery, who caused a national firestorm when he said that all Muslims are terrorists. Woolery attempted to bail out of the conversation when I sent him a link to a History Channel documentary on the Ku Klux Klan and asked him to talk about their use of Christianity, with the same gusto that he was going after Muslims. When I called him out for making such a hasty retreat, he stated that he opposed the KKK and everything they stood for. I responded by telling Woolery to think about the fact that the KKK is a terrorist organization whose ideology is based on a religion that they hijacked. Woolery quickly changed the subject with his next tweet.

We would have to brace ourselves for another assault on civil liberties as a result of the Boston bombing. Xenophobes and racists had already mobilized. Reporter Amina Ismail stood up at a White House press briefing the previous week and asked Press Secretary Jay Carney if he considered a U.S. bombing earlier that month in Afghanistan, which killed 11 children and a woman to be a terrorist act, since the Boston bombing had been classified as terrorism. The latest wave of U.S. xenophobia and bigotry was cloaked in "patriotism."

May 2013

The Connecticut General Assembly passed *the Penn Act* advisory board's toothless amendments to the racial profiling law. This legislation was literally passed by the state Senate under the cover of darkness with no prior notice that the bill was coming up for a vote. The advisory board bill focused solely on data collection with only a cursory nod towards enforcement, despite the fact that a Department of Justice investigation found that the East Haven police were engaging in racial profiling of Latinos. Instead of crafting legislation aimed at preventing a reoccurrence of this crime, which was the focus of an avalanche of gun control bills that were introduced following the Newtown school shooting, Gov. Dannel Malloy, Office of Policy and Management Undersecretary Mike Lawlor and the CGA continue to portray racial profiling as a theory which must be proven as fact. Our position is that this disparate reaction underscores a racial double standard at the State Capitol. The passage of the advisory board bill kills all of our enforcement language, which was passed last year, including our traffic stop receipt provision that was scheduled to go in effect July 1. Our immigration provision, which would ban patrol officers from harassing motorists and their passengers about their immigration status, was also left out of the bill.

Rep. Matt Ritter was the only lawmaker who has publicly supported our bill language; he promised to continue to work with us to get our amendments restored to *the Penn Act*. The advisory board bill was passed unanimously by the House on May 22 and is scheduled to go in effect January 1, 2015, so we would have to push for our amendments to be added after the 2013 legislative session ended. I believe that the sole purpose of the advisory board (our concept but hijacked by the Malloy administration) which includes ACLU legal director Sandra Staub, African-American Affairs Commission Executive Director Glenn Cassis and Latino and Puerto Rican Affairs Commission acting Executive Director Werner Oyanadel, was to kill our bill language and protect the police. I also think that members of the legislature such as

53

Judiciary Committee co-chair Senator Eric Coleman, who I chastised during a *Penn Act* public hearing last year for not returning my phone calls while the legislature was killing our bill in 2011, were complicit in this objective. As I have mentioned previously, State Representative Gary Holder-Winfield has stated publicly that the CGA killed CP's racial profiling legislation two years ago because the police did not like it.

The Senate sneaking through the advisory board's sham legislation while no one was looking is an example of the Access of Evil issue, which I will continue to talk about in this space. CP's *Penn Act* amendments were killed because of political and personal reasons, which have absolutely nothing to do with the bill itself. Blacks and Latinos in this state will continue to be left vulnerable to the type of police abuse, which occurred in East Haven. This is because the Malloy administration, lawmakers like Coleman, members of the Black and Puerto Rican Caucus and advisory board members, such as the ones I have named, are more interested in using the racial profiling issue as a political football than in actually protecting people of color. Activists such as Father James Manship, who initially agreed to work with me last year on the racial profiling issue and then inexplicably stopped responding to my phone calls and emails, have been conspicuous by their silence. Father Manship exposed the EHPD's harassment of Latinos, but for some reason is unwilling to support CP's *Penn Act* amendments. In my opinion, he has a lot of explaining to do. Others, such as New Haven police officer Shafiq Abdussabar, who came out of the woodwork last year to criticize CP's racial profiling bill AFTER it was passed by the Senate, were missing in action in 2013.

During a Hartford gun violence forum that was reported on by Hartford News editor Andy Hart, Malloy provided lip service instead of talking honestly about some of the root causes of urban violence; e.g. poverty fueled by President Bill Clinton's 1996 welfare "reform" bill and Black mass incarceration generated by racist Clinton backed drug laws, and the necessary solutions. The CP's *Ban the Box* amendment, which Democratic Party Labor and Public Employees Committee members

54

refused to discuss with us before passing a feel-good bill regarding job discrimination against formerly incarcerated individuals, would effectively deter this practice. During the forum Malloy said, "Once a person has that first conviction, they will probably be unemployed for a large portion of their life. We're working to prevent that first conviction." Instead of writing off Blacks and Latinos who have been convicted of a crime and consigning them to the prison industrial complex, Malloy and the Democrats should have supported a statewide Ban the Box conditional job offer provision, which would provide applicants who have a legal history with a fair shot at a job!

June 2013

The Connecticut General Assembly passed a $37.6 billion, two-year budget on June 3. Here are "highlights" from the budget, courtesy of *Connecticut Mirror* reporters Keith Phaneuf and Jacqueline Rabe Thomas.

"Connecticut's working poor would lose $21 million next fiscal year as the state Earned Income Tax Credit shrinks by one-sixth, from 30 percent of the federal EITC to 25 percent. The credit would be partially restored, to 27.5 percent of the federal EITC, in 2014... This new budget reduces aid to hospitals by more than $500 million in total over the next two fiscal years, including about $400 million cut from the grants used to reimburse hospitals for the provider tax they pay. It eliminates the 7 percent luxury tax on boat purchases, replacing it with the regular sales tax rate of 6.35 percent. And it also exempts boats from the sales tax if they are going to be docked in Connecticut for less than 60 days each year... The two-year plan includes a raid on the transportation fund, shifting its resources to general-fund expenditures, just as motorists prepare for one of the largest gasoline tax hikes in history.

It also refinances operating debt from the last recession, spends over $220 million from the current year's surplus and launches a new Keno lottery game. Further complicating matters, that shift leaves the transportation fund with $104 million less than the funding it would need to maintain current services in 2013-14, and $84 million less in 2014-15."

Phaneuf and Thomas noted that Gov. Dannel Malloy's campaign pledge to adopt the Generally Accepted Accounting Principles (GAAP) guidelines for financial accounting turned out to be yet another lie.

"The new budget again postpones the state's conversion to GAAP beyond Malloy's current term—and into the 2015-16 fiscal year. It marks the second significant delay of a process Malloy insisted, as a candidate back in 2010 would begin right away. Malloy promised to sign an executive order on his first day requiring agencies to report in compliance with GAAP standards. But the order he signed only ordered his budget office to study the matter. If GAAP standards are used, state finances are deep in the red. Fiscal analysts estimate that differential at $1.2 billion. And because of inflation, that number can grow over time."

Comptroller Kevin Lembo weighed in, releasing a statement on the Connecticut Senate refusing to pass a transparency bill, which would regulate corporate welfare.

Comptroller Kevin Lembo's press release on the CT Senate killing HB 6566 *An Act Concerning Transparency in Economic Assistance Programs*:

COMPTROLLER LEMBO STATEMENT ON FAILURE TO ADOPT TRANSPARENCY IN ECONOMIC ASSISTANCE

"I am concerned by the state Senate's failure to raise HB 6566, An Act Concerning Transparency in Economic Assistance—despite unanimous support by the House of Representatives, broad public support, bipartisan consensus and the bill's clear public policy value. Our state invests hundreds of millions of dollars every year in economic assistance and tax credits designed to promote economic development and job growth.

This legislation would have established key transparency and open government measures related to these dollars. "This legislation would have required the state to establish a publicly searchable database for economic assistance and tax credit programs. The database would have allowed the public to quickly and easily review the performance of these programs and credits—including key data, such as the number of jobs created or retained as a result of the assistance and compliance with the conditions of the assistance.

When hundreds of millions of dollars are spent or foregone every year to promote economic development, the public has a right to know how these transactions are performing. Most importantly, it would have compelled, by law, that state government disclose important details about the investment of taxpayer dollars—rather than rely on the discretion of any given administration. The bill would have put the state on a path toward performing regular tax incidence analyses. In addition to the right of every taxpayer to see how their tax dollars are spent, this would have provided legislatures and policymakers with more information about the impact of tax policy so that they can make informed policy decisions. Which groups are actually bearing the burden of each of our major state taxes? Do certain taxes disproportionately impact specific populations? A tax incidence analysis will help to answer these questions and lead to more informed tax policy decisions in the future. Establishing a clear and concise law requiring these disclosures would be ideal. However, the good news is that government already has the authority to establish this database—and disclose this state tax credit and economic assistance data—on its own in the absence of legislation, which I hope the administration will do and I will continue to urge. In the meantime, I'm incredibly grateful for the overwhelming support from advocates, the House and significant support within the Senate—a bipartisan group of thoughtful legislators who worked cooperatively to find common ground on this initiative."

Activist Benjamin Reyes submitted an op-ed to the Hartford News on the legislature's passage of a medical marijuana bill and the so-called War on Drugs:

"The problem with marijuana law is not that there are sick people who can't get ahold of marijuana. Now this is not to say that patients don't deserve access to cannabis. Quite the contrary, patients do deserve the right to have cannabis, as do we all. Cannabis has beneficial and medicinal qualities. However, it is not medication. Restricting its availability to only the sick and dying as the new law does; would be akin to limiting vitamins and healthy plants like garlic to terminal cancer patients. We can all benefit from using it responsibly. No, the real problem with marijuana law is the unquantifiably [sic] high cost of prohibition. By prohibiting a substance that is proven to be used by millions worldwide, our federal government has effectively created a billion dollar a year business; the prison industry. $1.2 billion a year, to be specific, is the cost to taxpayers to fund this cockamamy [sic] marijuana prohibition. There are 59,300 incarcerated Americans serving time for marijuana related drug charges at any given time, 37,500 of which are serving sentences for marijuana charges alone with no other drugs involved. A whopping 15,400 of these marijuana offenders are locked up for simple possession without sale. It's also worth mentioning that most of these inmates are minorities; their arrests are taking place in their homes and neighborhoods.

Communities of color have especially been ravaged by Hurricane DEA. I've likened the drug war to a social weapon of mass destruction of Black/ Latino neighborhoods. Its fallout affects us to this day. Bar none, the most used illegal drug, cannabis makes up 80% of the drug war budget, leaving just 20% to stop coke, meth, Rohypnol (the date rape drug), heroin and the myriad of other drugs on the black market. These figures don't even take into account the cost to run and maintain prisons, the emotional cost to thousands of broken families or the cost to our overburdened justice system. So where does medical marijuana play into all of this? Simple. Before medical marijuana, anytime anyone mentioned cannabis, it was in relation to the aforementioned issues. Now whenever you hear about marijuana, you think about sick patients who aren't getting their medicine. Medicinal marijuana doesn't do anything to solve the actual problems of prohibition. It is little more than a political tar pit, distracting the legalization movement from the real issues. My beef with the legalization movement is their misguided belief that medical marijuana will somehow help the legalization effort, when nothing suggests this at all.

The Connecticut General Assembly voting for medical marijuana after 30-plus years of smearing the plant as a harmful narcotic is like a bad joke. Medicinal marijuana to them is the perfect vehicle to renege on the lies they so furiously spread to keep cannabis illegal. It's silly to expect us to believe that a dying patient can handle the effects of marijuana, but a perfectly healthy adult cannot. Further confusing things, the medical marijuana bill allows palliative use but still restricts sales and growth. This begs the question; if individuals are not allowed to sell marijuana or grow it, then where is it coming from? Worse still, through medical marijuana the legislature has found a way to make one substance straddle two of our biggest, most corrupt moneymaking industries; prison and health care. All at once, they are telling us that this plant is both good and bad for you. Something has got to give."

October 2013

The Affordable Care Act (ACA) aka Obamacare health insurance exchange website, which had been beset by glitches since its October 1 launch, became the political football being tossed around in Washington. Tea Party Republicans caused a shutdown of the federal government in protest of a health care law that was devised by the conservative Heritage Foundation and first implemented in 2006 by then-governor Mitt Romney, a Republican, in Massachusetts. Senator Ted Cruz (R-Texas), the shutdown ringleader, is being hailed as a hero by conservatives and is the early favorite to be the Republican candidate in the next presidential election. The Democrats and their liberal base are tenaciously defending a right-wing concept, which led to a federal bill that was written by health insurance industry lobbyists. The World Health Organization (WHO) currently ranks the United States number 38 in quality of health care. France, which uses a single payer health care system, is ranked #1. While Barack Obama was running for president, he promised to pursue a universal health care system (Medicare for all) if he was elected and the Democrats took control of the House of Representatives and the Senate. You can view then-senator Obama's single payer campaign promise here.

During the first two years of Obama's term, the Democrats controlled the House and the Senate. Obama did not pursue a single payer system and in fact excluded single payer advocates from his 2009 health care summit. Candidate Obama promised that health care reform discussions in Washington would be televised nationally on C-SPAN. That didn't happen either.

The ACA debate underscores the harm that liberals and conservatives inflict on themselves and the rest of this country's citizens by blindly supporting Democratic and Republican Party policies, which are against all of our best interests. Medical bills are the number one cause of bankruptcy in the nation. The ACA will leave a projected 31 million people uninsured. The United States is the only industrialized country with a for-profit health care system. The logical move would be to study the health care systems in France and the other countries that are ranked highly by WHO and utilize universal health care and figure out how to effectively adapt it for use in the United States. Vermont is currently in the process of implementing single payer. I recently spoke with a doctor who educated me about the Medicare payment process, which can be extremely frustrating for health care providers. The American Medical Association (AMA) and other organizations representing these providers should have substantial input on how a single-payer system would work here.

Of course, none of this is happening because of the health insurance industry's control of Obama and Congress. Bruce Dixon of the *Black Agenda Report* listed the top 10 things the ACA gave us versus what we gave up:

"1. We got a Swiss cheese system that exempts many large corporations from having to insure their employees.

2. We got a Medicare expansion which can be thwarted at will by current or future Republican controlled state governments.

3. We got a chaotic and confusing "marketplace" in which patients with little information are encouraged to conflate low insurance premiums with low-cost quality insurance.

4. We got an initially unworkable internet front end for our chaotic and confusing "marketplace."

5. We gave an ongoing river of cash to private health insurance companies. Millions more are now forced to buy their crappy product, with the premiums funded by billions annually in public subsidies.

6. The ACA gives us little or no cost control over medical care and even bans most measures that would lower the cost of prescription drugs.

7. ACA only covers about half the nation's total uninsured. It leaves two thirds of the blacks and single mothers, along with half the low-wage employed currently without health insurance untouched.

8. We have to wait till 2016, when the Obama Administration is on its way out of office for all the provisions of the ACA to take effect.

9. Making health insurance and health care privatized commodities instead of human rights granted certain permanent rights to those profits under the currently popular conservative legal "takings" doctrine.

10. ACA's scheme of privatized health insurance paid for by public dollars was originally devised by one arm of the ultraconservative Heritage Foundation, and is opposed today by another arm of that same organization. Go figger [sic]."

November, 2013

Seattle, Washington provided some positive news for the left, as (gasp) socialist Kshama Sawant was elected to the Seattle City Council on November 15. Sawant's platform issues were a $15 an hour minimum wage and rent control. Sawant did indeed spearhead a campaign to pass the minimum wage increase, an effort that was supported by Mayor Ed Murray. Indian newspaper *India West* reported on the outcome.

"The Seattle City Council June 2 unanimously approved a $15 minimum wage over the next seven years—the highest in the nation—thus fulfilling a campaign vow made by Indian American council member Kshama Sawant to boost pay for the city's lowest-paid workers.

The Seattle Times said the outcome was 'not in doubt as a progressive mayor (Ed Murray) and city council throughout the spring vowed to address the national trend of rising income inequality and a city that has become increasingly unaffordable for many of its residents.'

'We did this. Workers did this, said Sawant, whose election in November on a $15-an-hour minimum platform helped spur the Seattle effort. 'Today's first victory for (the 15 Now campaign) will inspire people all over the nation,' she added.

Under the $15 minimum-wage law, minimum-wage workers will get raises beginning April 1, 2015. Employees of businesses with over 500 workers will start at $11 an hour and reach $15 in 2017. Large businesses that provide health care will have an additional year.

Businesses with fewer than 500 workers will be required to pay $15 in 2019. Small businesses that claim a credit for tips and benefits will reach $15 an hour in 2021. Wages increase each year under all plans. By 2025, according to city projections, all workers will be earning a minimum wage of $18.13 an hour, nearly double Washington State's current $9.32 an hour," The Seattle Times said. The victories in Jackson and Seattle showed what a focused, cohesive social justice movement could accomplish."

Meanwhile in Connecticut, Pelto narrowed the focus of his increasingly popular blog, as he railed against Malloy's efforts to privatize education in Connecticut. Pelto reported on the attempted corporate takeover of Clark Elementary School in Hartford.

Achievement First, Inc. the large charter school company that was co-founded by Governor Malloy's Commissioner of Education, Stefan Pryor, is continuing its campaign to get the Hartford Board of Education to close the Clark Elementary School and hand it over to the charter school operator.

In response, Hartford parents, teachers and community residents are fighting back. According to a press release from the coalition formed to fight off the Achievement First attack, 'Scores of neighborhood residents, civil rights activists, education advocates, teachers, classroom support personnel, and legislators joined together last week to speak out against proposed displacement of Clark School students.'

The event, last week, was put together by the Clark School's Parent-Teacher Organization (PTO) and School Governance Council (SGC).

According to Clark School PTO President and SGC member Lakeisha McFarland, 'Many of our parents are upset because we feel our school is being snatched from us. It's very painful for our parents. Our kids are succeeding and they're making it seem like they're failing.'

Joneisha Brown, the parent liaison at the Clark School for the district's Title I Program added, 'I can't support a scheme that breaks-up families or disrupts our children's education. I don't think it's fair to the children to ignore the good things that are happening at Clark; we have a long way to go, but let us keep going.'

One of the issues Clark parents are raising is Achievement First's apparent inability or unwillingness to provide services to Hartford's Latino children or children who requires extra special education services.

Year	Achievement First % English Language Learners	Hartford % English Language Learners
2010- 2011	4.6%	17.7%
2009-2010	4.8%	17.5%
2008-2009	0%	14.4%

As the above table reveals, Achievement First has completely failed to take its fair share of students who face language barriers such as needing extra help with English.

A grassroots group of Clark Elementary School parents, SAND Elementary School parents and local public school advocates joined forces to fight back against the corporate takeover of both schools by Achievement First, Inc. and Capital Preparatory Magnet School, respectively. The showdown took place at the monthly Hartford Board of Education meeting. Parents said that their chief complaint was that they were being excluded from conversations about the direction of Hartford schools such as Clark SAND and Rawson, the site of the Board of Education (BOE) meeting. Rawson Principal Gerald Martin claimed that he has been making an effort to reach out to parents. Martin said that he had no personal opinion on the charter school concept and that the decision on privatization should be left up to Malloy and the parents.

The previous week, Hartford Mayor Pedro Segarra announced that he would not support an Achievement First takeover of Clark School. However, that didn't mean this plan was dead; the BOE made that clear at the meeting. During the public comment portion, city resident Hyacinth Yennie accused the BOE of pitting parents against each other "with so called choice." She brought up the "blue ribbon"

Dwight School, which was shut down as an example of the BOE using "failing schools" as a ruse to justify privatization. The crowd at Rawson roared in approval when Yennie urged city officials to "put a leash on Dr. (Steve) Perry." Perry is the principal at Capital Prep. BOE Chairman Matt Poland was unconvincing as he denied being a pawn of the charter school power brokers and attempted to demonize public school advocates. Achievement First was co-founded by Stefan Prior, Malloy's Commissioner of Education. Perry was the central figure in the plan to privatize SAND School. Segarra and the BOE allowed Perry to take a quasi-paid leave of absence from his taxpayer-funded job (he had been absent 20% of the school year and arrived late or left early numerous times) so he could act as an agent for the charter school industry. Charter schools are big business. Really big business. *Democracy Now!* co-host Juan Gonzalez reported on the charter school hustle in 2010. He explained how Wall Street investors are reaping huge windfalls from school privatization.

"One of the things I've been trying now for a couple of years is to try to figure out why is it that so many hedge fund managers, wealthy Americans, big banks and executives of Wall Street banks have all lined up supporting and getting involved in the development of charter schools. And I think I may have come across one of the reasons: there's a lot of money to be made in charter schools. And I'm not talking just about the for-profit management companies that run a lot of these charter schools.

It turns out that at the tail end of the Clinton administration in 2000, Congress passed a new kind of tax credit called a New Markets Tax Credit. And what this allows is it gives an enormous federal tax credit to banks and equity funds that invest in community projects in underserved communities, and it's been used heavily now for the last several years for charter schools. And I focused on Albany, New York, which in New York state [sic] is the district with the highest percentage of children in charter schools. Twenty percent of the schoolchildren in Albany are now attending charter schools. And I discovered that quite a few of the charter schools there have been built using these New Markets Tax Credits.

And what happens is, the investors who put up the money to build the charter schools get to basically virtually double their money in seven years through a 39 percent tax credit from the federal government. In addition, this is a tax credit on money that they're lending, so they're collecting interest on the loans, as well as getting the 39 percent tax credit. They piggyback the tax credit on other kinds of federal tax credits, like historic preservation or job creation or Brownfields credits. The result is, you can put in $10 million and in seven years double your money.

And the problem is that the charter schools end up paying in rents the debt service on these loans. And so, now a lot of the charter schools in Albany are straining paying their debt—their rent has gone up from $170,000 to $500,000 in a year, or huge increases in their rents, as they strain to pay off these construction loans. And the rents are eating up huge portions of their total cost. And, of course, the money is coming from the state.

So, one of the big issues is that so many of these charter schools are not being audited. No one knows whom are the people [sic] making these huge windfall profits as the investors. And often there are interlocking relationships between the charter school boards and the nonprofit groups that organize and syndicate the loans. And so, there needs to be sunlight on this whole issue. And the state legislature right now is considering expanding charter school caps, but one of the things I press for in my column, there has to be the power of the government to independently audit all of these charter schools, or we're not going to know how public dollars are ending up in the coffers of Wall Street investors."

BAR commentator Dixon wrote a column on charter schools. Dixon talked about the true socioeconomic and political purpose of school privatization.

"Doug Henwood, a radical economist and founder of Left Business Observer, says it as succinctly as anyone when he sums up the goal of bipartisan corporate education reform imposed on poorer neighborhoods as "low cost privatized holding tanks leading to McDonalds jobs for the lucky, or to prison for the not so lucky" along with classes delivered by computers rather than unionized teachers. But as useful as this summation is, it leaves out one element worth noting. You can't run a global empire without a military class, any more than you can run a prison without prison guards. Before the era of corporate reform there was at least one achievement of genuine small democratic education reform pushed through by the administration of Chicago mayor Harold Washington in the 1980s. Since then parents in every public school have been allowed to elect parent councils, with reps from among rank and file teachers, which have veto power over Title I funds and principals' contracts, which are limited to two years.

The 'innovative' answer of downtown bureaucrats, corporate elites and subsequent mayors to parents taking a hand in running the schools has been to simply close Chicago public schools and replace them with charters over which parents have no say. What mayor, and what alderman really wants organized parents running their own neighborhood institutions? It's bad for business if you're a privatizer, or a politician who takes cues and campaign contributions from privatizers. Ultimately, habits of local democracy are bad for empire."

Pelto exposed how Perry used workplace bullying to further his attempt to take over SAND School and start his own charter school management company. Jonathan reported that Capital Prep teachers came forward to complain about Perry's administrative team pressuring them to write letters to the BOE supporting Perry's plan. Administrators told teachers to use their work emails to send these letters and to copy Perry on the emails, which would provide Perry and his team with a record of which teachers were playing ball. Jonathan pointed out that Perry using his subordinates to lobby the BOE was a clear violation of BOE policies, which prohibit the use of work emails for political activity. The school board voted 5-3 against the SAND proposal. Mayor Segarra said he would not support the plan due to a lack of support by the parents.

Perry was at the center of controversy following the Hartford Board of Education's decision to reject Perry's proposal to create his own charter school management company and take over SAND Elementary School. The day after the board's decision Perry posted a message on Twitter. Perry said, "The only way to lose a fight is to stop fighting. All this did was piss me off. It's so on. Strap up, there will be head injuries." I was among those who called for Perry's suspension. After reading Perry's defiant tweets, I came to the conclusion that he was correct when he said that his opponents should not fixate on him. Even a broken clock is right twice a day.

What public education advocates should have done was use the events of the previous week to amplify their general message about the racist, profit-driven charter school industry that Perry represents. There should be more discussion about how Wall Street uses Blacks like Perry as cover while they exploit low-income communities of color, and how

66

Wall Street is using Blacks like Perry as a weapon in their war against public employees. Perry is a pawn (albeit a well-paid one) in the Wall Street campaign to privatize city and state services and drive down wages and benefits.

Public education advocates do an excellent job of making their case against charter schools. Perry had been playing the martyr on his Twitter page, using the outrage over his tweet to enhance his image as the Black man who is persecuted by whites because he is articulate. Perry painted whites who oppose charter schools as racist. That's an interesting claim from someone who is staunchly anti-union and is working diligently to privatize education, considering the fact that unionized public sector jobs such as teaching comprise the largest source of employment for people of color.

The website politic365.com reported on the importance of public sector jobs to Blacks and Latinos during their coverage of the federal government shutdown.

"Government jobs remain a major source of employment for African Americans and a much smaller but still significant front of work for Latinos. Steven Pitts, an economist and labor policy specialist at the University of California Berkeley, has said repeatedly that government employment—be it at the local, county, state or federal level-together constitute the largest single employer of black men and women living in the United States. Between 2008 and 2010, nearly a quarter of all working African Americans were public sector employees. White workers are employed by a wider variety of industries.

The steady spate of government job cuts since the end of the Great Recession has also contributed mightily to the nation's still critically elevated black and Latino unemployment rates."

The charter school industry has been rocked by a scandal involving Beverly Hall, a champion of school privatization. *Black Agenda Report* commentator Glen Ford reported on the indictment of Hall on charges of racketeering, theft, influencing witnesses, conspiracy and making false statements.

"Hall was a high-rolling player in the nationwide criminal enterprise to destroy public education and replace it with a privately managed, but publicly financed, system. She wound up being hoisted on her own petard, her career wrecked by the same high stakes testing regime that she supported to the hilt, and on whose altar she had sacrificed-fired-90 school principals and countless rank and file teachers. Hall was caught in the minefield of No Child Left Behind and President Obama's Race to the Top, trapped in a web of deceit.

A key purpose of high stakes testing is to 'prove' that conventional public schools are inferior to the charter model, and that incompetent or uncaring teachers and their unions are the heart of the problem. The testing regimen is designed to fail large numbers of schools, so that they can be replaced with charter operations. Beverly Hall carried out a reign of terror in her overwhelmingly Black Atlanta district. Every public school teacher understood the rules: if your students get a low score, you are out the door. In return for torturing her teachers, Superintendent Hall was awarded accolades and goo-gobs of bonus money and lucrative speaking engagements. She was a kingpin of the privatization gang, not too many notches below Michelle Rhee.

But Beverly Hall was trapped in a contradiction. In order to fulfill her commitment to the corporate charter school mob, she had to use her powers as superintendent to disrupt the educational process and make teaching a living hell. However, if she was to further her personal reputation as a school administrator, Hall needed the students in her district to register ever higher scores on the tests. She had to prove, by the numbers, that Race to the Top worked—when clearly, it does not—or wind up in the same trash heap into which she was so eagerly throwing her teachers.

Since the students could not facilitate her crime by actually achieving the impossible scores, Beverly Hall had to rely on the lowly, terrified teachers to work her scam. Thus, she became the Superintendent of Cheating, and is now free on $200,000 bail."

The Walton family, who owns the Wal-Mart chain, has invested huge sums of money in charter schools. The Waltons are notoriously anti-union; they closed a Wal-Mart store in Canada when workers there tried to unionize. Wal-Mart employees in this country who have organized reported vicious retaliation from Wal-Mart management, including termination. Actor Aston Kutcher recently called out Wal-Mart for their low wages, which has resulted in workers being forced to rely on cash assistance. This issue was underscored when a Wal-Mart store in Canton, Ohio started a food drive to benefit employees who can't afford food as the Thanksgiving holiday approaches. *The Huffington Post* reported on a study by members of Congress.

"Walmart wages are so low that many of its workers rely on food stamps and other government aid programs to fulfill their basic needs, a reality that could cost taxpayers as much as $900,000 at just one Walmart Supercenter in Wisconsin, according to a study released by Congressional Democrats.

Though the study assumes that most workers who qualify for the public assistance programs do take advantage of them, it injects a potent data point into a national debate about the minimum wage at a time when many Walmart and fast food workers are mounting strikes in pursuit of higher wages."

Wal-Mart workers nationwide are once again organizing Black Friday strikes to protest the company's poverty wages. It's easy to connect the dots, as the Walton family is making big bucks while they impose their business model on this country's education system.

Public schools have serious problems, including segregation and discriminatory disciplinary rates. However, the charter school industry is not the cure. If charter school advocates and investors truly were acting in the interests of Black and Latino children, they would be working on the local, state and federal level to eradicate poverty. Poverty is a huge factor in the performance of public school students in communities of color. You will rarely even see the word poverty on Perry's Twitter page. The child poverty rate in Hartford is 53%. Blacks and Latinos earn approximately 60 cents for every dollar whites make and possess about 10 cents of net wealth for every dollar whites have. A community resident who posted a response to a Washington Post editorial on Perry's tweet made an insightful observation on how charter school supporters, Democrats and Republicans have avoided talking about poverty and racial economic disparity.

"Just one more example of why, when it comes to the school reform movement, it is necessary to abide by that old truism: if it sounds too good to be true, it probably is. I just came back from a meeting in DC where I heard House and Senate committee staffers, both Democrat and Republican, blather about school reform. Of course, none of them had any actual experience in education. So depressing. No one actually wants to try to understand the effects of poverty on children, their brain development, and the really long and hard work required to overcome them (or why schools cannot single handedly solve the social pathologies arising from extreme income disparity). Instead, both D's and R's spout their magic one-size-fits-all solutions: vouchers, charters, privatization, or whatever. They just want to declare victory and move on—until the problem comes back around again."

I have presented facts which show that school privatizers will only exacerbate racial and class inequity in this country. Steve Perry is a megalomaniacal, profiteering workplace bully, and he should be held accountable for his behavior. However, public school advocates should not allow themselves to become so consumed by their justifiable anger toward this man that they lose sight of the big picture. The community must be educated about Perry's puppet masters, who are using racialized politics and parents' understandable desire to see their children prosper as a means of undermining democracy, rolling back the gains of workers and turning education into just another profitable commodity for a corporate state.

Perry fired up his Twitter spin machine as he denied both the effects of poverty on children and the tremendous profits being generated by the charter school industry. Perry totally avoided any discussion of the racist impact of his repugnant attack on public sector jobs, the largest source of employment for Black men and women living in this country. Perry declared that citing the need to eradicate poverty as a component of improving Black and Latino students' school performance "hurts kids". Perry said, "Using the poverty argument to explain failure implies that poor people are less intelligent or less capable of learning. That's offensive." Perry's Wall Street masters have obviously coached him in the art of using a wall of words to respond to facts that they don't like, which provides them with cover to pursue their right-wing corporatist agenda.

A report by National Public Radio (NPR) on the effect of poverty on children in Philadelphia examined the impact of economic conditions on a child's ability to learn.

"Studies show that in some cases, kids living in poverty are more than two years behind their privileged counterparts. They're more likely to have fewer books in the home, have more health problems and miss more school days. Many kids come to school hungry, and then they can't focus and learn.

"They can't concentrate as well, and children who are food insecure don't perform as well on math and language arts tests. They don't do as well in school", says Mariana Chilton, director of the Center for Hunger-Free Communities at Drexel University's School of Public Health.

Chilton says that at the height of the Great Recession, nearly half of all families with kids in this city reported 'food hardship'—or increased hunger. She says the research is overwhelming: Poverty and hunger undermine children's cognitive, social and emotional development.

'They also have a hard time getting along with their peers and with their teachers,' she says, 'and so it's strongly related to how well a child can do in school.'

Some parents in the swaths of concentrated poverty in North and West Philadelphia consistently don't have enough (money) for food, heat, rent, running water or electricity. That often means their kids can't do homework, think or read in a comfortable place.

Neighborhood violence and crime only add to their sense of vulnerability."

Contrary to Perry's preposterous claim, no one is saying that these children are stupid. The premise of the NPR report is that students who live in areas of concentrated poverty obviously face external stressors, which distract them from learning. Perry's Wall Street masters desperately want to minimize the poverty and racial economic disparity issue, because an examination of socioeconomic factors, which lead to poor school performance, contradicts their claim that "failing" schools and unionized teachers are totally at fault. The response from Perry on Twitter was that poverty is a cop-out used by the left. One of his sycophants added that the poverty issue is too big and addressing it won't help children to perform better in school. In other words, poverty is a problem that Black and Latino kids should get over already; they should ignore minor annoyances like hunger and having no heat or electricity and just hit the books. Perry also tried to distort the facts about the profits that are being generated by the charter school industry. Perry said, "Magnets, charters & online schools make less than 20% of all schools.

Stop trying to pin decades of failure on the urban success stories." Of course, Perry's claim does not address the facts about how much dough Wall Street charter school investors are raking in. *Democracy Now!* co-host Juan Gonzalez exposed the multiple tax breaks that investors exploit and the subsequent huge profits (e.g. doubling a $10 million investment in seven years). The result is public dollars being funneled to Wall Street coffers. Perry's propaganda is a prime example of how Wall Street uses Blacks to exploit low-income urban communities.

The Black Misleadership Class, a term coined by BAR, has zero interest in addressing the root causes of poverty and its socioeconomic ripple effect in Hartford, because that would require holding the Democrats accountable for doing nothing about the issue. These "community leaders" can't hold the Democrats accountable if they continue to act as stooges for the party. Connecticut Voices for Children reported on the latest poverty statistics from the US Census. "Estimates of poverty rates varied significantly across Connecticut's cities: Bridgeport (25.3%), Danbury (9.3%), Hartford (38.0%), New Britain (24.1%), New Haven (26.1%), Norwalk (10.3%), Stamford (7.7%), and Waterbury (24.9%). The percentage of children under 18 in poverty in Connecticut cities was also reported for Bridgeport (37.6%), Danbury (11.0 %), Hartford (53.1%), New Britain (31.0%), New Haven (37.9%), Norwalk (13.0%), Stamford (9.7%), and Waterbury (40.0%)." My challenge to Hartford nonprofits such as A Better Way Foundation (ABWF) is to take on poverty and its accompanying issues, including Black/Latino unemployment, racial economic disparity and police containment of low-income communities of color. Blacks and Latinos earn about 60 cents for every dollar whites make, while they possess 10 cents of net wealth for every dollar whites have. There have been over 200 homicides in Hartford during the past decade. Poverty is a root cause of gun violence in this city.

Unemployment engulfs the Black community. Dixon talked about the refusal of the Black political class to speak up about this issue, especially since the beginning of Barack Obama's presidency. "For as
72

long as the stats have been kept, since well before the enforcement of the Voting Rights Act and the election of thousands of black faces to offices high and low across the country, black unemployment has never been less than double white unemployment. As recently as the 1970s and 1980s black politicians used to inveigh about fighting for full employment and something they used to call 'a Marshall Plan for the cities' to turn it around. But now, with the numbers and supposed influence of black politicians at an all-time high, addressing black unemployment isn't just off the table, it's somewhere out of the building. Both catastrophic black unemployment and the silence of the Black Misleadership Class on the issue have been normal for a good while now.

"Whenever the general unemployment rate drops a tenth or two of a percent nowadays, the talking heads at MSNBC and other outfits whose job is cheerleading for this administration fall over themselves to praise this president and his administration for their wise and far-seeing economic leadership. That's normal as well. But underneath those small reductions in unemployment is something ugly, something that's becoming another new normal.

Incremental reductions in unemployment, now more than ever before, seem to be driven by people giving up the job search as hopeless, people dropping out of the labor market to do whatever it is poor people do when they can't find work on the books. This has routinely become a large part of current reductions in unemployment, a new and disturbing normal in this, the supposed age of black political empowerment. If this were true under a white Republican, our black political leaders would be up in arms, at least long enough to mobilize us to vote one of their own into office. But in this, the age of the first black president, at what we are told is the pinnacle of black political power, is a new age, and there is a new normal."

Year after year, the poverty issue in this state is swept under the rug, while superficial political gestures such as a small increase in the woefully insufficient minimum wage are passed off by the Democrats as an example of their commitment to helping the poor. In November 2013 fast food workers nationwide staged strikes, demanding a $15 per hour minimum wage and the right to unionize without retaliation. Wal-Mart workers organized Black Friday strikes to protest their poverty wages. This growing revolt by oppressed workers should be supported by the

Democrats through comprehensive public policy initiatives. "Community leaders" aren't advocating for low-income communities of color; they're containing these neighborhoods by passing watered down legislation, which gives Black and Latinos the illusion of progress.

It's time for the Black Misleadership Class in Hartford to act in the interests of communities of color; grow a spine and a conscience. Speak out and organize to combat Black/Latino unemployment, racial economic disparity and police containment of low-income communities of color. Hold the Democrats accountable for ignoring structural racism. Talk about the fact that neither Malloy nor Obama have given a speech about poverty during their time in office. Stop apologizing for a president whose record clearly reflects a total disregard for the Black community, which has provided him with overwhelming support. Obama has publicly endorsed New York Police Department commissioner Ray Kelly, a staunch proponent of the racist stop and frisk policy, for the vacant Secretary of Homeland Security position. Stop and frisk opponents have warned that Kelly will attempt to implement stop and frisk on the federal level if he gets the Homeland Security job. In December 2013, Obama and Attorney General Eric Holder won a court decision, which will result in the continued imprisonment of thousands of Blacks who were sentenced under the federal crack cocaine law.

BAR's Dixon weighed in on this story. "First, it was the Obama-Holder Justice Department which first refused to retroactively reduce the unfair crack cocaine sentences under the law the president signed and the attorney general praised. Secondly, it was the Obama-Holder Justice Department, which went to court to keep those people in prison. They lost when the trial judge ruled they should be released. And third, the same Justice Department run by the same first black attorney general under the first black president appealed the order to reduce those sentences, instead seeking and obtaining yesterday's ruling by the Sixth Circuit Court of Appeals.

"On mass incarceration in general and the reduction of these unfair, unjust sentences, our first black president and attorney general are howling hypocrites, saying one thing and doing another. Their hypocrisy is enabled by traditional black civil rights organizations like the NAACP-LDF, who refuse to make a political issue out of Obama's and Holder's hypocrisy. The 'civil rights' establishment is in a bind. They claim to oppose mass incarceration and the prison state, although they've only just learned the phrase 'mass incarceration' and cannot fix their lips to say 'prison state.'

But since their first priority is boosting the political fortunes and careers of their peers in the black political elite, who we affectionately call our Black Misleadership Class, they are unable to call the devil in charge of mass incarceration by his name, if that devil has a black face."

February 2014

Barack Obama gave his State of the Union address on the eve of the one-year anniversary of the murder of Hadiya Pendleton. Obama talked about gun violence in malls, movie theaters and Sandy Hook but did not mention low-income communities of color. Hadiya was shot in Chicago, Obama's hometown, days after performing at his inauguration. Obama didn't mention her either. I must give the power structure in this country credit. When they selected Obama to run for president they knew what they were doing. No matter how many times Obama betrays Black people; they still worship him like a god.

Obama can sign the *National Defense Authorization Act* into law, allowing citizens to be thrown into jail without charges or evidence, go to court with Eric Holder to keep the federal crack cocaine sentencing amendment from being imposed retroactively (keeping thousands of Blacks in jail), and Black people still love him. White liberals and leftists are no better. Liberals support this imperialist warmonger as long as he addresses some of their pet issues. Leftists try to get Blacks to join campaigns such as Occupy Wall Street, but won't reciprocate by supporting Black led mass movements. The left is a joke.

March 2014

President Obama spoke at Central Connecticut State University as part of his campaign to raise the federal minimum wage to $10.10 an hour. Last Sunday the Fox CT Capitol Report program included a debate on the proposed minimum wage hike, following Gov. Dannel Malloy's comments to the national media on this issue. Malloy, who two years ago would not support a minimum wage increase in this state even after the bill was gutted, spoke with election year gusto to the national press about the need to raise the minimum wage to $10.10. City Council President Shawn Wooden and Democratic Party strategist Tanya Meck repeated the party line that raising the minimum wage to $10.10 will lift people out of poverty, which is a lie. The poverty line is based on a formula from the 1950's, which used the cost of purchasing food items considered staples at the time to set the poverty threshold.

An updated study of poverty by David Cooper, economic analyst at the Economic Policy Institute (EPI), finds that a single mother with one child would need a wage of $48,000 per year to maintain a "modest, secure standard of living." This study supports the argument for a $15.00 minimum wage.

Capitol Report panelist Jodi Latina, a Republican, said that she supports raising the minimum wage to $15.00 in exchange for tax breaks for small businesses. My problem with Latina's concept is that the current definition of "small business" is bogus. A 2012 report on Bush-era tax cuts by Rebecca Theiss, a federal budget policy analyst for EPI, explains this deception.

"The way that small businesses are defined for tax purposes has been put to use in this debate in a manner that is misleading. The default definition of 'small business' in the tax debate can often identify many entities that are neither small nor even businesses. Claims that raising the top two marginal tax rates will stifle small business growth are unfounded, largely relying on overly broad and misleading definitions of small businesses. Policies intended to support actual small (and new) businesses should focus on expansionary fiscal policy (for example, through fiscal stimulus) and a stronger social safety net. If anything, reductions in the top tax rate have been associated with an increasing concentration of income at the top of the income distribution and not necessarily associated with productivity growth."

I would support Latina's compromise after the definition of "small business" is amended to apply to businesses that are truly small. Seattle Mayor Ed Murray, a Democrat, is pushing for a $15.00 minimum wage in his city. If the Democrats were sincere about lifting people out of poverty, they would support the Fight for 15 movement. The party, which claims to be a friend of the poor, is just using poverty as a political football. Obama and Malloy, who both have avoided talking about poverty since they were elected, are now tossing the word around every day. Don't believe the hype, voters.

In November 2013, Mayor Pedro Segarra accepted Kennard Ray's withdrawal from the Deputy Chief of Staff position; following Segarra's announcement that he hired Ray, sensationalized corporate media reports about Ray's legal history dominated the local news cycle. A few days later Segarra issued this statement:

> "Sadly, we must accept Mr. Kennard Ray's withdrawal for the position of Deputy Chief of Staff after learning information that was not initially disclosed. Mr. Ray is a qualified individual with solid references from former supervisors and community leaders. However, public servants, especially those in leadership positions, must be held to a higher standard."

On March 7, 2014, the Hartford Internal Audit Commission released their report on Segarra's hiring practices. The report found that Segarra had hired several appointees without any kind of screening; no background check, no drug tests, no job application, nothing. Let's just cut to the chase, as it is pretty obvious how Segarra got himself in this jam.

First, the Segarra administration announced Ray's hiring prior to performing a background check. The corporate media then aired sensationalized reports about Ray's legal history. I contacted Maribel La Luz, Segarra's communications director, after the story broke. La Luz said Segarra acknowledged that his office made a mistake by announcing the hire prior to conducting the background check. Ray had done nothing wrong. The Hartford Ban the Box (BTB) ordinance stipulates that a city job applicant does not have to discuss their legal history during the interview process.

The whole point of BTB is to provide a level playing field for formerly incarcerated individuals and others with legal histories.

When the corporate media confronted Segarra with their findings about Ray, he had two choices. He could have admitted that his office jumped the gun by announcing Ray's hiring, but that Ray came highly recommended from the Connecticut Working Families Party, where he was the organization's legislative and political director. After checking out Ray's legal history, Segarra could have cited BTB as the reason why he was going to stick with his decision to hire Ray, who has clearly turned his life around. Segarra could have talked about how BTB was crafted specifically for individuals such as Ray, who should be held up as an example to young men of color in Hartford of what can happen if they strive to overcome their past mistakes. Segarra could have cited the city's Black/Latino unemployment rate as a reason why BTB is so important to disenfranchised young males in urban neighborhoods.

Instead, Segarra hit the panic button. He allowed Ray to withdraw from the position. The official story is that Segarra did not ask Ray to give up the job, but Segarra clearly wanted Ray to go away. Ray did not publicly discuss Segarra and was the focal point of a City Hall rally where activists called for his reinstatement. Now Segarra looks like the ultimate hypocrite since the audit report findings have been released. Most elected officials are so obsessed with playing the political game that their actions in situations such as this defy common sense. Segarra threw Ray under the bus for the sake of political expediency. Now Segarra's the one who's wearing self-inflicted tire marks. He can't talk his way out of this one; it is what it is. I contacted La Luz via email to get Segarra's response to the auditor's report and the obvious contradiction of his explanation for un-hiring Ray. I did not get a response. The simple fact is that the "higher standard" Segarra used as an excuse to give Ray the boot obviously does not apply to Segarra's cronies. Shameful.

Segarra squandered a golden opportunity to show that his support of BTB wasn't just lip service. He had egg on his face the size of an omelet. None of this was surprising to me. This debacle is an example of why this city, state and country are in the toilet. Politicians are serving their masters in the ruling class and themselves, instead of serving the people. Their primary objective is to look like they're doing the right thing, instead of actually doing what's right. I think it's time for Segarra to hold himself to a "higher standard." Let's see if "community leaders" such as ABWF Policy Director LaResse Harvey, a Segarra ally, and Democratic Party politicians such as Rep. Brandon McGee who say that they "Stand with Kennard" will ever speak up. There wasn't a peep from Harvey or McGee on their social media pages about the audit report and its obvious connection to Ray.

Mayor Segarra's March 10 State of the City Address did not mention the word poverty once, even though Hartford annually has one of the highest poverty rates in the United States. Segarra also did not mention the serious problem of Black and Latino employment. Segarra talked a lot about improving public safety, but the lack of economic opportunity in low-income communities of color is obviously a root cause of gun violence in this city

If Black and brown people can't find jobs, they will turn to the street economy (drug trade), where violence is an occupational hazard. Reading the text of Segarra's address made me feel the loss of Jackson, Mississippi Mayor Chokwe Lumumba even more. Lumumba died suddenly last month at the age of 66, eight months into his first term. Lumumba, a Democrat who was a disciple of Fannie Lou Hamer and Malcolm X, was truly this country's most revolutionary mayor. Lumumba talked about participatory democracy and economic human rights, words that you will not hear come out of Segarra's mouth. Lumumba was a proponent of using employee owned cooperatives to boost economic development. This model has been successful in Massachusetts, California, Ohio, and Oregon, among other states. Despite Lumumba's death, plans went forward for Jackson to host the Jackson Rising New Economies Conference May 2-4. Lumumba's son, Chokwe Antar Lumumba, became a candidate in the April 8 mayoral special election; his plan was to continue the movement that was led by his father.

Following Lumumba's death, *Democracy Now!* aired a 2013 interview with Lumumba following his victory in the Jackson mayoral election.

AMY GOODMAN: In our last segment today, we end in Mississippi.

MEDGAR EVERS: Don't shop for anything on Capitol Street. Let's let the merchants down on Capitol Street feel the economic pinch. Let me say this to you. I had one merchant to call me, and he said, "I want you to know that I've talked to my national office today, and they want me to tell you that we don't need nigger business." These are stores that help to support the White Citizens' Council, the council that is dedicated to keeping you and I second-class citizens. Now, finally, ladies and gentlemen, we'll be demonstrating here until freedom comes to Negroes here in Jackson, Mississippi.

JUAN GONZÁLEZ: Those are the words of the civil rights leader Medgar Evers in May 1963. Just a few weeks later, on June 13th, 1963, Evers was shot dead by a Klansman in his driveway in Jackson, Mississippi. Medgar Evers was the state's first NAACP field secretary. He was killed just hours after President John F. Kennedy delivered a nationally televised speech in which he proposed the Civil Rights Act of 1964. At the time of his death, he was carrying NAACP T-shirts that read "Jim Crow Must Go." Commemorations are being held this month to the mark the 50th anniversary of the assassination of Medgar Evers.

Well, Jackson, Mississippi is back in the news this week after veteran Black Nationalist and civil rights attorney Chokwe Lumumba was elected mayor of the city. He describes himself as a "Fannie Lou Hamer Democrat," and he surprised many political observers by winning the Democratic primary last month, despite being outspent five to one. Lumumba then easily won the general election on Tuesday. Over the past four decades, Lumumba has been deeply involved in numerous political and legal campaigns. As an attorney, his clients have included former Black Panther Assata Shakur and the late hip-hop artist Tupac Shakur.

Two years ago, he helped win the release of the Scott sisters, two young women from Mississippi who received double life sentences for a robbery that netted them $11. They were released after 16 years in prison.

AMY GOODMAN: As a political organizer, Chokwe Lumumba served for years as vice president of the Republic of New Afrika, an organization which advocated for "an independent predominantly black government" in the southeastern United States and reparations for slavery. He also helped found the National Black Human Rights Coalition and the Malcolm X Grassroots Movement and worked with the Jackson Human Rights Coalition to help pressure the state of Mississippi to retry the person who murdered Medgar Evers. In 2009, Lumumba was elected to the Jackson City Council. Chokwe Lumumba, mayor-elect of Jackson, Mississippi, joins us now from Jackson.

Welcome to *Democracy Now!* Congratulations on your victory. What do you attribute it to, after all these years? And why did you decide, from going—being involved with grassroots organizing for so many decades, to get involved with electoral politics?

CHOKWE LUMUMBA: Thank you for having me, and a shout out and thank you to your listening audience.

I attribute the victory that we had this last week to the people, the people of Jackson, who were more than ready to have leadership that was forward-looking and ready to raise Jackson to a different level of development, ready to embrace the ideas that all government should do the most to protect the human rights of the people in that jurisdiction. And we were very pleased with the out-coming of people to vote, with their participation, and with their continued support.

We have—I am now running for the mayor—or have, in fact, won the mayor of the city of Jackson, because I think it's necessary. We are a population here now in the need of a lot of development. Development is one of the tracks or one of the roads to human rights and to the recognition of human rights, especially our economic human rights. And some of that development is going to take the kind of leadership and the kind of consistency that we had in the struggle for voting rights and other kinds of rights, which has been unique to our history.

JUAN GONZÁLEZ: Well, Chokwe Lumumba, I'm not sure that many people around the country understand the symbolic—the symbolism of Jackson, Mississippi, as a center of racism and racial oppression over the—really, over centuries. The very name of the city—the city was named after Andrew Jackson by the white settlers when Jackson in 1820 was able, as Indian commissioner, to basically pressure the Choctaw

Indians to give up 13 million acres of land and move to Oklahoma in the Treaty of Doak's Stand. And that's why the white settlers named the city after Jackson, because of his success at ethnic cleansing. And then, of course, its history throughout the—through slavery and Jim Crow.

How did this change occur? How were you able to put this together, this coalition to be elected, given your history as a radical and an activist in the black liberation struggle?

CHOKWE LUMUMBA: I think it's a tribute to our consistency. It's a tribute to our refusal to say that we would bow to the oppression that was around us. It's a tremendous story of our people. You talked about Medgar Evers, but the continuation since Medgar Evers of fighting against oppression, fighting against economic oppression, fighting against the kinds of things which have surfaced in our decades, which are similar to the kinds of things you cite in the distant history of Jackson, we have been persistent. And with that persistence, see, our people now are ready to move to a different level of development.

And I should say that people should take a note of Jackson, because we have suffered some of the worst kinds of abuses in history, but we're about to make some advances and some strides in the development of human rights and the protection of human rights that I think have not been seen in other parts of the country. And I want to caution folks that we've got to be careful now when we talk about any one particular place in the United States. All over, we've seen intense oppression. I'm from Detroit, initially, and we've seen a lot of oppression there, historically as well as currently. New York has certainly seen its share. Washington, D.C., has seen its share. So, we don't want to be like people on different plantations arguing about which plantation is worse. What we have to do is to correct the whole problem, and we're about correcting the problem here in Jackson. And we're going to be inviting people to come here, and people want to come here, in order to participate in the struggle forward. And this is not a phony struggle. We're not just putting a false face on—we tell you we've had real problems, and we still have some real problems, but we're solving these problems, and we're going to try to solve a lot of them through economic development, which is going to involve the masses of the people, not just a few folks.

AMY GOODMAN: Can you tell us about your platform and the Jackson-Kush Plan?

CHOKWE LUMUMBA: Well, the platform is to advance the ideas of development and to advance the ideas of empowerment of the populations which exist in the city of Jackson, specifically. We have a population, the demographic here, 80 percent of the population is black, about 20 percent is white. And we have with us brothers and sisters who are of East Indian origin, as well as some Asian and some Hispanic folks coming in. Our slogan was "One city, one aim, one destiny." And the idea is to blend these populations into a struggle forward.

There are some people historically who have always tried to separate the populations and to have a certain portion of the population oppress the rest of the population. We're not going to tolerate that. We're going to move ahead. We're going to let everyone participate in this movement forward. We're going to invite everyone to participate in this movement forward.

And we have formed like a people's assembly, that's key to what we've done here, where we have—every three months, the population can come out and participate in an open forum to say what's on their mind. They can come out and learn some of the problems that the city is facing and some of the solutions that some of the problem solvers are supposed to be offering. And this will bring about more public education and political education to the population of the city, make our population more prepared to be motivated and organized in order to participate in the changes which must occur in the city of Jackson in order to move it forward. We say the people must decide. "Educate, motivate, organize." That's the slogan we use for it.

JUAN GONZÁLEZ: And in terms of the city council, as well, in Jackson, were there other folks who ran on a platform with you? And do you expect much difficulty in getting measures passed through your local city council?

CHOKWE LUMUMBA: Well, no, no, no. I think we're going to do quite well. And let me say that there's only one other person who actually ran from the same bases of organization that I come from, which is the Malcolm X Grassroots Movement. She was not successful in winning election, but we have really a pretty good city council—I mean, a very good city council, I think, has come into place. We've got three young men on the city council who are in their thirties, bright, forward-thinking, very progressive. We have an older brother who is an old school teacher, and he is a person who I think is going to make a contribution to what we're doing. We have a person from Ward 7, who is a white Democrat, and she has always been consistent in supporting a forward movement. And we have one Republican on the city council from Ward 1, and he is a person who I think understands the political climate and is going to move forward, too.

AMY GOODMAN: Chokwe Lumumba—

CHOKWE LUMUMBA: So I think we're going to be all right.

AMY GOODMAN: We just have 30 seconds. I wanted to ask you quickly about the news in this past month that Assata Shakur has been the first woman to be placed on—

by the FBI on the terrorists list. You represented her decades ago. Your thoughts? They've also increased the bounty for her—she took refuge in Cuba—to $2 million.

CHOKWE LUMUMBA: Well, I've always felt that Assata Shakur was wrongfully convicted, so she shouldn't be on a wanted list at all. She never should have been in prison. She was actually shot herself and wounded and paralyzed at the time that the person who she was convicted of killing was shot.

So she obviously couldn't have shot him. And she also was arrested, which caused the incident for about eight different charges which she later was found not guilty of or were dismissed. So I think it's unfortunate. Assata Shakur, I believe, will historically be proven to be a hero of our times, just like—

AMY GOODMAN: Chokwe Lumumba, we're going to have to leave it there.

CHOKWE LUMUMBA: Thank you.

AMY GOODMAN: Mayor-elect of Jackson, Mississippi. Thanks for joining us.

April 2014

In 1993, the rap group Wu Tang Clan released their classic single, "C.R.E.A.M. (Cash Rules Everything Around Me)." This is definitely the case in the world of politics. On April 2, the U.S. Supreme Court ruled on *McCutcheon v. FEC*. Plaintiff Shaun McCutcheon, the founder and CEO of Coalmont Electrical Development Corporation and major donor to the Republican Party, wanted to exceed the limits on donations to federal candidates. On June 22, 2012 McCutcheon and Republican National Committee filed a suit against the Federal Elections Commission in the U.S. District Court for the District of Columbia, obviously expecting a favorable ruling based on the legal precedent of the 2010 SCOTUS (Supreme Court of the United States) decision on *Citizens United v. Federal Election Commission*. However, on September 28, 2012 the court granted the FEC's motion to toss out the complaint. McCutheon and the RNC filed an appeal to the Supreme Court on October 9, 2012; the court agreed to hear the case on February 19, 2013.

The SCOTUS voted 5-4 to strike down limits on the amount of money that a person could contribute to federal candidates, parties and PACs (political action committees). The court ruled that limits on donations are unconstitutional. Chief Justice John Roberts wrote in the legal opinion that "The right to participate in democracy through political contributions is protected by the First Amendment, but that right is not absolute. Our cases have held that Congress may regulate campaign contributions to protect against corruption or the appearance of corruption. See, e.g., *Buckley v. Valeo*, 424 U.S. 1, 26-27 (1976) (per curiam). Congress may target only a specific type of corruption—'quid pro quo' corruption... Spending large sums of money in connection with elections, but not in connection with an effort to control the exercise of an officeholder's official duties, does not give rise to quid pro quo corruption. Nor does the possibility that an individual who spends large sums may garner 'influence over or access to' elected officials or political parties." The absurd influence of money in politics was given even more juice, courtesy of the highest court in the land.

Malloy took a victory lap in April after the Connecticut General Assembly passed a minimum wage bill. Malloy was cheered loudly as he signed the bill into law. However, the fine print will delay the increase to $10.10 until 2017. Imagine how you would feel if your boss said, "Congratulations, I'm giving you a raise. You just have to wait three years." The increase, which was insufficient to begin with, will be further watered down by 2017, due to inflation. Liberals of course hailed the bill's passage as a great victory. Fast food workers nationwide are fighting for a $15.00 minimum wage indexed to inflation. The day after signing the minimum wage bill, Malloy announced that he was running for reelection. Democratic Party politicians such as Majority Leader Rep. Joe Aresimowicz, the party's apologists and union "leaders" told state employees to forget 2011, while they dutifully remind workers of republican Wisconsin Governor Scott Walker's successful war on public employees in the state that is the mecca of unions. The American Federation of Teachers (AFT) CT chapter hosted an event featuring

Wisconsin public teachers, who talked about how Walker stripped their collective bargaining rights. There was no mention on their Facebook page about Malloy's attacks on public school teachers and unions.

The message was clear; public employees better vote for Malloy so a GOP governor doesn't take over. AFT CT supported Clark School parents group. How was AFT CT supposed to hold Malloy accountable for his school privatization campaign while they were simultaneously acting as agents for Malloy's re-election campaign? The memories of the actions of Malloy and the Democrats were still fresh in state workers' minds. Instead of encouraging the rank and file to vote for Malloy, union "leaders" urged workers not to vote for likely Republican challenger Tom Foley.

The 2014 gubernatorial election was a false choice. Both Malloy and Foley are union busters; the only difference is degrees. In 2013, Malloy introduced an anti-teacher, anti-union education bill which was mostly dismantled by the legislature. Malloy is a champion of charter schools, which are a commodity being used in the Wall Street campaign against public employees. The objective of course is to roll back these workers' gains in wages and benefits. The public sector is also the largest employer of Black people. Malloy was killing unions with a thousand paper cuts, while Foley would certainly use a sledgehammer if elected. Liberal activists did not have the guts to offend Malloy by using political action to push him to the left, because they wanted him to support their pet issues. Liberals' refusal to Malloy and the Democrats accountable resulted in worsening conditions for people of color, the working class and vulnerable populations in Connecticut.

Neil Vigdor of the Hearst Media Group reported that Pelto was considering a run for governor. Pelto did not deny the possibility. Malloy's abuse of public employees during his first term caught up with him, as many in this voter bloc embraced Pelto as an alternative. Malloy is the personification of the Democrats' habit of taking liberals/progressives for granted, using the specter of the big, bad Republicans as leverage.

Pelto appeared on the WFSB TV *Face the State* Sunday morning political talk show to discuss his possible candidacy for governor. Pelto said he would decide within the next month if he would enter the race as a Working Families Party or independent candidate. Program host Dennis House and Fox CT Capitol Report panelists, who also discussed Pelto, both avoided any mention of racial economic and criminal justice disparity issues impacting Hartford and other urban areas. I was disturbed to see that Pelto, who had talked about the poverty issue in Connecticut and publicly supported CP's racial profiling bill on his blog, did not mention racial justice issues once during his television appearances. If Pelto ran, would his message continue to be watered down? Would his talking points continue to be directed at white liberals and the Occupy Wall Street crowd? Was Pelto's feud with Malloy really about Malloy not giving Pelto a job in his administration? Pelto did say early in Malloy's term that he would accept a position if it was offered. Pelto was on the same page with his archrival Malloy, who did not discuss racial disparities during his Grab the Black Vote Tour in March; happy-go-lucky WYBC-FM DJ Juan Castillo of course did not dare ask any of those types of questions when Malloy appeared on his show. It appeared that even if Pelto entered the race, communities of color would continue to be faced with an election where no candidates were looking out for their interests. Likely Republican challenger Foley set up an urban-issues "think tank." This was obviously an election year scam, but Foley nonetheless was the only one of the current or possible gubernatorial candidates who has actually said the words "urban agenda."

It was telling that Patrick Scully, one of Malloy's media goons who wrote a hit piece on Pelto, is a privatizer. Scully referred to Pelto as a "union stooge." Isn't Malloy supposed to be the friend of organized labor? Unions provided Malloy with his narrow margin of victory over Foley in 2010. Union delegates were trying to convince members to give

Malloy a second term. Malloy appeared to be courting the right-leaning independents that he and his GOP opponent would be fighting over. Team Malloy had launched "Operation Lonesome" Rhodes as a pre-emptive strike against Pelto, who had been a huge thorn in Malloy's side. Pelto and public school teachers wasted time with their fixation on Perry, instead of educating residents in communities of color about the racist agenda behind privatization. The public sector is the largest employer of Black people.

May 2014

Days before the end of the 2014 legislative session on May 6, the Connecticut General Assembly passed a state budget bill, cobbled together by Malloy's administration and majority Democratic legislators after poor tax revenues blew a $300 million dollar hole in the budget. *The Connecticut Mirror* reported that there would be a built in $52 million dollar hole in the new budget, due to the failure to fund health care benefits that are contractually owed to retiring state prison guards. Tax breaks for teachers and consumers would be "pushed back" (translation: they ain't happening). State jobs would be frozen and eliminated in an effort to save $20 million dollars. *The Mirror* reported, "Gov. Daniel P. Malloy and Democratic legislative leaders announced a tentative budget deal Friday that postpones tax relief for teachers and consumers, repeals the launch of keno and relies on tens of millions of dollars in questionable assumptions about savings. Full details of the agreement—the product of hectic last-minute negotiations to counter shrinking tax revenue projections this week—were not released during a late morning press conference at the Capitol. Malloy's budget director, Office of Policy and Management Secretary Benjamin Barnes, confirmed that the agreement preserves $70 million in new grants to cities and towns, but that it suspends a new, $9 million tax break for municipalities. The deal also cuts about $20 million over several years from a new initiative to shore up the finances of the merged public college and university system. And this year's budget surplus, once projected at $505 million but reduced this week to $43 million, would be deposited in the emergency reserve, commonly known as the Rainy Day Fund."

The Democrats pulled a rabbit out of their hat, inserting in the budget document that they claimed would be $75 million in anticipated revenue from delinquent taxpayers. *The Mirror* reported that the Office of Fiscal Analysis could not vouch for the "Ante Up, the State is Broke and Needs Your Money" plan. "Nonpartisan legislative fiscal analysts not only declined to confirm the estimate, but added that 'we have sought, but not been able to obtain other information to support' the tax department's assertion." This plan was not mentioned at the budget press conference the day before. The Democrats again raided the transportation fund and the tobacco health trust and swiped cash from the so-called surplus. Money meant to finance the state's conversion to Generally Accepted Accounting Principles (GAAP) was also snatched. The Republicans added icing on the cake by introducing a budget, which included a provision to refinance the state's 2009 operating debt to remain in balance. The GOP had previously ridiculed this tactic as a Malloy budget gimmick. Connecticut Voices for Children predicted this debacle in their July 2013 report on the 2014-15 budget.

June 2014

Pelto officially turned the gubernatorial race upside down when he announced his candidacy on June 12 with this press release:

PELTO TO RUN FOR GOVERNOR—WILL CONVERT FROM EXPLORATORY COMMITTEE TO CANDIDATE COMMITTEE FOR GOVERNOR

Former state legislator Jonathan Pelto is announcing that he will be a candidate for Governor this year and that he and his Lt. Governor candidate, Ebony Murphy, will be converting their exploratory committee into a candidate committee for the office of Governor and Lt. Governor of the State of Connecticut.

"Since creating an exploratory committee for Governor a few weeks ago, I have been overwhelmed and incredibly humbled by the positive response I have received," said Pelto, who represented the Town of Mansfield in the Connecticut General Assembly for five terms from 1984 to 1993.

"With the help of volunteers across Connecticut, we are creating a grassroots campaign that can have a profound impact on the 2014 election." Pelto added.

Pelto says his campaign has over 100 volunteers out collecting petition signatures and that they have already collected approximately 2,200 signatures in the past few days. Pelto projected that the number of people collecting signatures will reach nearly 200 people by the end of the week and he is confident that the campaign will reach the 7,500 signatures needed to get on the ballot.

"I said I would only run for governor if I could be a credible candidate," Pelto said. "Having spent the last several weeks talking with voters across the political spectrum and with people willing to volunteer to help with our campaign, I am confident that we can utilize this opportunity to focus the electorate's attention on a number of important issues such as a fair and equitable state tax system, adequate funding and support for our teachers, students, parents and public schools, and an economic development strategy that is focused on supporting small businesses and creating real jobs rather than on giving out millions of dollars in Corporate welfare."

Pelto added, "As a third-party candidate for Governor, I recognize that the campaign system is rigged to make getting elected as difficult as possible, but I see a clear path forward and I am indeed running to win."

Some key issues the Pelto campaign plans to highlight include:

• Middle Income Tax Reform: Connecticut's middle class are already overburdened with taxes and in order to close the projected $1.3 billion budget deficit and maintain vital services, the income tax must be made more progressive by increasing the income tax rate on those making more than $1 million.

• Ending Corporate Welfare: Connecticut must close corporate tax loopholes and end Governor Malloy's "First Five" corporate welfare program that has given hundreds of millions of public funds to successful companies, essentially picking winners and losers in the private, free enterprise system.

• Supporting Connecticut's Public Schools: Gov. Malloy's 2012 education reform legislation proposed eliminating teacher tenure and unilaterally repealing collective bargaining for teachers in "turnaround" schools. Malloy's decision to hand Connecticut's public education system over to Charter School advocate, now

90

Commissioner of Education Stefan Pryce, has ushered in an unprecedented attack on teachers, local school districts and the professionalism of the State Department of Education. Rather than attacking them, it is time that the state provides Connecticut's public school students, families, teachers and administrators with the resources and training support that they need to ensure that all our children have an opportunity to receive a high quality education. This effort would include reaching a settlement on the CCEJF V. Rell School funding lawsuit rather than try to get it dismissed as the Malloy administration has done as this provides the best vehicle for adopting a fair school funding formula that provides public schools with the resources they need while reducing the burden on the local property tax.

• Rejection of Common Core and Common Core standardized testing scheme: Rather than placing further burdens on school systems, teachers and students brought on by the significant financial and time demands created by the implementation of the Common Core Standards and its Common Core standardized testing scheme, it is a time to devote greater time and energy to actual school work and instruction rather than teaching to the test.

• Restoring Support for Connecticut's Public Colleges and Universities: Despite claims to the contrary, the Malloy Administration has pushed through the deepest budget cuts in state history at Connecticut's public colleges and universities. At UConn, for example, prior to Malloy taking office, the Connecticut state budget accounted for 33% of the total cost required to operate the University of Connecticut. Three years into his term and after his record budget cuts at UConn, Connecticut State University and at the State's Community Colleges, the state now only provides 27.9% of the amount necessary to keep UConn operating. As a direct result of Malloy's budget cuts, the burden on students and their families have INCREASED by 17.3%. It is time for the state to restore its commitment to Connecticut students and families by supporting our public colleges and universities to make a high quality college education more affordable and accessible for everyone.

• Renewed Emphasis on Government Transparency: State government under the Malloy Administration has become increasingly secretive resulting in the loss of public accountability and an increase in the use of no-bid contracts. It is time to return Connecticut' oversight commissions including the State Ethics Commission, the State Freedom of Information Commission and the State Elections Enforcement Commission to their independent status and provide them with the resources they need.

Paid for by Pelto 2014, Ted Strelez, Treasurer, Christine Ladd, Deputy Treasurer, Approved by Jonathan Pelto

Ebony Murphy—a 31-year-old Black teacher who grew up in Hartford—was obviously being counted on to enhance Pelto's appeal to the disgruntled public school teachers and the urban community.

When asked by reporters about the points Pelto made in his announcement Malloy said, "I don't need to respond to what Jonathan says."

A glaring omission from Pelto's platform was an urban agenda, which meant that Foley remained the only gubernatorial candidate who publicly acknowledged low-income communities of color. Pelto's silence ensured that the plight of black and brown communities would remain invisible during the election. Foley's "urban think tank" could only be viewed as a gimmick, considering the GOP's overwhelming whiteness and their history of totally ignoring the socioeconomic issues which affect urban neighborhoods, such as poverty, unemployment, racial wage/wealth disparity, mass incarceration and felony disenfranchisement. Well, that's not totally true. Republican Congressman Paul Ryan had this to say,

"We have got this tailspin of culture, in our inner cities in particular, of men not working and just generations of men not even thinking about working or learning the value and the culture of work, and so there is a real culture problem here that has to be dealt with… you need to get involved, you need to get involved yourself, whether through a good mentor program or some religious charity, whatever it is to make a difference. And that's how we resuscitate our culture."

Ryan is clearly a student of the Southern Strategy, which was explained by GOP strategist Lee Atwater.

"You start out in 1954 by saying, 'Nigger, nigger, nigger.' By 1968, you can't say 'nigger'—that hurts you, backfires. So you say stuff like, uh, forced busing, states' rights, and all that stuff, and you're getting so abstract. Now, you're talking about cutting taxes, and all these things you're talking about are totally economic things and a byproduct of them is, blacks get hurt worse than whites. 'We want to cut this,' is much more abstract than even the busing thing, uh, and a hell of a lot more abstract than 'Nigger, nigger'."

Ryan launched a so-called War on Poverty, which consisted of shredding the remaining strands of the safety net; his plan was Atwater's wet dream. Ryan's House budget was a continuation of his war on the poor. The Center on Budget broke it down. "For several years now, Chairman Ryan (R-WI) has proposed annual budgets that would deeply cut programs for the poor. The Ryan budgets have consistently secured between 60 and 67 percent of their budget cuts from programs for low to moderate income people."

Pelto needed 7500 petition signatures by August 6 to appear on the ballot as the "Education and Democracy Party" candidate; he told the Hartford Courant that a squad of 200 volunteers had already collected 2200 signatures since he launched a petition drive the previous week. Pelto told the Hartford Courant his thoughts on Democratic Party critics who warned that Pelto would be throwing the election to the Republicans. Malloy and Foley were tied in the most recent poll. "That's the Democratic process. We are better off as a nation, a state, and a society when you have more candidates bringing in more issues. Democracy has repercussions. What we're going to witness here in Connecticut are the effects of a democratic system." The problem is that Pelto didn't bring in "more issues" regarding low-income people of color. He also engaged in tokenism by naming a Black woman as his running mate. Pelto was behaving exactly like his archrival Malloy. He was obviously only interested in being a gubernatorial election alternative for white liberals. Pelto had said that he wouldn't run if he couldn't win; that position morphed into a broad definition of being a "credible" candidate who would provide an alternative perspective on major issues. The Democrats whined about Pelto being selfish, but they clearly brought his candidacy on themselves by continuing to embrace a center-right, corporatist agenda.

Connecticut Mirror political reporter Mark Pazniokas laid out the challenge Pelto would face as a third-party candidate. "General-election ballot access is relatively easy: He must gather 7,500 signatures of registered voters, less than required to qualify for a Democratic or

Republican primary. But qualifying for public financing requires raising $250,000 and gathering 111,000 signatures, and the payoff is smaller: one-third of the $6.5 million available to major-party nominees. 'As a third-party candidate for Governor, I recognize that the campaign system is rigged to make being elected as difficult as possible, but I see a clear path forward and I am indeed running to win,' Pelto said. If Pelto really wanted to win, he would have been proactive about reaching out to the underserved, overlooked urban community. The last time we spoke, Pelto promised that he would adopt an urban agenda the same way that a lazy husband promises that he will take out the garbage. Disappointing, but not surprising..."

The possibility of a four-way race for governor loomed as Tea Party member Joe Visconti collected petition signatures in his bid to run as an independent. If Visconti's bid was successful, the GOP gubernatorial nominee would also face the possibility of a third party candidate siphoning votes. The Tea Party was still basking in the glow of economic professor David Brat's shocking June 10 victory over House Speaker Eric Cantor in the Virginia primary. Cantor became the first sitting House majority leader to lose a primary since 1899, when the position was created. Cantor raised $5,447,290 compared to Brat's $206,663 total, a mammoth 40-1 spread; a post-election analysis revealed that Cantor had spent more money eating at steakhouses ($168,637) than Brat spent on his entire campaign ($122,793). While Cantor would now have plenty of time to check out lunch specials, his colleagues had to deal with the repercussions of a defeat that shook the GOP to its core. Meanwhile the Democratic/Republican duopoly in Connecticut was being challenged from the Left and the Right by Pelto and Visconti, respectively. Foley faced a three-way GOP primary against former state Senator John McKinney and Danbury Mayor Mark Boughton, a candidate with a history of inflammatory remarks about immigrants. The long anticipated Malloy vs. Foley II sequel was being altered by a Democratic Party dissident and three conservatives who obviously didn't get the memo about Foley's scheduled coronation.

94

As the Connecticut gubernatorial race heated up, a firestorm erupted in Hartford that underscored how arrogant and out of touch the Democrats are. On June 4, Segarra and City Council President Shawn Wooden announced a deal to bring the New Britain Rock Cats, the Double A farm team of the Major League Baseball Minnesota Twins, to the capital city. The deal included a plan to build a $60 million stadium downtown. Community residents were outraged. The "leaders" of one of the poorest cities in the country were about to commit an act of fiscal insanity. Debra Cohen of Activate CT, a group of local activists, reported on the raucous June 9 city council meeting, which followed the Rock Cats announcement:

"I arrived at the Hartford City Council meeting too late last night to sign up to speak on the Rock Cats stadium plan but I was there to hear some great testimony from others. The overwhelming majority of people who I heard speak were in opposition to building the stadium and their reasons included the following: Lack of transparency in the process of this decision- citizens of Hartford knew nothing about it until it was announced to be in the works. One person who stated this is a representative of the district in which the stadium is planned to be built! I am sorry I don't remember his name (Hartford Cityline reported that this was Rep. Angel Arce). One speaker demanded to see an audit type of report from every group responsible for development of this plan.

"The money planned to be spent on the stadium should be used to address other needs in the city. Many people spoke about improvements that are needed at the Martin Luther King, Jr. Elementary School. Another speaker brought an impressive list of specifics that could be addressed by 60 million dollars including the hiring of teachers, school renovations, early education opportunities for city youngsters and more. Parking-no provisions have been made for adjacent parking. Reports that stadium building rarely brings in the revenue that they are meant to bring in.

"Several people challenged the idea that Rock Cat games would be a boon to the restaurant and hotel industry in the city, pointing out that the idea of thousands of people coming to games from out of town and choosing to stay at a city hotel is unrealistic. A challenge was made to the claim that the stadium would result in 600 new jobs. One person raised the important issue of consequences of closing the existing stadium in New Britain to that city.

"The meeting room was full—more full than I have ever witnessed. When the period of public comment was finished there was a lot of continued conversation in the hallway and several people were interviewed for TV. I do not recall the channels that were represented but it was obvious that this topic is a big deal. The next meeting for public comment will be in July (Hartford Cityline reported that the date is July 21). Apparently, this is not a 'done deal' but we must watch very closely to be sure that no further decisions are pushed through in secret as has been the case with developments so far."

The motivation for Segarra, Wooden and the council board was simple. The plight of the poor does not keep elected officials in Connecticut up at night, but their Boston/New York inferiority complex does. The Red Sox, Patriots, Celtics and Bruins get busy to our north, the Yankees, Mets, Giants, Jets, Knicks, Nets and Rangers do likewise to the south. Hartford's professional sports scene is not quite as glamorous. The Hartford Whalers were this city's only major league sports franchise.

The Whalers played in the World Hockey Association from 1972-79, and then joined the National Hockey League in 1979, along with the Edmonton Oilers, Quebec Nordiques and Winnipeg Jets as part of the WHA/NHL merger. The Whalers played in Springfield, Massachusetts from 1978-80 due to the Hartford Civic Center roof collapse.

The team won a league championship and qualified for the playoffs every year during their time in the WHA, but struggled after joining the NHL. The Whalers won only one division title and missed the playoffs ten times. They were ridiculed throughout the NHL for their Brass Bonanza fight song. The Whalers were also demeaned as the team that played their games in a mall. Still, the franchise had a loyal fan base until owner Peter Karmanos moved the team to North Carolina in 1997.

Since the Whalers left town, politicians in Connecticut have tried to fill the void. In 1998 Gov. John Rowland attempted to lure the New England Patriots of the National Football League to Hartford. Rowland and Patriots owner Bob Kraft came to a verbal agreement to relocate the franchise here. Two days before the deal became binding Kraft backed out; apparently, Hartford was used by Kraft as leverage to get the Patriots a new stadium in Massachusetts. Rowland was left with egg on his face.

Now the New Britain Rock Cats were the object of desire. The team was viewed by the Hartford Democrats as an opportunity to bring some prestige to the city. The proposed $60 million dollar baseball stadium would be worth six times more than the most expensive ball park in the Double-A Eastern League, where the Rock Cats play. A specious claim that the stadium will generate 665 "full time equivalent jobs" is being used to justify the deal. Don't get it twisted, this was the equivalent of your neighbor who never talks to you, buying an outrageously expensive TV, and then inviting you to come over and watch the game, so he can rub his purchase in your face. Malloy, a notorious publicity hound who was running for re- election, was quick to distance himself from the Rock Cats announcement. Malloy said that the city should not count on getting funds from the state to pay for the new stadium. Roger Noll and Andrew Zimbalist:

"In our forthcoming Brookings book, *Sports, Jobs, and Taxes: The Economic Impact of Sports Teams and Stadiums*, we and 15 collaborators examine the local economic development argument from all angles: case studies of the effect of specific facilities, as well as comparisons among cities and even neighborhoods that have and have not sunk hundreds of millions of dollars into sports development. In every case, the conclusions are the same. A new sports facility has an extremely small (perhaps even negative) effect on overall economic activity and employment. No recent facility appears to have earned anything approaching a reasonable return on investment. No recent facility has been self-financing in terms of its impact on net tax revenues. Regardless of whether the unit of analysis is a local neighborhood, a city, or an entire metropolitan area, the economic benefits of sports facilities are de minimus."

While tone-deaf sportswriters like Jeff Jacobs of the Courant mock critics of the Rock Cats deal and hail the arrival of a professional sports team, the economic reality in Hartford remains unchanged. Hartford's poverty rate annually hovers between 30% and 40%, one of the highest in the nation. Black and Latino unemployment is still at

Depression-era levels; the unemployment rate for young Black males in some areas of Connecticut is as high as 50%.

People of color earn about 60 cents for every dollar whites make and possess about 10 cents of net wealth for every dollar whites have. The median wealth for single Black women is $100, $120 for single Latino women, and $41,000 for single white women. It's a shame that residents had to tell Wooden and the council board the obvious; throwing money they don't have at a luxury item like a sports facility is a bad idea. The Hartford Democrats' showed the entire state that their top priority was themselves. The Major League Baseball Hall of Fame is located in Cooperstown, New York. You can find Hartford's Hall of Shame at 550 Main Street.

June 9

WFSB TV reported that Department of Transportation officials were studying a plan to revive tolls, or "congestion pricing" as the DOT now euphemistically referred to the quasi-tax for travelling from point A to B. The tolls would be collected on two of the state's busiest highways— I-95 between New Haven and New York, and I-84 in Hartford. The DOT plan was to use revenue from the tolls to fund, repair and maintain these roadways. Because the state transportation fund had been raided multiple times by the Democrats to fill budget holes, some lawmakers wanted to amend the state constitution to stipulate that revenue from the tolls would be used exclusively for the fund. Manned tollbooths were phased out in 1985 after seven people perished in an automobile crash at an exit in Stratford.

WFSB reported that new technology had been developed to collect tolls:

"DOT officials said over the years, tollbooths have made a dramatic transformation, where booths have been replaced by electronic sensors mounted overhead on special framework.

'All of the systems that are being put into place generally do not have any manned toll booths,' DOT Chief of Planning Tom Maziarz said, adding that most booths use overhead devices, or gantries, where the speed limit passing under them can be between 60 and 70 mph.

This means no stopping or slowing down to pay, but some drivers said they aren't sure they can afford the new expense.

'My husband drives on the highways for his job, and I just don't think it would be a good idea,' said Marie Morley of Meriden.

The DOT is looking into other options, like congestion pricing, where higher toll charges would happen during peak demand periods. Another option is called managed lanes, which would give drivers a choice where regular lanes remain free of charge but the express lane requires paying the toll.

The congestion study is expected to be released in January of 2015, and any plans regarding tolls would not happen until after that."

Instead of exploring new, egalitarian ideas to generate revenue for the state, officials were reaching back 30 years for a concept that would have a negative impact on the working class and the poor.

June 13

The American Federation of Teachers CT rewarded Malloy for his attacks on public school teachers by formally endorsing Malloy's re-election. Malloy, who squeezed concessions out of teachers during his first term, added insult to injury by saying that education reform was needed, because teachers won tenure simply by showing up. During his State of the State address in February 2012 Malloy said, "It's been said by some that I won't take on the issue because it will damage my relationship with teachers. In today's system, basically the only thing you have to do is show up for four years. Do that, and tenure is yours." If there was any doubt that union "leaders" were in the pockets of the Democratic Party, the AFT endorsement served as official confirmation.

That same week, Foley employed a bizarre strategy as he walked around Church Street in New Haven with a microphone and camera crew, "interviewing" city residents. Foley found one woman who rambled on about people sitting back and collecting welfare when they should be earning a living. Foley told *The Mirror* that the stunt was his idea. It appeared as if Foley was attempting to change his image of being a stuffed shirt by mingling with the common folk. Foley told *The Mirror* that if he was elected he would not attempt to reopen the SEBAC concessions deal with Malloy; this was contrary to statements by his primary opponents McKinney and Boughton, who said that state workers should make more concessions in order to balance the state budget. Malloy had also promised not to ask state employee unions to return to the bargaining table.

Foley denied that he would attempt to change state laws regarding union membership, and assured public employees that he would not emulate Wisconsin Governor Scott Walker's scorched earth tactics, which have crippled unions in the mecca of organized labor.

In 2011, the Republican-controlled Wisconsin legislature passed Walker's "budget repair bill." The legislation restricted state and municipal workers' collective bargaining rights, as employees would only be allowed to negotiate regarding their wages. A cap on raises was implemented. Workers would have to increase their contributions to pensions and health care. Restrictions were placed on union dues collections from employees. These measures had a devastating effect on union membership in Wisconsin.

Foley up to this point had declined to participate in GOP debates. His spokesman told the press that Foley would be present at two debates prior to the primary on August 12.

Conservative voters who wanted to know Foley's position on gun control could not get a straight answer.

When asked about the gun control bill that was passed by the legislature following the Newtown school shooting (resulting in some of the strictest gun laws in the country), Foley would only say that the bill would have been "different" if he had been governor. Foley did say that the weapons Adam Lanza used in the spree killing were purchased legally, and that the gun bill would not have prevented the tragedy. Foley echoed the contention of gun control opponents who said that improving the mental health treatment system should be the focus of legislation.

June 16

Foley and Malloy spoke to Connecticut AFL-CIO union delegates in New Haven. *The Mirror* reported that Foley was laughed off the stage when he distorted the meaning of his remarks about Wisconsin. Foley had talked about the need for a "Wisconsin moment in Connecticut." Like a cheating husband caught in the act, Foley told the crowd that he was referring to one- party rule by the Connecticut Democrats; he assured everyone that he did not wish to bust the unions as Walker had done in Wisconsin. No one was buying it. However, Malloy, who had attacked unions throughout his first term as governor, was given a warm reception by the delegates. Did I mention that the unions are in the Democrats' pockets?

June 17

CNN hosted a live town hall with former Secretary of State Hillary Clinton, the likely Democratic Party presidential nominee in 2016. Clinton was promoting her memoir, Hard Choices. The event took place at the Newseum in Washington D.C. Host Christiane Amanpour asked Clinton the expected questions about foreign policy issues such as the September 11, 2012 attack by Islamic militants on a U.S. diplomatic mission and CIA annex in Benghazi, Libya. U.S. Ambassador J. Christopher Stevens and Sean Smith, U.S. Foreign Service Information Management Officer were killed in the attacks; Stevens was the first U.S. Ambassador killed on duty in 33 years. Iraq was another topic; at the time the Al-Queda offshoot group ISIS had just captured Mosul, Iraq's second largest city, and were moving in on Bagdad, the capital city. Clinton said she was "still looking for answers" about Beghazi, and blamed the U.S. puppet Iraqi government for not setting up an agreement to keep American troops in the country.

Clinton stuck to her liberal talking points. Members of the town hall audience asked Clinton about Obama's record number of deportations, the legalization of marijuana, gun control and same sex marriage. Clinton gave the usual lip service to "providing a path to citizenship" for undocumented immigrants while calling for undocumented children to be shipped out of the country. She passed the buck to the states regarding the legalization of marijuana (how about ending the racist, so-called War on Drugs entirely?), and expressed support for gun control and same sex marriage.

CNN political analyst John King said that Clinton sounded like a "states rights Republican" when she answered the marijuana legalization question. Clinton predictably was coy and ducked Amanpour's question about whether or not she would run for president. The program then degenerated into the typical corporate media ass kissing session; the town hall, which was billed as a forum where any question could be asked, was in reality an infomercial promoting Clinton's book and her candidacy for president.

BAR commentator Danny Haiphong talked about how a Clinton presidency would immobilize Blacks and white liberals, just as Obama had done.

102

"Hillary Clinton is a rabid Democratic Party imperialist whose record as Secretary of State makes her a welcome addition to the Oval Office of capitalist-imperialist treachery. In 2011, following the extrajudicial murder of Muammar Gaddafi by US-NATO bandits, Clinton reported to the media 'We came, we saw, he died.' This demonstration of Western imperial arrogance capped off the successful US-NATO overthrow of independent Libya by way of 'humanitarian intervention.' During this same period, Clinton staunchly advocated for the escalation of US-NATO involvement in Syria and continued pressuring Iran to open its economy to Western capitalist ruin with starvation sanctions and military threats. These moves made Obama's first Secretary of State a darling to US imperialism despite the loss of political points suffered from the embarrassing "blowback" experienced in Benghazi on Sept. 11th 2012."

Haiphong also pointed out Clinton's support of US military action against Iran, her comparison of Russian President Vladimir Putin to Adolf Hitler for his response to the coup in Ukraine, and her husband Bill Clinton's track record as president; in 1996 Clinton collaborated with Republican Speaker of the House Newt Gingrich to dismantle cash assistance. The former president also passed mandatory minimum sentencing legislation, which fueled Black mass incarceration.

Back in Connecticut, the AFL—CIO wrapped up their two-day convention with their expected endorsement of Malloy, but a diss of his education commissioner. *The Mirror*'s Mark Pazniokas reported on the convention.

"The Connecticut AFL-CIO's biennial political convention was a two-day infomercial promoting the re-election of Gov. Dannel P. Malloy, with one carefully choreographed note of discord: A rebuke to the Democratic governor's choice of Stefan Pryor as commissioner of education.

Before formally endorsing Malloy, the statewide labor federation adopted a resolution Tuesday calling for a requirement that an education commissioner hold the same credential as a school superintendent, a standard that Pryor does not meet.

'We're hoping the governor's listening,' said Melodie Peters, the president of AFT-Connecticut, one of the state's two major teachers' unions.

The resolution drawn up by the AFT, which separately endorsed Malloy ahead of the AFL-CIO convention, was a message to a Democratic governor and to labor's rank-and-file. It was meant as a gentle rebuke to Malloy, not a rejection; a way to soothe educators, not provoke them."

Pazniokas reported that Pelto was pissed because he was not invited to the convention to speak along with Malloy and Foley. AFL-CIO national president Randi Weingarten described Pelto as "a friend who has some important things to say, but his candidacy is a distraction and a danger that can only draw votes away from Malloy." Weingarten used the specter of Foley and a repeat of the events in Wisconsin as justification for her union endorsing Malloy. "The stakes here are whether you're going to have a Dan Malloy or a Tom Foley as governor, whether you are going to have a Connecticut that acts as Connecticut or that emulates Wisconsin."

Long term unemployed individuals continued to suffer in limbo, due to inaction by certain conservative lawmakers in Washington. A bipartisan Senate bill that would restore emergency unemployment insurance remained stalled in the House. The bill would provide retroactive benefits from December 28, 2013 to May 31. Another provision ended benefits for anyone whose adjusted gross income in the previous year was $1 million or more. A significant component of this legislation was a provision which would provide job seekers with referrals to employment services when they reached their 27th week of receiving Unemployment Insurance (UI) benefits. Senators Susan Collins (R-ME), Rob Portman (R-OH), Lisa Murkowski (R-AK), Mark Kirk (R-IL), Jeff Merkley (D-OR), Cory Booker (D-NJ), Sherrod Brown (D-OH), and Dick Durbin (D-IL) co-sponsored the bill. The Republican-controlled House, which included GOP members who accused unemployed people of sitting on their butts while taking a handout, refused to support a measure, which would provide assistance to individuals who were looking for work.

Center on Budget Chief Economist Chad Stone analyzed the ass-backward approach to unemployment by two GOP controlled states, Kansas and North Carolina.

"Kansas reduced regular state unemployment insurance benefits, but North Carolina is the poster child for cutting the program. It cut not only the maximum number of weeks of benefits but also the benefit level. That rendered North Carolina ineligible for federal emergency benefits starting in July 2013, six months before federal lawmakers let the entire federal program expire."

North Carolina lawmakers argue that by cutting jobless benefits, they generated a sharp decline in unemployment. Critics, however, note a continued slide in the labor force participation rate (the share of North Carolinians working or looking for work), suggesting that many people who lost benefits simply stopped looking for work. In fact, a careful statistical comparison of labor market trends in North Carolina and neighboring South Carolina and Virginia "does not appear to support findings of large effects from changes in [unemployment] benefits"—other than, of course, the gratuitous hit on workers struggling to find a job and their families."

June 18

What a difference two weeks and public outcry makes... On June 4, Hartford City Council President Shawn Wooden stood next to Mayor Pedro Segarra, as they proudly announced a deal with the owner of the New Britain Rock Cats to bring the minor league baseball team to Hartford. Since then community residents have voiced outrage and state legislators—including Sen. Eric Coleman, who Wooden was challenging in an August 12 primary, expressed dismay at the lack of transparency surrounding the deal. Wooden initially continued to defend the Rock Cats move, saying that community residents would understand after they got more information. Wooden officially flip-flopped on June 18, saying that he would not support the deal unless private investors put some money up.

Hartford Courant columnist Kevin Rennie opined that the Wooden/Coleman primary had become a referendum on Rock Cats-gate.

"Any sports team, but especially baseball, is a bauble politicians cannot resist. Decades of economic studies, however, have frequently concluded that their benefits are oversold to entice taxpayers into footing the costs of building stadiums for rich team owners.

A baseball stadium is a major investment and serious risk to city finances that requires meaningful public participation. Giving the people who are going to have to pay for the stadium a voice in how or whether to proceed appears to be what Segarra and his allies fear most. They trust a duplicitous Boston real estate developer but fear the people of Hartford. However you feel about the proposal, the manner in which it was shaped, presented and defended ought to give you pause. Thanks to Eric Coleman, thousands of Hartford Democrats will have a chance to express themselves in a meaningful way. A Coleman victory and Wooden defeat on Aug. 12 will send the kind of message politicians do not need translated."

Coleman was obviously seizing on a golden opportunity to throw some dirt on Wooden, who was endorsed by the Democratic Party over the longtime incumbent. Still, the latest development was great news for opponents of the stadium.

The Mirror reported that Mark Boughton announced he was ending his campaign for governor; difficulties obtaining public financing caused Boughton to pull the plug. Boughton told his fellow Republicans to support Foley. The party endorsed candidate. John McKinney remained as Foley's only primary opponent. The State Elections Enforcement Commission threw out a complaint alleging that Malloy illegally used an independent issues group to conduct a poll, and that a former staffer conducted campaign activities on behalf of Malloy before he formally announced his bid for re-election. The SEC gave Malloy the green light to receive $ 6.5 million in public campaign finance money. The SEC postponed a vote on Foley's application, due to issues surrounding the documentation of funds the Foley campaign had raised. Former Secretary of the State Susan Bysiewicz managed to keep a straight face while telling reporters why it was okay for her to run for state Senate in a district where she doesn't live. Bysiewicz, a longtime Middletown resident, had her eye on the 31st Senate District seat (representing Bristol) left vacant by David A. Roche, who resigned due to personal issues. Bysiewicz told *The Mirror* that she was already planning a move to Bristol when the Senate seat opened up. "Months ago, we checked out streets and neighborhoods in Bristol with friends. Fast forward to Monday morning, when Dave Roche put out something about not running. My friends in Bristol politics asked, 'If you are still interested in coming to Bristol, is this something you would be interested in?'" Yeah, right. Bysiewicz did not have to live in Bristol to run for the Senate seat, but she would have to be a resident of the town in order to serve, if she was elected.

Back in Washington, Rep. Alan Grayson (D-FL) called for an amendment to a defense spending bill which would prohibit the military from "gifting" surplus weaponry such as mine resistant tanks to the police. The *Off the Grid* website reported that the Pentagon's 1033 program has been providing law enforcement with weapons such as tanks for years.

"The Mine Resistant Ambush Protected (MRAP) vehicles were designed to protect troops in Iraq and Afghanistan from insurgents' homemade bombs, but now MRAPs are being given away to police departments in such communities as High Springs, Florida, population 5,350. The High Springs police paid the Defense Departments' Law Enforcement Support Office $2,000 for an MRAP that originally cost taxpayers $600,000, a local TV station reported. Even though the vehicles cannot be used in many places, around 165 MRAPs have been given away to police agencies all over the United States according to Fox News. The MRAPs were built for use in Iraq and Afghanistan, but since the Iraq War is over and the Afghan adventure is winding down, the US Army has been giving or selling the vehicles to local law enforcement agencies.

The program has led to "rampant fraud and abuse," Reuters columnists Michael Shank and Elizabeth Beavers discovered. In a special report the columnists called 1033 a flagrant waste of tax money. Some of their shocking discoveries included:

At least one officer sold military weapons he had been given through the program on eBay. Some police departments actually lost military equipment and weapons, including AR-15 rifles, they had been supplied with.

Some officers gave the military style weapons away to their friends.

There was so much fraud and abuse that the Pentagon actually suspended distribution of weapons to police forces. The distribution of other pieces of equipment such as armored cars and helicopters continues.

Some police agencies may have sold or auctioned off weapons to raise money for other purposes."

While Paul Ryan's budget cuts funding for vital social services and the Republican-controlled House holds an unemployment insurance bill hostage, the defense budget is so bloated that the Pentagon is giving away weaponry meant for military combat to police departments all over the country. What's wrong with this picture? President Dwight Eisenhower warned us about the growing influence of the military industrial complex. Dr. Martin Luther King said a country that spends more money on instruments of war than on programs to help its people is approaching spiritual death. A shift in priorities is long overdue in Washington. Rep, Grayson is one of the few lawmakers who are taking a stand against U.S. militarism. His amendment was rejected due to a procedural issue. Rep. Louie Gohmert (R-Texas) stood on the House floor after Grayson spoke and said that the U.S. doesn't engage in imperialism. Amazingly, he was not struck by lightning.

June 19

Raul De Jesus and Alexander Aponte were the latest councilmen to jump ship on the New Britain Rock Cats stadium deal; both said they would not support the construction of a stadium for the Rock Cats without funding from the private sector. City Council President Shawn Wooden claimed that he told Mayor Pedro Segarra's administration from the beginning that he wanted private investors to fund the stadium. However, Wooden never made this demand publicly when the deal was announced, which would have been to his advantage because he was challenging Sen. Eric Coleman in an August 12 primary.

108

Coleman pounced on the opportunity to throw jabs at Wooden as he talked to the Hartford Courant about the stadium controversy.

"That proposal was so bare and needed so much more analysis and thought and consideration. I just don't know what they were thinking holding a press conference on the steps of City Hall announcing with great glee and excitement: 'We're going to have a baseball stadium.' Then to follow that up saying this a done deal— that's completely out of touch with the sentiments and the feeling of the residents of the city of Hartford and the region."

Coleman said that Wooden's belated call for private stadium funding was a politically expedient response to public furor over the deal.

"I think congratulations are in order for the many Hartford residents who were outraged or up in arms about what was, until this point, a taxpayer-funded project. I'm sure their outrage and their actions led to this modulation of Mr. Wooden's support for the stadium."

Wooden appeared on the WFSB TV *Face the State* program with former major league baseball player and current ESPN analyst Doug Glanville, where he continued his spin job. The fact remains that Wooden didn't make his support conditional when he stood grinning next to Segarra three weeks before; he started using the word "if" after protests erupted over the deal. Wooden's claim would mean that he and Segarra proudly announced the stadium deal even though they both knew at the time that the city didn't have the money to pay for it. Segarra told the media that the stadium plan was a "done deal." It was clear that Wooden was a candidate for state Senate who was desperately trying to put out a fire before voters in Hartford hit the polls.

A component of this issue, which was lost in the sauce was a planned North Hartford supermarket that was in limbo because of the stadium deal. Thomas E. Deller, the city's Director of Development Services, said that the supermarket deal is still a priority. Food deserts are a serious problem in low-income communities of color.

Bysiewicz dropped her exploration of running for the 31st District of Bristol Senate seat.

In Washington, debate over the defense spending bill included the introduction of an amendment which would prevent President Obama from going around Congress and sending combat troops to Iraq. Three hundred "military advisers" were sent to Iraq, supposedly to beef up security at the US embassy. The al Queda offshoot group ISIS had taken control of several Iraq cities, including Mosul, the second largest, and was moving in on Bagdad, the capital city.

Independent media news program *Democracy Now!* reported on the resurgence of the U.S. war machine:

"The Obama administration is sending up to 300 military advisers to help Iraq's fight against the Sunni uprising that has taken over large parts of the country. President Obama announced the new U.S. contingent while ruling out the deployment of combat troops. But Obama also said he remains open to launching military strikes at the Iraqi government's request.

President Obama: 'Because of our increased intelligence resources, we're developing more information about potential targets associated with ISIL. And going forward, we will be prepared to take targeted and precise military action if and when we determine that the situation on the ground requires it. If we do, I will consult closely with Congress and leaders in Iraq and in the region.'

According to *The New York Times*, 'a senior administration official' said the potential U.S. bombing campaign 'could be extended into neighboring Syria.' In his remarks, Obama also said he is not pushing for the resignation of Iraqi Prime Minister Nouri al-Maliki, but renewed calls for Maliki to abandon a sectarian-focused rule. Secretary of State John Kerry will visit the Middle East and Europe this weekend for talks with U.S. allies. Iraqi troops, meanwhile, are massing north of Baghdad for a potential offensive to retake captured towns from Sunni militants."

Rep, Colleen Hanabusa introduced the amendment which prevents Obama from circumventing Congress and using military force against Iraq. Rep. Hanabussa spoke to *Democracy Now!*:

"The amendment passed last night by unanimous consent. In other words, there was no opposition. I believe it is the only amendment in what is now, the defense appropriation measures, which the House of Representatives will be voting on. What it says is, as you know, the president invoked the War Powers Resolution, which has in it certain conditions, so he has, for a period of time, the ability to do as he has done.

110

The resolution does not, in any way, prevent him from sending troops in—troops or anyone in to help the—an embassy situation or our citizens in Iraq.

That has no impact. And what he's done up to now, by invoking it, he has the authority to do. However, what the resolution then requires is—and the amendment re- affirms—is that anything past that, the president must come to Congress in order to get further authorization. And this amendment says that he cannot use any funds. So no funds shall be used in a situation where the president has not complied with the War Powers Resolution."

June 20

Jonathan Pelto, who had been collecting petition signatures in an effort to be added to the 2014 gubernatorial election ballot as an independent, met with Republican Party operative Chris Healy and gave him a petition. Healy of course circulated the petition among his GOP colleagues. Pelto claimed that he never expected Healy to do this, which is like me giving Bernie Madoff my ATM card and PIN number, then being surprised when my bank account was wiped out. Pelto's actions gave plenty of ammunition to his critics, who claim that Pelto is running for governor only so he can stick it to Malloy, who would not give Pelto a job in his administration. Mark Pazniokas of *The Mirror* reported on the Pelto/Healy meeting.

"A former Republican state chairman is gathering signatures to help get Jonathan Pelto, a Democratic critic of Gov. Dannel P. Malloy, on the ballot as an independent candidate for governor, telling GOP voters that Pelto will draw votes from Malloy.

Chris Healy, who stepped down in 2011 after four years as GOP chairman, wrote an email to Republicans in his hometown of Wethersfield urging them to sign a Pelto petition. He told *The Mirror* he was circulating a petition he obtained from Pelto, whom he has known for years, in a recent meeting over coffee.

Healy and Pelto give the same the account of that meeting only to a point: Pelto says he gave Healy the petition, but not with the intention that Healy get signatures. Healy says he explicitly told Pelto he would circulate the petition. 'I told him I would do what I could to help,' Healy said. 'I certainly did not ask nor would I expect any help or support from the Republicans. We're doing just fine on the petitions,' Pelto said.

Pelto, who tried and failed to get a job with the Malloy administration, has been a critic of Malloy since he took office in January 2011 as the first Democratic governor since William A. O'Neill left office two decades earlier. As the party's political director, Pelto played a role in O'Neill's last campaign."

June 21

Gov. Dannel Malloy and Lt. Gov. Nancy Wyman attended the Working Families Party convention. Mark Pazniokas of *The Connecticut Mirror* reported that Wyman thanked state workers for their votes in 2010. "Without you in 2010, we couldn't have survived and become governor and lieutenant governor," Wyman said, making the political personal. "Dan and I know we couldn't have done this without you." Malloy was singing a different tune during an interview with *The New York Times* reporter David M. Halbfinger in February 2011, three months after he was elected. "There is much skepticism in Hartford about whether Mr. Malloy will ultimately win what he needs from the unions, which provided critical support for his election. Even labor leaders question whether the governor will force concessions, he said. 'I've had people come up to me and say, 'We got you elected,' Mr. Malloy said. 'And my quick retort is, 'Yeah, and you're the reason it was so close.' Because lots of people voted against me as a way to express their anger against them."

You're welcome, Dan. I'm a state employee.

Pelto had the gall to rip off Martin Luther King while he spoke at the WFP convention; he used Dr. King's quote, "There comes a time when silence is betrayal." After promising me that he would formulate an urban agenda, Pelto rolled out a platform without one. Pelto betrayed communities of color with his silence on issues such as poverty, Black/Latino unemployment, racial wage/wealth disparity and police

112

containment. Pelto could have really made a difference; instead he was giving voters more of the same.

Hartford Public School teacher Stephanie Sans shared her thoughts on Pelto excluding an urban agenda from his platform.

"Does one need a platform on this issue if one is perhaps not running for governor but as a spoiler? Where is the education platform, especially for inner city schools given the achievement gap? While education was mentioned, it is very, very, vague—too vague for me as a Rocky Hill, Manchester, and Hartford Public School teacher.

Where was Mr. Pelto on the nights we coalesced on behalf of the community for Clark School and America's Choice at SAND? He was at home blogging about it, rather than showing public support. My former principal Steve Perry was front and center both nights. His tweets following both meetings made me quite uncomfortable, especially as the first HFT Building Rep in the history of C Prep. Politicians have agendas and certain groups carry the weight of those agendas. Perhaps we are just a platform for sound bites. Just food for thought.

In my life, I judge actions, not just words. Sometimes, it's up to an individual or small group to make a meaningful difference. It's not as easy but 'doing' is better than just talking. A heart with true intentions is compelled to act upon his/her words. Talking or blogging gets your message out to larger audience but then there must be a 'history' of actions behind the talk. Blogging about Clark Uprising was good but being there in support of the teachers and community was better. I know; I was there. I look around and it's so fascinating to see those who often shout the loudest run away the fastest when push comes to shove."

June 23

Secretary of State John Kerry arrived in Iraq to "fire" Prime Minister Nouri al-Maliki, as the militant group ISIS continued to seize towns in Iraq as they headed toward Baghdad. Kerry said, "We will help Iraqis to complete this transition if they choose it. If they want, they have an opportunity to choose leadership that can represent all of Iraq, a unity government that brings people together and focus on ISIL. And I am convinced that they will do so, not just with our help, but with the help of almost every country in the region, as well as others in the world who will always stand up against the tyranny of this kind of terrorist activity."

Democracy Now! spoke to Baghdad resident Ahmed, who was opposed to US military intervention.

"It cannot be solved through military intervention. It has to be solved through diplomatic and political channels. This is our message to Obama. We say to him that we do not want him to send reinforcements or an aircraft carrier. This cannot help us. The situation in Iraq is very critical, and it needs quick solutions." Another Baghdad resident Qassim Hashim asked for the US to intervene. "We hoped for such a stand. It is the American forces' duty to protect the Iraqi people and its institutions, as stipulated in the Strategic Framework Agreement." Anti-war protestors in Washington, DC spoke to *DN*'s MARA VERHEYDEN-HILLIARD:

"We're here today to stand in opposition to any new war in Iraq. The U.S. government, the Obama administration, has said that they are sending 300 advisers into Iraq. He said that he will consider bombing as he determines whether there are appropriate targets. And the simple fact is, what we're seeing in Iraq today is purely the result of U.S. militarism and U.S. intervention. This is a country that before the shock-and-awe invasion, the people of Iraq were not divided along sectarian or religious lines."

Peace protestor David Barrows told *Democracy Now!* that he wanted the US to intervene in the Iraq crisis.

"Well, I'm here because I don't want another war to start. I don't want bombing. I'm sick of these bombings. They do absolutely no good. You know, we're bombing in Yemen. We're bombing all over the place. We're killing women and children and men who have nothing to do with war. It really makes me sick. I mean, I was born in this country. I just wonder: what's going on with the American people? Wake up, America! You've got to stop doing this terrorism. That's what we're doing. We're becoming a people of terrorism."

Patrick Cockburn, Middle East correspondent for *The Independent* told *Democracy Now!* about the fear that gripped Baghdad.

"Well, Baghdad is a very frightened city. Nobody quite knows what's going to happen. You know, news keeps coming in of further gains by ISIS, or DAIISH, as it's always called here. The whole of Anbar province, this enormous province to the west, has fallen. And they're only—ISIS is only about an hour's drive to the north. Of course, Baghdad is a big, enormous city, six or seven million people. The majority are Shia. So

114

people say, "Well, they'll never break through because of all these armed Shia." But, you know, the fact remains that since the fall of Mosul, the government hasn't won any victories, and the— and ISIS has gone on taking more cities. You see militiamen in the streets of Baghdad. Prices of everything have gone up. A lot of people have got out of the city, big queues outside the passport office. So there's is an atmosphere of barely suppressed panic."

BBC reported that ISIS had seized the top Iraq oil refinery.

"Sunni rebels in Iraq say they have fully captured the country's main oil refinery at Baiji, north of Baghdad. The refinery had been under siege for 10 days with the militant offensive being repulsed several times.

The complex supplies a third of Iraq's refined fuel and the battle has already led to petrol rationing.

Insurgents, led by the group Isis, have overrun a swathe of territory north and west of Baghdad including Iraq's second-biggest city, Mosul.

They are bearing down on a vital dam near Haditha and have captured all border crossings to Syria and Jordan.

A rebel spokesman said the Baiji refinery, in Salahuddin province, would now be handed over to local tribes to administer.

The spokesman said that the advance towards Baghdad would continue.

The BBC's Jim Muir in Irbil, northern Iraq, says the capture of the refinery is essential if the rebels are to keep control of the areas they have conquered and to supply Mosul with energy. Neighbouring Iran says it opposes US intervention. Supreme Leader Ayatollah Ali Khamenei accused Washington of 'seeking an Iraq under its hegemony and ruled by its stooges.'"

Iran is by no means a bastion of freedom, but Khamenei has a point. The United States tried to blame their puppet government for the Iraq crisis, but the fact is that the U.S, invasion was the root cause. Yes, the people of Iraq suffered under the brutal dictatorship of Saddam Hussein. Since the U.S. invaded Iraq under false pretenses, removed Saddam from power and left, the people there are suffering even more. This country needs to bring the war dollars home. The U.S. cannot be the policeman of the world; they cannot "fix" Iraq. The ongoing U.S. quest for hegemony only brings violence and death to innocent people.

Meanwhile, back home, Jeff Cohen of WNPR reported that the City of Hartford had officially gone out to bid to find an owner's representative and an architectural and engineering firm, despite the fact that the Rock Cats stadium deal would not be approved by the city council for at least a couple more months, if it was approved at all. Cohen questioned Maribel La Luz, Mayor Segarra's spokesperson, about the moves by Segarra's team. La Luz said, "It's important for us to have a team of professionals in place who are ready to go and to be able to answer questions from Council and other stakeholders on how the project would be executed."

Tom Foley, who still faced an upcoming August primary against Sen. John McKinney, nonetheless revved up the Republican Party fundraising machine, beginning the process of filling up the GOP war chest for the gubernatorial election. Mark Pazniokas of *The Mirror* reported on the latest campaign development.

"Tom Foley has to win a primary in August to be crowned the Republican nominee for governor, but he already is using his endorsement by the GOP convention last month as a mandate to assert control over the state party's fundraising.

With an expectation to qualify for public financing, Foley has dispatched his finance director, Lauren Casper, to take over fundraising for the party in hopes of finding resources to expand the capabilities of the state GOP for the fall campaign.

By branding the party as an extension of his campaign, Foley is signaling donors to give to the GOP what they can no longer give to him as a publicly financed candidate. The strategy echoes Gov. Dannel P. Malloy's efforts in developing a more muscular Democratic Party."

Politifact.com examined Democratic Party Sen. Harry Reid's claim that the Dems didn't have a lot of billionaire donors. Current donation disclosure rules do not allow for a clear picture but this is what Politifact was able to find.

116

"We cross-checked the Open Secrets list of the top 100 individuals donating to outside spending groups in the current election against the Forbes list of the world's billionaires and found that, as of June 19, there were 22 individuals on the Open Secrets list who were billionaires. Of those 22 billionaires, 13—or more than half—gave predominantly to liberal groups or groups affiliated with the Democratic Party. The other nine gave predominantly to conservative groups.

Among the liberal-leaning donors are former New York City Mayor Michael Bloomberg and business magnate George Soros. On the conservative side are S. Daniel Abraham, who founded SlimFast, and Vincent McMahon, who owns World Wrestling Entertainment.

These lists aren't complete due to the disclosure rules protecting donors' identities. Both sides are spending more of this "dark money" than ever before, said Robert Maguire, a political nonprofit investigator at the Center for Responsive Politics." The report confirmed what we already knew; both parties are controlled by the ruling class. As much as they bicker publicly, the Democrats and Republicans have more similarities than differences. They both perpetuate structural racism in the form of the prison state, racial wage/wealth disparity, protecting Wall Street and the military industrial complex."

June 24

U.S. Secretary of State Kerry tried to pour cold water on speculation about U.S. military intervention in Iraq, as 90 more American military advisors were dispatched to the war torn country. John Kerry told the BBC's Kim Ghattas, "A united Iraq is a stronger Iraq."

Kerry has told the BBC there must be regional unity to expel Sunni rebels from the Isis group who have taken large swathes of northern and western Iraq.

He said there was no military solution, stressing the need for a new Iraqi government that empowered people in communities where ISIS had taken hold.

Kerry has been talking to Kurdish leaders in the northern city of Irbil.

117

The rebels continue to advance, and are fighting to take a key oil refinery. The insurgents, spearheaded by Islamists fighting under the banner of the Islamic State of Iraq and the Levant (ISIS), have overrun much of north and west Iraq, including the second-biggest city, Mosul.

Meanwhile, a United Nations human rights team in Iraq reported that at least 1,075 people were killed in Iraq so far in June, most of them civilians.

June 25

Iraqi Prime Minister Nouri al-Maliki rejected Kerry's call for him to take a powder; using the "c-word" in the process. CNN reported that both Syria and Iran had entered the fray; Syrian state media denied a CNN report of Syrian airstrikes against ISIS in the Anbar province. CNN also reported that Iran was using drones in Iraq for surveillance. McClatchy DC reported on al- Maliki's attempt to retain power.

WASHINGTON—Iraqi Prime Minister Nouri al-Maliki on Wednesday denounced calls to form an emergency unity government as a "coup against the constitution and an attempt to end the democratic experience."

Maliki, who is Shia, has faced criticism from the U.S. and rival Iraqi politicians for failing to include minority Sunni and Kurdish groups in the political process.

But in his weekly television address, the BBC reports, the prime minister wouldn't agree to give religious or ethnic minority groups greater representation. Maliki said that a "national salvation" government wouldn't be representative of the results of April's parliamentary elections, which awarded his own party 92 of 328 seats.

At the same time, he urged "all political forces" to reconcile in the face of a fierce terrorist onslaught by radical Sunni fighters from the Islamic State of Iraq and Syria.

"We desperately need to take a comprehensive national stand to defeat terrorism, which is seeking to destroy our gains of democracy and freedom," Maliki said.

Back in America, Detroit was invaded by corporate criminals who controlled the city through economic martial law. *Black Agenda Report* commentator Margaret Kimberley made an effective comparison between Detroit and Iraq. Both have been occupied by hostile forces.

"A world away in Iraq, a nation is crumbling under the weight of eleven years of violent occupation by the United States. The once developing nation is now a ruin, with all of its infrastructure and systems from health care to education destroyed by western avarice. The prime minister who was chosen with America's blessing, Nouri al-Maliki, has now become an inconvenience and faces a bleak fate... Just as Iraq's infrastructure has been destroyed, Detroit residents now live without basic services which ought to be regarded as the right of every human being. In the United States, a country which boasts of its high level of advancement, residents of a major city must plead to the international community for the right to access water."

United Nations experts said that the city of Detroit's unconscionable plan to shut off water to about 3,000 residents was a violation of their human rights. The UN report condemned the heinous act by the city of cutting off some residents' water without warning:

"The Detroit People's Water Board is hearing directly from people impacted by the water cut-offs who say they were given no warning and had no time to fill buckets, sinks and tubs before losing access to water. In some cases, the cut-offs occurred before the deadline given in notices sent by the city. Sick people have been left without running water and working toilets. People recovering from surgery cannot wash and change bandages. Children cannot bathe and parents cannot cook."

Activists in Detroit told *Democracy Now!* that they are getting reports of shutoffs ranging from 3,000 a week to 3,000 a month, Detroit has become ground zero for disaster capitalism. A Wall Street engineered scheme of derivatives and loans which involved the now imprisoned Mayor Kwame Kilpatrick resulted in the city becoming insolvent. The banks who created the mess are now demanding payment. Emergency Financial Manager Kevyn Orr was installed to facilitate the payoffs to the corporate crooks in the form of a complex (but legal) derivatives scam, which allowed the aforementioned banks to gobble up Detroit's assets through bankruptcy proceedings.

As always it is poor people of color who suffer the most in these situations. Activists said that the water shutoff is nothing but extortion, which is part of a master plan by the city to privatize water services. *The Metro Times* website reported that Congressman John Conyers was taking steps to push back against the economic terrorists in Detroit.

"U.S. Rep John Conyers (D- Detroit) also took aim at the shutoff plan this week, saying in a statement that 'draconian water cutoffs are not a pathway to financial solvency. To the contrary, actions that deny residents the ability to bathe, hydrate, or prepare meals for themselves and their families create costly long- term public health challenges. These water cutoffs are not only inhumane, but economically short-sighted.' Conyers says he plans to introduce legislation to protect access to water during bankruptcy proceedings,' as well as work with members of the U.S. Congress to potentially tap federal emergency relief. Detroit filed the largest municipal bankruptcy in United States history last summer."

June 26

Republican gubernatorial candidates Tom Foley and Sen. John McKinney had a big love fest at the first GOP forum in Rocky Hill. To the surprise of absolutely no one; Foley and McKinney promoted a pro-business, anti-worker agenda. McKinney repeated his pledge to target public employees, while Foley ducked the question about going after more concessions from state workers. Keith Pahneuf of *The Mirror* reported on the forum.

"McKinney and Foley stake out slightly different ground when it came to cutting state spending.

The Senate leader said he would reopen negotiations with state employee unions and seek more concessions.

Despite concessions provided in 2011, state employees still receive a health care plan that is 'more expensive than the best private-sector plan out there,' McKinney said, adding he also would seek to replace the pension program with a 401(k)-style plan for new workers.

McKinney also said he would seek to reduce the state's reliance on public-sector workers to provide social services and turn to more cost-efficient private, nonprofit agencies. When asked whether he favored further concessions, Foley didn't address that point directly. But he said the cost of state employees' salaries and benefits 'is really only a third of the state budget'."

Shawn Wooden appeared on the WNPR *Where We Live* program, his latest media stop as he tried to put out the fire started by his flip-flop on the Rock Cats Hartford stadium deal. The day before an op-ed from Wooden was printed in the Hartford Courant. I decided to use a little humor to bring attention to Wooden's pre-election damage control campaign.

SHAWN WOODEN IN CONCERT—IT'S THE CONCERT EVENT OF THE SUMMER!

You've seen, read and heard Hartford City Council President/State Senate candidate Shawn Wooden all week, as he desperately tries to explain his flip-flop on the New Britain Rock Cats Hartford stadium deal. Now Shawn will be taking his performance to the next level as he spins live in concert!

The Corporate Media Spin Tour will feature Shawn performing his greatest hits:

I Always Wanted Private Funding (I Just Never Said It), Stadiums = Jobs, Baby, Forget About My Flip- Flop, Don't Take Your Vote Away, I Want Your Primary Love, Solid as a Rock Cat, Bonding with You, and Stop Dogging My Stadium Plan (Featuring DMX).

If you don't have money for a ticket, just borrow it like the City of Hartford does! This is a Politics as Usual production.

ISIS militants continued to advance in their attack on Iraq, capturing a town near the capital city of Baghdad. *Democracy Now!* reported on the latest developments:

"Sunni militants have seized a new Iraqi town just an hour from the capital Baghdad. Mansouriyat al-Jabal is home to four natural gas fields and is the latest in the north and west to fall under militant control. In a televised speech, the powerful Shia cleric Muqtada al-Sadr vowed to "shake the ground" underneath advancing Sunni militants and expressed concern about foreign involvement in Iraq. ISIS forces are reportedly setting their sights on Iraq's second-largest dam, in Haditha. *The New York*

Times reports Iraqi forces guarding the dam have been ordered to prepare for opening the floodgates, despite the potential for widespread damage. ISIS militants already control a major dam up the Euphrates River in neighboring Syria. Along with dangerously low water levels, that could threaten a new humanitarian crisis. On a visit to Iraq, Ertharin Cousin of the United Nations World Food Programme voiced concern for the estimated half a million Iraqis displaced in recent weeks.

Ertharin Cousin: 'These people didn't have any place else to go, and they are depending upon the international community and the generosity of the people of this community for their survival. The challenge is that we do not have the necessary resources to provide the assistance that is required for a sustained period of time. We need the international community to continue to support our efforts here so that no family who has now come to find refuge goes without the basic food, water and other assistance needs that U.N. community and WFP is working to provide to them.'"

During an event in Minnesota, Obama said that the U.S. would not send combat troops to Iraq.

June 28

BBC reported on the US employing armed drones in Iraq: "Although the US has confirmed it is flying armed drones in Iraq to protect US personnel on the ground, US officials say American troops are not directly involved in the hostilities." Iraq troops launched an offensive to retake the city of Tikrit from ISIS rebels. Shia cleric Grand Ayatollah Sistani called for the appointment of a new prime minister amidst calls for the creation of a unity government.

June 29

Wooden continued to be roasted in the local media for his flip-flop on the Rock Cats stadium deal. Hartford Courant columnist Colin McEnroe opined that the secret deal by Segarra and Wooden made them look like fools.

"Mayor Pedro Segarra announced the plan on June 4, with City Council President Shawn Wooden standing next to him. On June 8, Segarra said it was 'a done deal.' In other words, the time for your public input was never. Last week, my WNPR colleague Jeff Cohen reported that the city has already put the stadium architect job out to bid, even though the stadium itself hasn't been approved.

Meanwhile, the deal is falling apart. The voters don't like the largesse bestowed on the wealthy Rock Cats owners. Wooden is getting clubbed by state Sen. Eric Coleman, his opponent in a primary for Coleman's seat, for being a directionless tool. Wooden, who stood with Segarra and never objected to the 'done deal,' is now moving backward like a crawfish on crack and insisting on bigger private investment.

Here's why you don't sneak behind our backs and make a deal like this: You look like a bunch of rubes. The people you're dealing with are a lot shrewder than you, and they're taking you to the cleaners.

Advocates justify the construction of the stadiums with public subsidies and tax dollars in two very distinct ways. The first way points directly to economic benefits. Advocates say that a newly constructed sports stadium will revive the local economy and expedite its growth within the immediate region. Secondly, proponents say that a new stadium can act as a job creator and have multiplier effects on the local economy."

However, more often than not these claims turn out to be untrue. In order to understand the economics of sports stadiums one must separate fact from fiction. Cities believe that investing millions of public tax dollars into a stadium will improve cities' image and thus attract new investment and business dollars. However, Mark Rosentraub, an expert on sports economics says that using sports franchises as a way to stimulate economic development is a myth (as cited in Delaney & Eckstein, 2003).

In Jacksonville, team owners for a new NFL stadium projected that $130 million a year and 3,000 new jobs would be added to Jacksonville's local economy. In Baltimore, 1,394 new jobs were projected to be created with the construction of their new stadium. However, none of these projections were actually realized. The projections were only realized by one-tenth of what they were estimated. (Baade & Sanderson, 1997).

"Why are projections so far off? Consulting firms perform much of the promotional studies for team owners that contained flawed methodologies and unrealistic assumptions. A consultant who provided a report not consistent with favorable results was immediately fired or not given new contracts with team owners in the future. Therefore, these studies, more often than not, concluded adding a sports franchise will have a meaningful impact on the local economy. "

Haverford College report, The Economic Effects of Sports Stadiums and Franchises

It would have been nice if Wooden had put the same energy into talking about racial wage/wealth disparity in this city as he had doing his pathetic spin tour. Segarra and Wooden got played like racquetball by the Rock Cats owners because they were only thinking of advancing their own political careers. This myopia made them easy marks and their self-serving scheme blew up in their faces. If Segarra and Wooden were truly thinking about the best interests of Hartford residents, they would have never considered trying to foist this fraud on the people in the first place. This issue is emblematic of the mentality of corporatist Democrats who are so eager to impress their ruling class puppet masters, they become victims of the same element who put them in power. Meanwhile, a planned North Hartford supermarket that would actually help the community remained in limbo, because of Segarra and Wooden's delusional, elitist stadium plan.

If these two bunglers were sincere about putting a dent in Black/Latino unemployment, which hovers at Depression-era levels, they would have implemented egalitarian measures such as the Malcolm X Grassroots Movement's *Jackson Plan*. The *Jackson Plan* is based on participatory democracy in the form of the Jackson People's Assembly and worker owned cooperatives. The late Jackson, Mississippi Mayor Chokwe Lumumba, a self-described Fannie Lou Hamer Democrat, successfully launched worker cooperatives in that city. Worker cooperatives also thrive in Boston, western Massachusetts, southern Vermont, San Francisco Bay Area, Madison, Wisconsin, Canada, Mexico, Europe, the Middle East, South America and Asia. Concepts such as worker cooperatives are threatening to the corporate state. How are they going to get people to work for poverty wages at a fast food restaurant if a worker cooperative is available as an alternative? Capitalism needs poor people.

124

Dennis House mentioned on *Face the State* that the city was putting together a stadium proposal that would include other elements, including the planned North Hartford supermarket which initially was scrapped after the stadium deal was announced. The concern with this plan would be a lack of access for North End residents on days that the Rock Cats are playing or the stadium is in use for other events, due to traffic and parking issues. Councilman Larry Deutsch, who was a guest on *Face the State*, talked about the need for year-round jobs that pay a living wage. The city's revamped proposal should include a stipulation that jobs connected to the stadium, supermarket and any other businesses must meet these criteria. Deutsch said that he has asked the city's attorneys if $50 million will be placed in an escrow account, so that the city will have cash on hand if the Rock Cats move in four or five years and the city is stuck with an empty stadium. No one at this point had given Deutsch an answer.

House had a problem with Deutsch's plan to have a public referendum on the stadium, because of the city's low voter turnout. The number is low because residents in the poverty-stricken areas of Hartford see that their economic plight remains the same, no matter who gets elected. House would obviously prefer that Segarra and Wooden make the call with no input from community residents, which is what started this damn mess in the first place.

House's stance on the stadium plan is yet another example of what *Democracy Now!* host Amy Goodman refers to as the Access of Evil. House was acting as a mouthpiece for the city's power brokers, who wanted this stadium to be built on the people's dime.

While House and his colleagues at WFSB sat and smiled in front of TV cameras every day, all hunky-dory with their white privilege, people of color in this city were dying slowly. These community residents bravely endure poverty on a daily basis; if the on-air personalities at WFSB experienced these conditions for 15 minutes, they would jump out of a window. I'm talking about folks who stay outside all day during the summer. They're not out there, because they're enjoying the fine weather. They can't stay inside too long, because it's so damn hot and they don't have air conditioning. I submit that if House and his co-workers had to walk a mile in the shoes of the poor; their approach to journalism would change dramatically.

The only time that you will see a WFSB satellite truck in North Hartford is when a Black or Latino male is being chalked out in the street; they have no interest in covering a community meeting on the socioeconomic causes of urban street violence. WFSB regularly perpetuates the racist image of North Hartford as the area to be avoided at all costs. The truth is that the North End is filled with insightful people who see through the BS of city politics better than anyone else. House, why don't you actually talk to them and ask how they feel about the hustlers who work at 550 Main Street instead of blaming the people for the voter turnout numbers? I'm talking about the people who live on streets like Cabot, Enfield and Westland, the areas that WFSB uses to air their images of violence pornography. You could even have North Hartford residents as guests on your show. Talk to the people for a change, instead of the crooks and liars whose public policies have created the conditions that WFSB exploits every day.

June 30

Gubernatorial candidate Jonathan Pelto and his running mate Ebony Murphy both ducked CP member Mary Sanders' question about racial justice issues during a candidate forum on Monday. Sanders asked Pelto what his strategy was for dealing with poverty, welfare reform and mass incarceration. Pelto rambled on about the importance of Mary's question, and then pivoted to his talking points about Malloy.

Bruce Covert of *Think Progress* reported on Walmart being penalized for closing down a store in Canada after workers unionized.

"Walmart is known for resisting efforts to unionize its American workforce. But in Canada, one of its stores actually voted to join a union—and then six months later, the company shut the store down.

In September of 2004, the United Food and Commercial Workers Union (UFCW) was certified as a representative of employees in a store in Jonquiere, Quebec. In April 2005, just before an arbitrator was about to impose a collective agreement, Walmart closed the store.

On Friday, the Supreme Court of Canada ruled that Walmart violated Quebec's labor laws in doing so. It found that the company closed the store during a freeze period codified in the law, which limits a business's ability to change working conditions from the time that employees file to unionize to when they have a contract, go on strike, or are locked out. The court ruled that Walmart ran afoul of this law without a valid reason for closing the store, which never re-opened.

The company has said it didn't close the store because workers joined a union. In an email to the AP a Walmart spokesperson said, "We are disappointed by the decision."

An arbiter will now determine remedies for the 190 fired employees, including possible payment for damages and interest."

It's worth repeating that the Walton family; the owners of Walmart, are huge investors in the charter school industry, which targets unionized public school teachers as scapegoats of "failing" schools. The 'Walmartization' of education is part of the overall attack on state and municipal employees.

Meanwhile, back in Iraq, ISIS has declared the creation of an Islamic state. *Democracy Now!* reported on the latest developments.

"The Sunni militant group leading a rebellion against the Iraqi government has declared a Muslim caliphate in the parts of Syria and Iraq under its control. In a statement, the Islamic State in Iraq and Syria, known as ISIS or ISIL, said it will now be known as the "Islamic State." The group also called on Islamist factions worldwide to pledge allegiance, a potential challenge to its former ally, al-Qaeda. Iraqi lawmakers are holding a key session on Tuesday to begin selecting a new government. This comes as the Iraqi army has launched a new offensive to retake the northern city of Tikrit. Speaking in Geneva, a spokesperson for the United Nations refugee agency said aid officials have been unable to reach tens of thousands of displaced Iraqis.

Christiane Berthiaume: "There are hundreds of roadblocks which not only prevent us from joining people who need help to bring them assistance, but which also prevent people from getting out in order to join a distribution point. There is no freedom of movement. We can't join them, and neither can they join us.'"

July 2014

A Gambler's Budget: The Fiscal Year 2014-15 State Budget Wade Gibson, J.D.

This report on the two-year state budget approved by state lawmakers and the Governor in June warns that the "quick-fix" budget solutions adopted in the budget will deepen the state's long-term budget deficit and could ultimately endanger funding for child and family services. The analysis highlights the use of borrowing, one-time revenues, and fund transfers to close budget deficits and cover operating expenses. By relying on these measures, rather than recurring revenues to close the state's budget gap, the report by the Fiscal Policy Center at Connecticut Voices for Children concludes that state policymakers have opened up a larger revenue hole in future budget years.

The report, which examines the two-year budget plan for Fiscal Years 2014 and 2015, finds:

• Over the two-year period, the budget plan relies on almost $600 million in borrowing, over $400 million in temporary fund transfers, and $500 million in one-time revenues to pay for operating expenses. Because these funding sources will dry up at the end of the two-year budget, there is currently a projected state deficit of $712 million in Fiscal Year 2016 and comparable holes in 2017 to 2018. If state policy makers had instead used recurring revenues rather than one-shot revenues and borrowing, the long-term budget would be nearly balanced in these years.

• Reliance on debt and one-time revenues will further increase budget risks for the state if economic growth does not return quickly. The state's budget projections assume that robust economic growth will result in increased state tax revenues. With a nearly empty Rainy Day reserve fund, if this growth does not emerge, Connecticut would have little choice but to turn immediately to deep cuts, steep tax increases, and more borrowing.

• The state government has transformed over $1 billion in debt it owed itself and its employees into debt it now owes to bondholders, resulting in less flexibility and control of the repayment of that debt. While the state budget plan pays down funds owed to the state employee and teacher pension systems, it does so by borrowing money from private bondholders. In addition, the state has borrowed money from the private market to meet stricter accounting requirements under the rules of Generally Accepted Accounting Principles (GAAP). While in an emergency, state policymakers could ask employees and retirees for concessions to preserve vital public services, the state can expect less flexibility from the private bond market.

Malloy administration Chief of Staff Mark Ojakian responded to a reporter's question about the possibility of cutting the State Earned Income Tax Credit for the poor, which was already cut last year, by saying, "Everything is on the table." Well, not quite everything; a truly progressive income tax on the rich, closing corporate tax loopholes and implementing regulation of corporate welfare isn't on the table, in the room, in the house, or anywhere in the neighborhood as far as Malloy and lawmakers are concerned. The projected deficit following the November election was $1.32 billion. During a debate between Republican gubernatorial candidates (Tom Foley did not participate) there was a call for more "shared sacrifice" in the form of additional state employee concessions, layoffs and the repeal of collective bargaining rights. State employees have agreed to concessions, including a wage freeze, twice since 2009. During the debate over the budget bill GOP lawmakers read a laundry list of statistics, which they cited as proof that the state is headed in the wrong direction under Malloy and the Democratic Party controlled legislature. These conservatives conveniently left out one number; the $3.6 billion deficit that Malloy inherited from his predecessor, Republican M. Jodi Rell.

The common denominator in Connecticut's economic nightmare is the Democrats and the GOP.

While their failed economic policies consisting of coddling the rich and corporations at the expense of the working class and the poor, spending cuts, fund raids and shell games keep this state drowning in red ink, the national movement for publicly owned banks continues to grow. Elected officials on the left and the right realize that public banks are a common sense solution to state budget woes and can be a boost to local economies. Two of the public bank bills that have been introduced in over 25 states were sponsored by Republicans in Arizona and Virginia. North Dakota, the home of the country's only publicly owned bank, is a red state. Budget deficits are used as a pretext for the nationwide attacks on public employees. This corporatist agenda is all about using privatization to roll back the wages and benefits of all workers. Once again, lawmakers celebrated the end of another legislative session where the issue of poverty and racial economic disparity was ignored. Don't get it twisted; the $10.10 minimum wage bill, which doesn't go in effect until 2017, was an election year gimmick, which will not change the economic condition of low wageworkers. A comprehensive measure like the MXGM Jackson Plan is a true formula for economic justice.

Researcher and author Stacy Mitchell explained how public banks could revitalize state and local economies in a 2011 *Yes Magazine* article.

"There's no single solution to the thorny problem of how to restructure our financial system, but one of the most promising strategies involves creating state-owned banks that can bolster the lending capacity of local banks, helping them grow and multiply.

North Dakota is the only state, so far, that has a publicly owned bank. Founded in 1919, the Bank of North Dakota (BND) was a populist response to dynamics similar to those we face today. The state's struggling farmers, tired of being at the mercy of powerful out-of-state financial interests that controlled the availability and cost of credit, decided they needed a bank better aligned with their own interests.

BND is wholly owned by the state, which deposits all of its money, except pension funds, with the bank. BND does not compete with local banks; it does not solicit retail banking business and has no branch offices or ATMs.

Instead, BND partners with local banks to expand their lending capacity. Much of BND's $2.8 billion loan portfolio consists of 'participation loans.' These are business loans originated by local banks, which then invite BND to finance a portion of the loan (and share part of the risk). This enables local banks to make more loans and maintain more diverse portfolios.

Thanks largely to BND, North Dakota has a more robust community banking network than any other state. It has 35 percent more local banks per capita than South Dakota and four times as many as the U.S. average. Small local banks account for 60 percent of deposits in North Dakota, compared to only 16 percent nationally.

Inspired by the North Dakota model, activists and small-business owners in more than a dozen states backed bills this year to create state-owned banks.

Over the last decade, lending by North Dakota's local banks has averaged about $12,000 per capita (plus about $2,400 in participation lending by BND), compared to just $3,000 for community banks nationally. BND has also enabled local banks to maintain a higher loan-to- asset ratio than their counterparts in other states, which means they devote more of their assets to productive lending, rather than safer holdings like U.S. securities.

Although BND has some loan programs that accept a higher risk or lower return to meet specific economic objectives, such as its Beginning Entrepreneur Loan Guarantee Program, the vast majority of its lending decisions are made on a for-profit basis. It participates only in loans that make economic sense. As a result, BND has pumped $300 million in profit into the state's general fund over the last decade. (In a state like Illinois that has a population of 13 million, the equivalent return would be about $6 billion)."

In 2014, Elizabeth Warren (D-MA) who ran on a platform of reforming the banking system, launched a campaign to expand postal services to include banking for underserved communities. Low-income urban and rural communities lacked access to financial services. A white paper by the United States Postal Service (USPS) Inspector General entitled *Providing Non-banking Financial Services to the Underserved* explained the benefits of postal banking.

"The Postal Service is well positioned to provide non-bank financial services to those whose needs are not being met by the traditional financial sector. It could accomplish this largely by partnering with banks, who also could lend expertise as the Postal Service structures new offerings. The Office of Inspector General is not suggesting that the Postal Service become a bank or openly compete with banks. To the contrary, we are suggesting that the Postal Service could greatly complement banks' offerings. The Postal Service could help financial institutions fill the gaps in their efforts to reach the underserved. While banks are closing branches all over the country, mostly in low- income areas like rural communities and inner cities, the physical postal network is ubiquitous. The Postal Service also is among the most trusted companies in America, and trust is a critical element for implementing financial services. With affordable financial offerings from the Postal Service, the underserved could collectively save billions of dollars in exorbitant fees and interest. This could make a big difference to struggling families—on average, people who filed for bankruptcy in 2012 were just $26 per month short of meeting their expenses."

The consensus among supporters of postal banking was that congressional approval was not needed by the USPS, as they already provide financial services such as dispensing money orders. David Dayen of *New Republic* magazine reported that the IG conducted the study in collaboration with a team of international postal banking experts, along with a former Merrill Lynch executive. Dayen pointed out the international success of the postal banking system.

"In other countries, this market is served at the post office. Almost every developed nation in Europe and East Asia operates a postal banking system. A few have been privatized, including what was the world's largest savings bank, Japan Post.

And some operate as a private-public partnership. But countries like Israel, France, Switzerland, Russia, South Korea, South Africa and more all allow their citizens to perform simple banking tasks at the local post office. New Zealand's Kiwibank, a recent innovation, was established in 2002 specifically to protect citizens from financial predators."

The USPS actually provided financial services from 1911 until 1967, when they were squeezed out of the market by the big banks.

The National Association of Letter Carriers supports postal banking, but the USPS brass has not gotten behind the concept, choosing instead to come up with cost cutting measures like reducing the frequency of mail delivery from six to five days, and—get this—eliminating door-to-door mail delivery. Under the USPS plan, there would be a gradual shift to "centralized" and "curbside" delivery. Sounds crazy, right? This provision actually made it into President Obama's 2015 fiscal year budget plan. Progressive ideas, which would revitalize the USPS, clearly didn't interest Obama. The message from the President was, "Yes We Can make you drive to the mall to pick up your damn mail."

July 2

The Service Employees International Union endorsed Malloy... Foley qualified for public financing on his third try... Office of Policy and Management Undersecretary Mike Lawlor, Central Connecticut State University researcher Ken Barone and token black William Dyson of the so-called Connecticut Racial Profiling Prohibition Project attempted to spin the latest data on racial profiling in this state.

CONNECTICUT STOPS MINORITY DRIVERS AT HIGHER RATE

BY DAVE COLLINS

ASSOCIATED PRESS

HARTFORD, Conn. (AP)—New data show that Connecticut police pull over black and Hispanic drivers at disproportionate rates when compared with population numbers, but state officials caution the reasons aren't clear.

In the nearly 304,000 traffic stops made by police statewide from October to April, 14 percent of the drivers were black and nearly 12 percent were Hispanic. According to census figures, nearly 8 percent of Connecticut residents who are old enough to drive are black and 9.7 percent are Hispanic. Police pulled over about 256,800 white motorists during the same time period, representing 84.5 percent of all traffic stops. Whites 16 and older comprise about 84 percent of the state population. Asian drivers, meanwhile, got stopped at a lower rate when compared with the

133

population. About 1.1 percent of traffic stops involved Asians over 16, who comprise 3.6 percent of the population.

The numbers were compiled by researchers at Central Connecticut State University under a revamped state law designed to prevent racial profiling by police. A new computer system went live in November and began collecting a wide range of traffic stop data from all 106 police agencies in the state, including the race, ethnicity and sex of drivers, the reason for the stop and any enforcement actions taken.

"The question is what's driving it," said Michael Lawlor, state undersecretary for criminal justice policy and planning, referring to the higher minority traffic stop numbers. "You really have to drill down several levels (of data) to determine if there's a problem or not."

Those several levels of data are expected to be released next month in the first full report from the new information system. The report will include data from every police agency, and the public will be able to go online and view all the numbers. Officials released only the statewide totals on Thursday.

Kenneth Barone, a researcher at Central Connecticut State, said there could be many reasons why minorities are pulled over at higher rates. For example, he said, a police supervisor in one part of a city may place a stronger emphasis on traffic stops than a supervisor in another part, which could skew total numbers for the entire city.

Former state Rep. William Dyson, a Democrat from New Haven, said there is certainly a perception in minority communities that police target blacks and Hispanics for traffic stops more than they do whites. But he said it's too early to tell from the new numbers whether there are racial profiling problems in the state.

The racial profiling law was approved in 1999 and named after the late state Sen. Alvin Penn of Bridgeport, who pushed to require police officers to record the race and ethnicity of drivers they pull over. But the effort failed in the following years when less than a third of police departments in the state submitted the information as required to the state African-American Affairs Commission, which did not have the resources to process the data.

The legislature and Gov. Dannel P. Malloy overhauled the law in 2012.

I wrote a commentary in October 2013 on *the Penn Act* advisory board protecting the police in Connecticut. The lack of political power in low-income communities of color has been evident during the racial profiling issue in Connecticut. Keep in mind that the CP encountered

134

resistance to our racial profiling bill from a Democratic Party controlled legislature and a Democratic governor.

July 12

On June 12 WNPR—FM reported that activists were discussing a plan to collect the 1400 signatures needed to trigger a referendum on the stadium. Wooden, a panelist on the Fox CT Capitol Report Sunday morning political talk show, began to backpedal by stating on the program that the "private sector" now would have to step up and fork over some dough for the stadium; the original plan was for the city to borrow the money.

Part 2

Racism Report:

Penn Act Advisory Board

The members of the Connecticut Racial Profiling Prohibition Project, the puppet Alvin W. *Penn Act* advisory board of Gov. Dannel Malloy, have not mentioned the Department of Justice investigation of racial profiling by the East Haven Police Department during any of their meetings which were televised on the Connecticut Network, nor have they mentioned the 2012 DOJ indictment of EHPD officers David Cari, Dennis Spaulding, Jason Zullo and Sgt. John Miller or the trial of Cari and Spaulding on their website: http://www.ctrp3.org

Last week I left messages with advisory board members Ken Barone, American Civil Liberties Union legal director Sandra Staub and Redding Police Chief Douglas Fuchs asking for an explanation. Predictably, Staub did not return my call. Fuchs told me that informing the public about the East Haven case or studying the DOJ investigative report on the EHPD isn't something that the advisory board, which is supposedly working to stop racial profiling in this state, needs to do. "That's not our charge," Fuchs said. "Our job isn't to look backward. Our job is to collect traffic stop data in the best manner possible." I then asked about the disparity in the reactions to the Newtown school shooting and the East Haven case.

Following the spree killing at Sandy Hook, a legislative task force on gun violence was created. The task force visited suburban towns, including Newtown (while excluding gun violence plagued cities Hartford, New Haven and Bridgeport) to discuss possible solutions. The gun laws in Connecticut were subsequently strengthened. Police officers were assigned to selected schools. I pointed out to Fuchs that clearly the state "looked backward" at the Newtown shooting and implemented measures designed to prevent that tragedy from happening again. The reaction by the state, reflected by Fuchs' comments, to the East Haven case has been the exact opposite. After a lengthy pause, Fuchs reiterated his position that the East Haven case is not the advisory board's concern. After questioning my "professionalism" Fuchs would not respond when I asked him if he had anything to say to the Latino East Haven residents who have testified at the trial about being harassed and brutalized by Spaulding and Zullo.

Testimony by EHPD Sgt. Anthony Rybaruk supports residents' testimony against Zullo. The advisory board's stated purpose of data collection is to determine if racial profiling is happening in Connecticut (duh). The East Haven case is irrefutable evidence of biased policing which the board has chosen to ignore.

Barone, who has been the public face of the advisory board and is listed as the contact person on their website, would not answer my questions and ever so politely referred me to Bill Dyson, the advisory board chair/figurehead (and the Black guy). Dyson started off by totally contradicting Fuchs, as he said that the East Haven case was the impetus for the formation of the board, and that the board is formulating policies in direct response to the case. Dyson then said that he has not read the DOJ investigative report of the EHPD! Like Fuchs, Dyson had no answer for why the advisory board hasn't discussed the case during their televised meetings and community forums or during any legislative hearings and why there is no mention of the case on the advisory board's website. Dyson had a problem with my contention that he could not effectively develop policies to respond to the case if he didn't know squat about what actually happened. I submit that the board has not mentioned the DOJ investigation of the EHPD or the trial of Cari and Spaulding because their true assignment is to protect the police. My conversations with Fuchs, Barone and Dyson and Staub's display of

138

cowardice have strengthened my belief. In an astonishing display of arrogance, Dyson repeatedly asked me why the advisory board should study and discuss the DOJ report. I challenge Dyson to ask the Latino East Haven residents who have suffered at the hands of Cari, Spaulding, Zullo and Miller that question, if he has the guts.

Trayvon Martin, Political Football

The World Socialist website recently published a commentary entitled "Democrats Seek to Channel Mass Anger Over Killing of Trayvon Martin." The piece included the following assessment of the political reaction to Trayvon's murder. "Various politicians, both Democrat and Republican—including President Obama—have sought to express sympathy for Martin. Their aim is to forestall any discussion of the more basic social questions behind the killing, and to divert popular anger into safe political channels." The piece went on to give the example of a Trayvon Martin rally in Detroit where several speakers used Trayvon's killing as a reason for why Obama should be re-elected. This type of opportunism is not limited to the major political parties. Occupy Hartford, a group who I criticized in a recent column for ignoring the racial profiling bill which is currently being debated at the State Capitol, quickly climbed aboard the Trayvon bandwagon by posting articles about the shooting and promoting a rally in North Hartford, which featured Mayor Pedro Segarra, City Councilman Kyle Anderson and Democratic Party operative LaResse Harvey as speakers.

The lynching of Trayvon Martin was manipulated by Hartford Democrats and "community leaders." "Community leaders" participated in what were basically Democratic Party pep rallies, attended by Mayor Segarra and other Democrats. The World Socialist Website published a series of columns, including one entitled, "Democrats Seek to Channel Mass Anger Over Killing of Trayvon Martin." The columns examined how the Democrats and their operatives pimped Trayvon for political gain.

"Various politicians, both Democrat and Republican-including President Obama-have sought to express sympathy for Martin. Their aim is to forestall any discussion of the more basic social questions behind the killing, and to divert popular anger into safe political channels. Politically, the demonstrations have been dominated by supporters of the Democratic Party and officials in the Democratic Party. Typical was Detroit, where several thousand gathered, Reverend Horace Sheffield II spoke before the event at Detroit's Hart Plaza. He told the crowd, 'If you look behind any incident like this, there is someone who someone did vote for or someone who someone didn't vote for.' Several speakers openly called for what the rest implied—a vote for Obama. Racial inequalities exist and racism is promoted by sections of the ruling class. However, this is one particular expression of the fundamental division in society: class. Indeed, the most horrific levels of poverty and unemployment for black workers are to be found in cities overseen by black mayors, politicians, police chiefs and businessmen. There is popular anger over the acquittal (of Zimmerman), seen as a travesty of justice that also sets a dangerous precedent. Sections of the Democratic Party, however, have sought to exploit the tragic case for their own ends."

"Activists" who have never cared about the killing of Black youth are suddenly showing tremendous interest in the Trayvon Martin case, a display of hypocrisy, which can only be described as pathetic. While there are many people who are involved with the Trayvon Martin movement who are sincerely outraged and seeking justice, there are just as many who are simply using Trayvon as a vehicle to advance their own agendas. The social issues that the World Socialist Website alluded to, certainly include racial profiling, police violence in communities of color, racist criminal justice policies, including the so called War on Drugs which is actually a war on low-income urban neighborhoods, black unemployment, racial economic disparity, racialized politics and racism in the mainstream media. This confluence of factors has resulted in a nationwide perception of young Black males as a threat that must be dealt with accordingly. The right wing has capitalized on this stereotype by launching a smear campaign, which portrays Trayvon as a foul-mouthed, weed-smoking jewel thief. Glen Ford of the *Black Agenda Report* pointed out in a recent commentary that the racist policies of national and local governments gave George Zimmerman the impression that American society would approve of his actions. Ford noted that during his 911 call to police Zimmerman proclaimed that "assholes" like Trayvon "always get away," a ludicrous statement given the facts about black mass incarceration in this country. It should be noted that none of Zimmerman's 46 911 calls since 2004 resulted in any arrests or the need for further action by police. Since the start of 2011, Zimmerman's calls primarily focused on what he considered to be "suspicious" people in his neighborhood. Almost all of these "suspicious" individuals were black males, including one whom Zimmerman described in a 911 call as being "7-9" years old.

Democrat President Bill Clinton was instrumental in fueling black mass incarceration through his support of racist criminal justice policies and the "welfare reform" law, which has continued the cycle of poverty in black communities. President Obama refused a 2009 demand, by members of the Congressional Black Caucus, that he initiate targeted job creation in communities of color, where black unemployment has reached Depression-era levels. The unemployment rate among young black males in some areas of Hartford is as high as 50%. Hartford has one of the highest poverty rates in the United States at 31.9%. These are the types of connections that the Democrats and their gatekeeper sycophants in North Hartford do not want you to make to the lynching of Trayvon Martin.

The lead homicide investigator in the Trayvon Martin shooting wanted to charge Zimmerman with manslaughter on the night of the killing, but was overruled by the Florida state's attorney. The Sanford police reportedly tagged Trayvon's body as a John Doe, despite the fact that a police report filed February 27 at 3:07 a.m. lists his name, city of birth, address and phone number. The cops did not contact Trayvon's parents until his father filed a missing person report later on the 27th. Why did the police hide Trayvon's body from his parents?

Zimmerman's father, a retired judge, told a Florida TV station that he talked to the police and the state's attorney's office after his son shot Trayvon. What did they discuss? Mary Cutcher, a witness to the shooting, which took place in her backyard, told Florida TV station *WFTV* that Zimmerman was the aggressor, and that it was Trayvon who was screaming for help, before he was fatally shot. Cutcher said that the police only took a brief statement from her and that they have repeatedly blown off her attempts to talk further with them about what she saw and heard. The police did not take a statement from Trayvon's girlfriend, who was on the phone with Trayvon when the confrontation with Zimmerman took place. His girlfriend had offered to come in for a sit down interview. The Orlando Sentinel reports that voice experts have refuted Zimmerman's claim that he is the one who is heard calling for help on the 911 tape. A legal analyst for *WFTV* says that Zimmerman disobeying the order from the 911 dispatcher not to follow Trayvon negates his self-defense claim. Yet Zimmerman had not been arrested at that time.

The Democratic Party is using operatives such as Al Sharpton to contain the national Trayvon Martin justice movement, while simultaneously promoting the criminalization of Black youth, which directly led to Trayvon's death. As I have reported above, a MXGM report found that Blacks are killed every 28 hours by the police, security guards and self-appointed vigilantes such as George Zimmerman. The Trayvon protests, which have involved Democratic politicians, totally avoid the topic of police containment in black/brown communities, which includes harassment, brutality and murder as tactics, and ignore facts such as the MXGM *Operation Ghetto Storm* report's finding that Blacks are killed at a rate of one person every 28 hours by police, security guards, and vigilantes like Zimmerman, who was studying law enforcement at the time he lynched Trayvon. The Sanford, Florida police did not arrest Zimmerman until global protests forced the hand of the State's Attorney.

During a protest against the Zimmerman acquittal in Hartford, Mayor Pedro Segarra spoke vaguely about how "our government has failed us." He added that a conversation must begin to "bring justice and peace."

Okay Mayor, let's talk about President Obama endorsing New York Police Department Commissioner Ray Kelly for the vacant Secretary of Homeland Security job. Kelly's racist stop-and-frisk policy currently has Blacks and Latinos in New York under siege. The Atlantic Wire laid out the statistical proof of this racism in a May article on David Floyd's stop-and frisk lawsuit against the City of New York. Floyd was subjected to a stop-and- frisk in 2008.

"That stop was one of the 540,000 times that year that the police performed a stop-and-frisk procedure. It was one of the 444,000 times that year that the person being frisked was Black or Latino. It was one of the 474,000 times that year that the person being frisked was not arrested for having committed a crime. For the next three years, those figures would grow."

Obama said, "Ray Kelly's obviously done an extraordinary job in New York." The first Black President clearly supports Kelly's law enforcement policies, which include stop-and-frisk. MXGM pointed out on their Twitter page that naming Kelly to the Homeland Security post would lead to nationalizing the stop-and-frisk practice. Obama is talking out of both sides of his mouth. While he talks about how Trayvon would have looked like his son and how he could have been Trayvon 35 years ago, Obama is giving his stamp of approval to the racist police tactics, which created the climate that led to Trayvon's murder. Black Youth Project blogger Mo Green discussed Obama's hypocrisy in a recent column.

"See, while Obama is busy telling black people that he feels their pain while simultaneously explaining that pain to white people, his administration is doing the work of ensuring that the white supremacy that led to Trayvon Martin's death and his killer's acquittal remains functioning. Now, Kelly may never be nominated, but the very fact that he has been linked to the administration in this way is once again a reminder, to me at least, that having a black head of state is insufficient for dismantling the very system that violently impacts black people's lives on a daily basis. Kelly shouldn't even be an option."

Black Agenda Report commentator Glen Ford weighed in:

"The president has high praise, and possibly a powerful appointment in store, for Ray Kelly, the New York City Police Commissioner who has overseen and defended over five million stop-and-frisks since 2002, overwhelmingly targeting black and brown men. Obama is looking for a new head of Homeland Security. 'I think Ray Kelly is one of the best there is,' Obama said. Kelly proudly justifies his management of the Mother-of-All-Stop-and-Frisk operations, as intended 'to instill fear' in young Blacks and Latinos that they may be patted down by a cop whenever they leave their homes. Kelly also created a massive program to spy on Muslims, not only in New York City but in other localities, and arranged for CIA agents to be embedded in the NYPD to conduct domestic surveillance—which is illegal."

Will Segarra and Council President Shawn Wooden talk about the fact that the Democrats are using Trayvon's death as a tool to recruit black voters? The World Socialist Web Site reported on how the national protests that were organized by Sharpton turned out to be a pep rally for the Dems.

"Demonstrations were held in cities throughout the United States over the weekend in response to the acquittal of George Zimmerman, who killed Trayvon Martin in Sanford, Florida, last year. There is popular anger over the acquittal, seen as a travesty of justice that also sets a dangerous precedent. Sections of the Democratic Party, however, have sought to exploit the tragic case for their own ends. The demonstrations were relatively small, with the largest in New York attracting more than a thousand people.

Several hundred gathered in other cities, including Los Angeles, Washington, D.C., Miami, Detroit, and Pittsburgh.

The protests were organized by National Action Network (NAN), founded by Al Sharpton. Sharpton and the NAN are an integral component of the Democratic Party establishment, seeking to use racial politics to divert opposition over disastrous social and economic conditions back into the Democratic Party.

A primary demand promoted by the organizers, who cast the issues entirely in racial terms, was for Obama's Justice Department to bring charges against Zimmerman on civil rights grounds. Sharpton, who spoke at the New York event,

144

praised Obama for his remarks at a press conference Friday, when the president equated himself with Trayvon Martin.

The lineup of Democratic politicians was so deep at the New York rally that the person introducing speakers felt compelled to state that it was not an election rally. In Detroit, mayoral candidate Krystal Crittendon took to the megaphone, saying, 'One thing we can all do for Trayvon is show up at the ballot box and vote. We need to let them know that we will not stand for this. We can take control by voting.' "

CP is calling on Segarra and Wooden to publicly denounce the Democrats for pimping Trayvon Martin in an effort to increase the party's voter base, and to call out Obama for his public support of Kelly for the Secretary of Homeland Security position. Kelly's appointment would certainly lead to the federal implementation of stop-and-frisk. This policy and the feds' "Secure Communities" anti-immigrant program are Black and Brown community containment tactics. CP's Jashon Bryant/Trayvon Martin Act is aimed at abolishing this law enforcement policy. Ending police containment and racial economic disparity is the way to "bring justice and peace" that Segarra called for at the Hartford rally. Let's see if Segarra and Wooden have the guts to spark this conversation.

Like the Trayvon Martin case, the 2013 murder of black teen Jordan Davis by Michael Dunn, continued the pattern of injustice related to the extrajudicial killing of Black males. I wrote a commentary on the Jordan Davis trial verdict February 22, 2014.

The Jordan Davis murder trial ended last Saturday, as a Florida jury convicted Michael Dunn of three charges of attempted murder and another charge of firing into an occupied vehicle. Judge Russell Healy was forced to declare a mistrial on the first-degree murder charge after the jury said it was deadlocked. The circumstances of this case are well documented; the verdict definitely sent a mixed message. Dunn faces 60+ years in prison when he's sentenced in March. For the 47-year-old Dunn, that's obviously a life sentence. Nancy Grace of HLN reports that Dunn will not be eligible for parole. However, Dunn was not convicted of lynching Jordan, who was unarmed when he was shot by Dunn while sitting in the backseat of an SUV, according to the testimony of eyewitnesses. Dunn showed no emotion when the verdict was read.

The Black community is rightfully angered by the jury's inexplicable failure to convict Dunn on the murder charge, but they should express the same level of interest in the routine extrajudicial killing of Blacks in the United States. More on this shortly.

Apparently, the Mister Rogers sweater Dunn wore during his testimony was enough to offset the fact that Dunn fled the scene, never called police or discussed the shooting with his fiancée. Rhonda Rouer testified that Dunn also never mentioned Jordan having a firearm, which totally contradicted Dunn's claim that Davis was armed with a shotgun and Dunn acted in self-defense. After the shooting, Dunn returned to a hotel with Rouer and ordered a pizza. The obvious rhetorical question is would Jordan have been able to spend the night in a plush hotel munching on fast food if he had shot a white, middle-aged software developer? Not bloody likely. Even if Dunn had been convicted of murdering Jordan, the systemic issues, which led to the killing remain. If a Black person is killed by a police officer, security guard, or vigilante every 28 hours, aren't armed vigilantes like George Zimmerman and Dunn simply imitating the behavior of killer cops who routinely get away with executing Black males?

Dunn's attorney produced a few character witnesses who testified about what a "peaceful" guy Dunn is. The jury never heard about Dunn's racially charged jailhouse letters or Dunn's neighbors, who told the Davis family lawyer about Dunn's history of violence, fraud, drug use and racist behavior. Charles Hendrix said that Dunn attempted to solicit him to do a hit on a man who was suing Dunn's software company. Hendrix added that he reported this crime to the local police, who showed no interest. Hendrix's wife said Dunn used the word "nigger" on two occasions, and she had to admonish him not to use racial slurs in her home. Mrs. Hendrix went on to say that when her husband told her about Dunn shooting Jordan, her first thought was that Dunn always wanted to shoot someone. Jordan's parents at least know that their son's killer will spend the rest of his life behind bars. Unfortunately, the extrajudicial killing of Black people remains rampant and Dunn was not held accountable for lynching Jordan. The State of Florida will retry Dunn on the murder charge. I totally agree with Grace, who said that Dunn must be retried on principle. The record should show that Dunn is guilty of murder.

Zimmerman and Dunn were simply imitating the behavior of killer cops who routinely get away with executing Black males. The CP's Trayvon Martin Act is designed to address the extrajudicial killing of Blacks.

Trayvon Martin Act Bill Language

It's time to take action to stop racial profiling and police containment in Black and Brown communities here in Connecticut.

Trayvon was shot and killed after being approached on the street by Zimmerman, an armed neighborhood watch leader. Dunn shot Jordan Davis during an argument about loud music. Former Bay Area Rapid Transit police officer Johannes Mehserle murdered Oscar Grant in 2009 with no provocation or reason. Since 2010, over 1500 Black people have been killed by police. A few of the more recent victims include Tom Yancy, Yvette Smith, John Crawford, Tamir Rice (12 years old), Tanisha Anderson, Jason Harrison, Gregory Lewis Towns, Michael Brown, Kaldrich Donald, Robert Baltimore, Cameron Tillman (14 years old), Hallis Kinsey, Ray Paul Kemp, David Andre Scott, Eugene Williams, Robert Storay, Ezell Ford, Emanuel John-Baptiste, Victor White, Lashano Gilbert (from New London, CT), Eric Garner, Akai Gurley, David Yearby, Latandra Ellington, Wllie Hsarden, Rumain

Brisbane, Mathew Walker, Tyree Woodson, Charles Smith, Darrien Hunt, DeAndre Lloyd Starks, Denis Grigsby, Samuel Shields, Ernest Satterwhite, Kenneth Lucas, Jerry Brown, Dontre Hamilton, Jeremy Lake, and Sandra Bland.

We've had many unnecessary deaths right here in CT as well. CP's *Trayvon Martin Act* is aimed at addressing this public safety crisis.

The Trayvon Martin Act calls for the creation of a legislative task force on police misconduct and includes some of CP's original racial profiling bill language. The CT legislature passed some of our provisions in 2012 and they were scheduled to go in effect July 1, 2013. Last year our traffic stop receipt language was repealed in favor of a version emphasizing electronic data collection and analysis, instead of a copy of the mandated "Traffic Stop Report" going to the motorist. We believe this copy is the only way for motorists to know how their race is being represented and is a proven factor in undetected biased policing. We sat in on testimony of dozens of motorists of color from around the state who were stopped, harassed, given tickets with race recorded as White, and heard of many other biased law enforcement actions.

Problem: Drivers do not get a copy of the Stop Report which has allowed some officers to lie about the race of the people they stop. Some victims of profiling may not complain because they don't know officers are covering up the profiled stops. As we mentioned previously our traffic stop language was passed by lawmakers in 2012 but was repealed due to pressure by the police before it was scheduled to become law in 2013.

Addition to current law:

"1) Traffic Stop Reports are to be filled out in duplicate so that each motorist receives a copy of the completed form from the officer, in addition to any ticket or summons if one is issued. 2) The copy of the report should be given to the driver as well as the information on filing complaints if motorists believe they have been profiled. 3) If the reports are entered into an electronic data collection system a copy will be immediately available to the detained driver."

Problem: Drivers and their passengers are being asked for identification and questioned about their immigration status even when they are clearly not involved in criminal activity.

Addition to current law:

"1) The driver shall only be asked for a: Driver's License, the Vehicle Registration and Proof of Insurance and no other identification or questions about immigration status; 2) Passengers shall not be asked for any identification or questions about their immigration status unless they are being arrested for criminal activity."

Problem: Men of color are stopped and frisked or worse in every corner of our state; community residents have reported to us that if they dare challenge police officers in their neighborhood, they are often thrown to the ground, cuffed and arrested, and then charged with resisting arrest.

This happens to our teenagers in schools as well as on our streets. Many have been beaten or shot by police or others with "authority," often fatally as the MXGM report shows.

Addition to current law:

"1) Create a Legislative Task Force which would serve in the following capacities: a) investigate complaints of misconduct of state or local police officials, b) provide training and oversight to public school guards, university and transportation police, c) provide training and oversight of neighborhood watch organizations and properly screen and monitor persons functioning in these roles; 2) the Task Force will reserve spots for urban lawmakers whose constituents are disproportionately affected by these issues; 3) the Task Force will conduct monthly public hearings around the state, days and evenings, which would also be broadcast by the Connecticut Network for television or online viewing; 4) the Task Force will create a process whereby people could file formal complaints about profiling and harassment by police or other law enforcement authorities through their legislators' offices or CHRO."

Part 3

July 2014

Oh, the horror... It's the return of... campaign ads. Pazniokas of *The Mirror* reported on Foley buying TV time. The brainwashing of the public begins.

"The low-key Republican primary for governor is about to get a higher profile: Tom Foley's campaign has purchased about $40,000 of time on three broadcast stations in the Hartford-New Haven market, with the first commercials scheduled to air Monday.

Records on file with the FCC show that Foley's campaign reserved the time Tuesday, the day before the State Elections Enforcement Commission approved his application for public financing, providing him with a quick infusion of more than $1.35 million.

A spokesman for the elections commission said Foley is free under the law to reserve the TV time before winning approval of public financing so long as he does not incur expenses that exceed the $1.35 million primary grant and the $250,000 in qualifying contributions.

Participants in the voluntary public-financing program must abide by spending limits of $1.6 million for a primary and $6,500,400 for the general campaign.

His opponent, John P. McKinney, has applied for public financing and says he is optimistic his grant would be approved next week."

Pazniokas reported that GOP Sen. John McKinney and his running mate David Walker were close to obtaining public financing for their campaign.

"The Republican ticket of John P. McKinney and David M. Walker said Friday that an initial review of its application for public financing by the State Elections Enforcement Commission has raised questions about just $4,600, leaving them with hopes of still winning approval next week.

A gubernatorial campaign must submit $250,000 in qualifying contributions of no more than $100 each to obtain public financing, and each must be accompanied by paperwork detailing each donor's name, home address and employer.

This morning we received a report that the SEEC review of our application for grant funding will only require follow-up on about $4,600 in contributions in order to qualify for the state grant. The required paperwork will be submitted expeditiously," the campaign said.

By contrast, the SEEC validated only $220,000 of the $264,000 originally submitted by the GOP convention-endorsed candidate, Tom Foley, leaving him $30,000 short of the qualifying threshold.

Foley twice failed to meet the qualifying threshold, but he exceeded the mark Wednesday after submitting $16,549 in additional donations and further documentation for other contributions."

July 4

It was an eventful week between the CP and Pelto's camp. Gubernatorial candidate Jonathan Pelto and his running mate Ebony Murphy both ducked CP member Mary Sanders' question about racial justice issues during a candidate forum on Monday. Watch for yourself at the 1:26:21 mark of the video.

In response to my pointing this out, Ebony Murphy replied:

July 4, 2014 at 12:13 pm

Hi David. At least you're not calling me a 'token' this week, so that's something to be pleased about this Fourth of July. Is being a 'token' the flipside of being 'uppity?'

How dare I, some teacher from Laurel St, ponder running for public office? I deal with issues of racial justice on a personal level daily with two brothers ages 19 and 25 who are both in that 'targeted for incarceration' demographic. I worry about them every time they get behind the wheel of their cars. I have had my own experiences being pulled over and 'accused' of stealing my own car most recently as August 10, 2013, in Manchester. I also happen to be a black person myself, and have been for almost 32 years, though you may not have noticed because I happen to be a WOMAN at the same time as being black, so even I 'wanted' to dodge issues of racial justice, racism, and sexism, which I don't, I could not. You know what's funny is my entire adulthood, and before then, too, I have been 'accused' of talking too much about race and then simultaneously 'accused' of being a 'token' or not being black enough. These are experiences I am sure you can relate to, David.

Obviously, I care about the profound economic disparities in our cities and in our state at large, and the issues such as mass incarceration and access to education and training, that intersect with racism and poverty. The reason I became a teacher all those years ago at a GED program for pregnant and parenting teens is because I see clearly how all these issues come to together to affect the lived experience of young people and their families and communities. So 'ducking?' Nope, here I am.

Ebony and Pelto's sycophants clearly had their orders to start spinning. Pelto still hasn't responded to my comments about him welshing on his promise to me to include an urban agenda in his platform. I guess Pelto was too busy handing out his petition to Republicans. As for the rest of the yapping from Pelto's camp, all I will say is that a video is worth a thousand words.

My Conversation with Jonathan Pelto re: Urban Agenda

Below is a series of Facebook message exchanges between myself and independent gubernatorial candidate Jonathan Pelto. As I mentioned above, Pelto welshed on his promise to me to include an urban agenda in his campaign platform. Note that Pelto did not respond to a message from me reminding him of that promise. Pelto told me that he would draft a racial justice plan covering economic and criminal justice issues, and share it with me prior to releasing it publicly.

From me to Jonathon Pelto:

I'm going to call a spade a spade. Even a broken clock is right twice a day. After observing Steve Perry critics for the past few months, I now believe that he is correct when he says that race is a factor in the campaign against him. When I started out criticizing Perry on my Twitter page, whites were retweeting me, becoming followers and interacting with me. When I started talking about the need for folks to stop fixating on Perry and educate the public about what he represents (Wall Street's war against public employees, systematic oppression of workers through bullying), whites became offended and acted like they didn't understand what I was saying.

I see that I'm still being kept on the outside by you and others who started the campaign against Perry. I'm not going to allow myself to be used as a token while a predominantly white led coalition goes after a Black target. One of my pet peeves is phony white liberals and I'm definitely seeing what I consider to be a racist element in the strategy whites are employing against Perry.

You used to be a lawmaker. You know that changing public policy is the only way to improve the conditions in this country. Even if the Board of Education got rid of Perry TODAY, you know that the profit driven charter school system and the attacks on public schools and teachers will continue. The Community Party is working on legislation which would address Perry's bullying of teachers and you have done nothing to support the bill. I told you weeks ago that we're holding a public event this month which will give teachers and parents an opportunity to share their complaints with a lawmaker; you never responded. Buttering me up with a blog post and a flowery holiday email cannot obscure what I'm seeing. I am insulted.

David Samuels

Founder, Community Party

January 15, 5:56am

Jonathan Pelto replied on January 18, 1:53am:

David, I'm sorry I certainly didn't intend to keep you on the outs. I'm trying to work on as many pieces of this corporate education reform stuff as possible and still work on all the other issues. I've tried support your work on the profiling stuff and I on the workplace bullying. If I dropped the ball I'm sorry and hope we can resolve the problem.

To which, I replied,

Are you going to promote Matt Ritter's town hall on your blog? Are you going to email your coalition and encourage them to attend? Will you attend and bring some teachers with you to tell Matt how they have been bullied at Capitol Prep? Are you going to publicly support our effort to expand the Safe Work Environment Act to cover city employees such as public school teachers?

154

Pelto responded,

Yes, will publicize, will share with teachers, will do all I can to support.

I asked Pelto,

Do you know about this bill? It would allow charter school employees to unionize.

http://www.cga.ct.gov/asp/cgabillstatus/cgabillstatus.asp?selBillType=Bill&bill_nu
m=5066&which_year=2014&SUBMIT1.x=12&SUBMIT1.y=13

Bill Status

http://www.cga.ct.gov

Connecticut General Assembly Official Legislative Site for Bills, Legislation, Statutes,
and sessional activity. Visit our site to find all your legislative information

Pelto replied,

NOPE, THANKS!

On February 2, 7:07am, I messaged Pelto,

No problem. This bill would provide employees with some protection against
workplace bullies like Perry.

On April 6, 2:43pm, I sent another message to Pelto,

You wrote a column about how the state is playing Clark School parents, but it seems
like members of your coalition (AFT CT, Hartford Rising) are also playing them.
What's up with that?

Pelto responded,

Fair question—I'll start looking.

To which I replied,

I'll be doing the same.

Later in April, on the 20th at 3:07pm, I messaged Pelto again,

I suggested months ago that you run for governor; you should definitely do it. Blogging is not enough. The Democrats take voters on the left for granted. The people need an alternative and the Democrats must be challenged from the left. A third party candidacy would give liberal/progressive voters a real choice.

And a week later,

I'm deeply disturbed that since you've been discussing your possible gubernatorial candidacy you haven't talked about racial justice issues, specifically poverty, Black and Latino unemployment and racial wage/wealth disparity in Hartford and other urban areas. You've talked about poverty often in your blog; I've quoted you multiple times in my Hartford News column. You have also talked about the Community Party's racial profiling bill, which I sincerely appreciate. That being said, I'm going to have a lot to say about any gubernatorial candidate who ducks racial justices issues. I know how candidates water down their message for the sake of political expediency.

Tom Foley has created a think tank on urban policy. That's a smokescreen, but at least he said the word "urban." If I don't hear any talk about urban policy from gubernatorial candidates on the left, I'm going to have a big problem with that. I'll call a spade a spade; I think it's good you've been holding Malloy accountable for the past few years but I see that like other liberals (Black, Latino & white) you avoid talking about the layered aspects of structural racism, which I know is the reason why you tend to distance yourself from me. I'm just going to give you fair warning that I will hold you accountable if you don't use your platform to talk about race and how structural racism impacts the economic and criminal justice systems in this state. You should also know that a few months ago an urban legislator asked me to ghostwrite a public message to 2014 gubernatorial candidates, demanding that they include an urban agenda as part of their platform.

Pelto did not respond, so, the next day, I wrote,

Malloy ignoring you for four years did not work for him; I don't know why you think that will work for you. Have it your way; it's on.

The following day, Pelto replied,

David, the fault is simply being overwhelmed with things, and still trying to make a living and raise a family. I assure you I will not run without a breakthrough urban platform and will not develop one without sitting down to discuss and include the work you and the Community Party are doing. Politicians like to use words like 'promise,' but I promise you that I have it on my top tier to do list.

Jonathan

> I replied,

Jonathan, I've been hearing this from you for years. We're all overwhelmed in our own way. I'll believe what you're saying when I see it.

> Pelto responded,

Fair enough. I'll put things down on paper and share them with you.

> On June 15, I wrote to Pelto,

I just heard on Fox CT that you're running; there weren't any reports on the media outlets I check daily on Twitter. I don't see an urban agenda listed on your platform. I haven't received the plan for low-income communities of color that you promised.

> Pelto still has not responded.

July 7

Foley's campaign ad debuted. The Greenwich billionaire was portrayed as a "regular dad." Foley was shown fixing a car with his oldest son (apparently his on-call mechanics had the day off) and playing with his 2 ½ year old twins.

Back in 2003, the U.S. attempted to crush an uprising by Iraqi workers after successfully overthrowing Saddam Hussein and occupying the country. The U.S. Coalition Provisional Authority busted unions and banned strikes as they slashed workers' wages back to the levels that were in place under Hussein. Guess who was an integral part of these worker suppression tactics? *Democracy Now!* interviewed *Progressive* reporter David Bacon about his article "The Occupation's War on Iraqi Workers." Bacon explained that $87 billion in funding would not be used to improve the conditions of Iraqis.

"Remember that the $87 billion is on top of the $60 billion that was appropriated to fight the war. So, we have a total of $147 billion that is being spent, or is set to be spent in Iraq—and this money is going to be spent not on improving conditions for the Iraqi population. For instance, there is no unemployment benefit system in Iraq. If you lose your job, if you are one of those lucky people who has a job and you lose it, you're in deep trouble because there is no unemployment benefit system.

These new unions being formed in Iraq are all calling for an end to the Occupation as part of what they see will improve conditions for Iraqi workers and also give them some voice over the direction of the Iraqi economy. Right now, workers have no voice over these privatization plans.

They're simply being announced by Americans, by people from the United States like Tom Foley, who is the Occupation Authority's representative for private sector development. He gets into the newspapers in Baghdad and announces the industries that will be privatized.

But there is no process, even, of consultation with Iraqi workers, let alone any process in which they can decide over whether or not the property of the Iraqi government is going to be sold off or turned over to private owners."

Foley's "Father Knows Best" TV ad did not include any mention of his tenure in Iraq.

During an interview with Pazniokas, McKinney laid out his economic plan should he be elected governor. You know the Republican drill; spending cuts, tax cuts (especially for the rich), coddling of big business and attacks on public employees. While Foley has said that he would keep spending flat, McKinney told Mike Savino of *the Manchester Journal Inquirer* that he will make cuts. Savino reported that Foley would have to cut spending by $893 million during the next fiscal year in order to maintain the state's $19 billion 2014 spending level. McKinney plans to demand more concessions from state workers, who have agreed to concessions twice since 2009. Twenty-two hundred state positions would be cut under a McKinney administration. New state employees would have a 401 (k) program shoved down their throats, instead of having a pension. McKinney told Savino that he will impose a hiring freeze. While McKinney would eliminate the practice of workers boosting their pensions with money earned working overtime and retired employees would no longer be able to return to work (collecting a pension and a salary), the hypothetical new governor would not go after companies who sock away far more cash by using a tax loophole to ship their profits out of state. McKinney would implement income and estate tax cuts.

How effective are tax cuts in stimulating state economies? Michael Leachman and Chris Mai of the Center on Budget and Policy Priorities present Kansas as a case study.

"As other states consider large tax cuts, they should heed these key lessons from Kansas:

Deep income tax cuts caused large revenue losses.

Kansas' tax cuts this year are costing the state about 8 percent of the revenue it uses to fund schools, health care, and other public services, a hit comparable to a mid-sized recession. State data show that the revenue loss will rise to 16 percent in five years if the tax cuts are not reversed.

The large revenue losses extended and deepened the recession's damage to schools and other state services. Most states are restoring funding for schools after years of significant cuts, but in Kansas the cuts continue. Governor Sam Brownback recently proposed another reduction in per-pupil general school aid for next year, which would leave funding 17 percent below pre-recession levels. Funding for other services—colleges and universities, libraries, and local health departments, among others—also is way down, and declining.

The tax cuts delivered lopsided benefits to the wealthy. Kansas' tax cuts didn't benefit everyone. Most of the benefits went to high-income households. Kansas even raised taxes for low-income families to offset a portion of the revenue loss; otherwise the cuts to schools and other services would have been greater still.

Kansas' tax cuts haven't boosted its economy. Since the tax cuts took effect at the beginning of 2013, Kansas has added jobs at a pace modestly slower than the country as a whole. The earnings and incomes of Kansans have performed slightly worse than the U.S. as a whole as well. (An exception is farmers, whose incomes improved as the state recovered from a drought.) And so far there's no evidence that Kansas is enjoying exceptional business growth: the number of registered business grew more slowly last year than in 2012, and the state's share of all U.S. business establishments fell over the first three quarters of last year, the latest data available.

There's little evidence to suggest that Kansas' tax cuts will improve its economy in the future. No one knows for certain how Kansas' economy will perform in the years ahead, but it isn't likely to stand out from other states. The latest official state revenue forecast, from November 2013, projects Kansas personal income will grow more slowly than total national personal income in 2014 and 2015."

No matter who was elected, Connecticut would continue to be subjected to the conventional economic policies which keep this country in the toilet.

Martha Page, executive director of Hartford Food System and Rex Fowler, executive director of Hartford Community Loan Fund, the two organizations working to bring a full-service supermarket to Hartford, wrote an op-ed to The Courant. Page and Fowler advised against the city's revamped stadium plan, which would include a grocery store.

"We needed an operator with a unique skill set for a Downtown North store. We found one in Connecticut, one with decades of experience operating successful, community-oriented supermarkets in cities, serving highly diverse customer groups. The operator was eager to incorporate the supermarket into a larger vision for a 'Healthy Hartford Hub' that might include a community teaching kitchen, an in-store nutritionist, a walk-in health clinic, a pharmacy and a culinary training program for city residents.

Following the announcement of the city's new vision for Downtown North, no longer to be anchored by a supermarket but instead by a baseball stadium/entertainment venue, our operator and investors indicated the proposed development's change in orientation increased the risk of our project too much. Many if not most of the supermarket's projected shoppers would still be driving to a Downtown North store and might understandably opt to buy food in the suburbs on game days to avoid stadium traffic.

That doesn't mean supermarkets and stadiums can't co-exist. The risk is mitigated in cities such as Boston and San Francisco, where good public transportation systems allow stadium patrons to take a subway to a game rather than drive, or where supermarket customers are more likely to walk to the store rather than take their cars. Hartford isn't there yet."

The letter by Page and Fowler is yet another effective argument against the stadium. North Hartford needs an accessible supermarket to address the food desert problem in that area. This stadium plan is just a vanity project for the city's power brokers.

July 8

Immigration advocates protested in Washington DC in support of children fleeing murderous chaos in Central America. CNN reported that families in Guatemala were being terrorized through extortion, kidnapping and murder, including the murder of children. Children from Honduras were fleeing the murder capital of the world. President Obama, dubbed the Deporter in Chief by his critics, did not disappoint. While liberal media pundits railed about House Republicans' obstruction on immigration reform, they avoided mentioning an inconvenient fact; Obama has deported more undocumented immigrants than George W. Bush. Right-wing immigrant bashers certainly don't want to talk about an Immigration Policy Center report, which found that undocumented immigrants pay more in taxes than the wealthy.

Democracy Now! reported on the protests in DC.

"In the United States, immigrant advocates gathered at the White House to criticize the Obama administration's treatment of immigrant children fleeing violence and poverty in Central America. More than 52,000 unaccompanied children from Guatemala, El Salvador and Honduras have been seized at the U.S. border since October, about double the amount over the same period last year. Protesters say many of the children are trying to rejoin their families.

The Obama administration is poised to ask Congress for $2 billion to pay for more detention centers and immigration judges to handle the influx. The White House said Monday most of the children are unlikely to qualify for humanitarian relief and would be deported. According to the U.N. high commissioner for refugees, 58 percent of unaccompanied children detained by the United States could be entitled to refugee protections under international law.

Obama asked for $3.7 billion. In a classic case of doubletalk, Obama described this situation as an "urgent humanitarian situation" in his letter to Congress, while simultaneously planning to limit the rights of the children at court hearings. This will make it easier to deport them. Immigrant advocates were rightfully pissed. The Associated Press reported that Senate Democrats were skeptical of Obama's immigration flim-flam.

'Everybody's very concerned. I'm one of them,' said Sen. Dick Durbin, D-Ill. 'I just want to make sure that at the end of the day we're being fair, humane and doing this in an orderly way.'"

July 9

The United Nations called on the United States to accept most of the Central American migrants as refugees. Meanwhile, Obama came to Texas to do fundraising for Democratic Party congressional candidates. The President also found a little time to deal with the border crisis, as he visited with Republican Gov. Rick Perry. Perry had been a vocal critic of Obama's immigration policy. While the corporate media fixated on the "should Obama visit the border and look concerned" question, Obama held an evening press conference where he reiterated the U.S. position that most of the children would be deported.

Democracy Now! reported on the UN appeal for the U.S. to accept most of the migrants as refugees.

"As the White House vows to speed the deportation of migrant children, United Nations officials are calling for most of them to be accepted into the United States as refugees. A report by the U.N. high commissioner for refugees in March found that 58 percent of unaccompanied children detained by the United States could be entitled to refugee protections under international law. The United Nations renewed the call ahead of a meeting Thursday in Nicaragua between the United States, Mexico and Central American countries. The agenda includes updating a 30-year-old declaration on state obligations to aid refugees. The UNHCR says: "The U.S. and Mexico should recognize that this is a refugee situation, which implies that [children] shouldn't be automatically sent to their home countries, but rather receive international protection." President Obama is in Texas today meeting with Republican Gov. Rick Perry on the border crisis."

Meanwhile, in Chicago, eighty-two people were shot, 14 fatally, during the July 4 holiday weekend. While the corporate media focused on gang violence in the city, *the Chicago Reader* examined the root cause of violence in urban communities; poverty. Affluent neighborhoods are not the scene of gangs and street violence, In low-income communities of color, the local gang is the biggest employer. Unemployment among young Black males is as high as 50%. Latino unemployment hovers at Depression-era levels. Lacking opportunities, Black and Latino males turn to the underground economy to get paid, where violence is an occupational hazard. Steve Bogira of the Chicago Reader talked about the disparate rates of violence between rich and poor neighborhoods. Not surprisingly, *the Chicago Reader* report found that disease and death also occur far more often in poverty-stricken communities.

"Every life lost to homicide is a tragedy, of course—and a sense that the life was unfairly taken often heightens the pain. Compounding the unfairness, residents of certain neighborhoods are far more likely to suffer that fate. We illustrated this last month by comparing homicide rates in two sets of Chicago communities—the five poorest and the five least poor. The homicide rate in the poorest neighborhoods was 11 times the rate in the least-poor neighborhoods. And if that isn't unfair enough, poverty—and especially the concentration of poverty that segregation causes—kills disproportionately in nonviolent ways as well.

Using the same two sets of communities, we extended our analysis beyond homicide—the eighth-leading cause of death in Chicago—to other, more common causes of death. Our comparison shows that poor African-American neighborhoods should come with a surgeon general's warning. When it comes to the leading causes of death in Chicago (cancer, heart disease, diabetes-related illnesses, stroke, and unintentional injury), the mortality rate in the five poorest neighborhoods—Riverdale, Fuller Park, Englewood, West Garfield Park, and East Garfield Park—was far higher than in the five least-poor neighborhoods—Mount Greenwood, Edison Park, Norwood Park, Beverly, and Clearing. For diabetes-related deaths, it was almost double; for unintentional injury, it was more than double. The infant mortality rate—the rate of death in the first year of life—was two and a half times as high. And the death rate from all causes was 60 percent higher than in the wealthier counterparts, and 43 percent higher than the citywide rate."

Jesse Jackson called on Obama to fund economic development and jobs in high crime Chicago areas. Jackson said that Obama should find money to address gun violence in Chicago just as quickly as he did in response to the border crisis. "If we can find $4 billion for those children—and we should—we can find $2 billion for Chicago. There are more children involved, and more have been killed, and more have been shot." Obama has not mentioned Black/Latino unemployment once during his two terms in office.

Back in Connecticut, petitioning independent gubernatorial candidates Jonathan Pelto and Tea Party member Joe Visconti crossed paths outside a state board of education meeting. They exchanged petition signatures and spoke about their united opposition to the Common Core curriculum standards. Visconti's platform also included so-called gun rights. The legislature passed a sweeping gun control bill during the 2013 session, a response to the infamous spree killing at Sandy Hook Elementary School in Newtown. Visconti hoped to use that issue to differentiate himself from Foley, who had been evasive regarding his opinion on the gun bill, and McKinney, who voted for it. McKinney's district included Newtown. McKinney and his running mate David Walker announced that they qualified for public campaign financing. The pair taped their first campaign ad, which was expected to air soon.

Campaign ads are the most visible representation of money in politics. These ads show candidates telling you how they will return (insert name of state here) to prosperity. The candidate is shown in a factory talking to workers and helping senior citizens cross the street. What you usually won't see is any mention of the candidate's actual policy positions. Attack ads can sink their targets (see Mike Dukakais) but they do not guarantee victory (see Linda McMahon vs. Chris Murphy). George W. Bush's ad squad successfully used racism with the infamous 1988 Willie Horton ad against Dukakis, in order to paint Dukakis as being soft on crime. Dukakis was also hurt by the Bush campaign's "Dukakis in the tank" ad, which was a case study in how a public relations blunder could come back to harm a candidate. Campaign

164

ads are simply vehicles of misinformation. Candidates are being sold, like all other products.

July 10

CNN's website posted an opinion piece on urban policy by Foley and Ben Zimmer, the executive director of Foley's Connecticut Policy Institute. The commentary included the usual GOP propaganda about deregulating businesses, privatizing education and locking up more Black people, cloaked in a message about "solutions" for low-income communities of color. The Malcolm X Grassroots Movement Jackson Plan is a truly egalitarian blueprint for addressing the economic plight of black and brown neighborhoods.

July 11

Obama's $3.7 billion emergency spending bill to deal with the refugee crisis on the country's southern border was moving swiftly through the Democratic Party controlled Senate but had stalled in the House, where the Republicans held the majority. GOP leaders balked at the cost of the bill... House Mayor Pedro Segarra withdrew a proposal to bond up to $60 million for a stadium. Segarra said that the project would have to be financed by the private sector. The much needed North Hartford supermarket that was originally planned remained derailed by the stadium proposal.

A *New York Times* article by Benjamin Mueller on the stadium plan was arguably the best written piece about this issue. Mueller raised several important points, including the need for the North End supermarket. "A 2012 study showed Hartford to be eighth worst in the nation for access to healthful, affordable food when compared with cities of similar size." Mueller talked about the lack of transparency around the stadium plan, pointing out that the people involved with the supermarket proposal were never told about the stadium negotiations, which took place over a period of eighteen months. Mueller interviewed a community resident who was unimpressed with Segarra's decision to have the private sector finance the stadium.

"'Calling the city's emphasis on private financing a 'rhetorical shift,' Jamil Ragland, a North End resident opposed to the plan, said city leaders were misguided. 'The grand goal seems to be to bring in white suburbanites from the outside,' he said, 'as opposed to actually addressing the needs of people in the city. Sitting in his North End apartment on a recent afternoon, Mr. Ragland, 28, said the priorities of the city's politicians were misplaced. Boutique fragrance shops and upscale groceries that have recently opened in Hartford seem like a bid for the business of 'mobile, middle-class, white people,' he said. 'If we don't have money to spend on $30 soap or $9 spaghetti sauce or handcrafted beer from a brewery,' Mr. Ragland said, 'we just don't exist then. You don't want me here.'"

Finally Mueller talked about the slim chance of the stadium becoming a reality; even with the shift in emphasis to obtaining private sector funds.

"Hartford's push for private financing did not surprise industry analysts, who said that the team-friendly deals that once sailed through city governments were now wilting in the face of concerns over tax increases and cuts to social services. As minor league baseball expansion slows and cities face more trouble drawing outside visitors to stadiums, baseball executives said, Hartford's plan to draw private investors faces steep hurdles.

'To think they could even come up with a third of stadium costs is not possible,' said Miles Wolff, the commissioner of the Can-Am League and the American Association, two independent baseball leagues. 'Ballparks don't make money. That's why they're public facilities.'

Richard Foley, a former state Republican chairman who now heads a political consulting firm, said, 'I would be surprised if it ever gets built.'"

Mueller's article underscored the Hartford Democrats' total disregard for the poverty stricken North End, and the anger residents in that neighborhood felt when they observed the elitist, tone deaf indifference of Segarra and Wooden. Many people in North Hartford don't have disposable cash that they can donate to the Democratic Party war chest, so elected officials aren't checking for them. As Ragland said, poor people in Hartford are invisible to the likes of Segarra and Wooden; the interests of low-income communities of color don't factor into the policy decisions being made at City Hall and the State Capitol. I'll keep it real; I was rooting to see Wooden lose the August 12 primary against Sen. Eric Coleman, because it's obvious that Wooden is a mercenary who is only concerned about his political career. That being said, conditions in the North End have only worsened during Coleman's time in office; his criticism of Wooden regarding the stadium plan, while accurate, is clearly self-serving. North Hartford would lose no matter who won the Coleman vs. Wooden primary.

July 14

The Connecticut Mirror reported on independent gubernatorial candidate Jonathan Pelto's budget plan. Pelto, who claims to be an alternative to Malloy, Foley and McKinney, rattled off the stale Democrat talking point about how he would stand up for the middle class. Pelto did not mention poverty or low-income communities of color once. It was hilarious to hear Pelto, who gave former GOP chairman Chris Healy a petition to get himself on the ballot in November, talk about lying Democrats and Republicans while referring to himself as a "truth- teller." Pelto should pursue a stand-up comedy career after the elections are over.

Last week CNN's website posted an opinion piece on urban policy by Foley and Ben Zimmer, the Executive Director of Foley's Connecticut Policy Institute. The commentary included the usual GOP propaganda about deregulating businesses, privatizing education and locking up more Black people, cloaked in a message about "solutions" for urban neighborhoods. The Malcolm X Grassroots Movement

Jackson Plan is a truly egalitarian blueprint for addressing the economic plight of the black and brown community...

Malloy's first campaign ad debuted. The biggest lie was Malloy's claim about fixing the budget. Yes, the current $1.4 billion shortfall was less than the $ 3.7 billion deficit Malloy inherited from former Republican governor M. Jodi Rell. However, the ad failed to mention how Malloy's $500 million "surplus" for the fiscal year ending June 30 shrunk to $43 million, due to a tax revenue shortfall of more than $450 million. Malloy's "balanced budget" was achieved by the Democrat controlled legislature raiding funds (e.g. transportation, tobacco health trust) and other smoke and mirrors tactics.

Finally, McKinney's first TV ad consisted of his usual public employee bashing and the claim about how he's going to reduce the size of state government. Here's a reality check from Connecticut Voices for Children. "Connecticut's state and local government has not grown as a share of the economy since 1970. Connecticut's state and local government is the 5th smallest in the country, relative to the size of its economy."

Have I mentioned that the 2014 gubernatorial election was a false choice?

President Obama's Justice Department gave Citigroup a barely audible slap on the wrist for selling toxic mortgage products during the mid-2000s. Erika Eichelberger of Mother Jones reported that the DOJ fined Citigroup $7 billion, which only affected the company's second quarter profits while their overall earnings remained in the black. No executives went to jail, as usual. Citi shareholders, not the company brass, had to eat the loss. Despite the fact that Citi committed fraud, the DOJ pursued a civil case instead of hitting the company with criminal charges. Just another day at the office for the 'Too Big to Jail' banks.

Eichelberger went on to describe the DOJ speed bump.

"The settlement deal is simply the 'cost of doing business,' says John Taylor, the president and CEO of the National Community Reinvestment Coalition, a housing advocacy group. Citi will 'pay these fines and move on.'

The Citi deal is one of several lukewarm settlements the government has entered into with banks in recent years over financial crisis-related wrongdoing. In November, JPMorgan Chase agreed to pay a record $13 billion for selling toxic mortgage products in the run-up to the financial crisis. Some experts say the fine should have been 22 times higher. Last year, Sen. Elizabeth Warren (D-Mass) sent a letter to the Justice Department, noting she was concerned that the Obama administration was letting big banks off too easy: 'If large financial institutions can break the law and accumulate millions in profits, and if they get caught, settle by paying out of those profits, they do not have much incentive to follow the law.'"

Law Professor Erwin Chemerinsky's 2012 commentary on three strikes law reform in California underscores the disparity in the punishment the so-called justice system dishes out to the big banks and us peasants.

"Individuals have been sentenced to life in prison under the three strikes law for stealing a slice of pizza or a pair of batteries or a handful of videotapes. For example, my client, Leandro Andrade, was sentenced to life in prison with no possibility of parole for 50 years for stealing $153 worth of videotapes from K-Mart stores. He received this sentence under California's three strikes law even though he had never committed a violent felony. His only prior convictions were for three burglaries of unoccupied homes that occurred many years earlier. On November 6, California voters approved Proposition 36, which reforms California's three strikes law to require that a third strike be a serious or violent felony. Additionally, it allows re-sentencing of many of those whose third strike was a minor offense.'"

July 15

Asean Johnson, a 10-year-old student activist who lives in Chicago, responded to a piece by columnist Roland Martin, who suggested that the National Guard be deployed in the city. During the July 4 holiday weekend, 84 people were shot, 16 fatally. Martin talked about declaring martial law, as community residents would be subjected to searches and seizures. The daily street executions of Blacks must be kept in mind when considering Martin's plan.

Jasiri X of the Black Youth Project reported on Asean's assessment of Martin's National Guard strategy.

"According to Asean, sending the National Guard to Chicago would just, 'escalate the violence'. Challenging Roland Martin's assertion that Chicago residents are walking around in 'perpetual fear' Asean, who lives in Roseland, said his community is a 'very welcoming and loving community, we just don't have the resources'. Asean's mom Shoneice spoke in even more specifics, 'we need affordable housing, wellfunded schools, wrap around services with counselors and social workers. We haven't been invested in in decades.' Asean called Roland Martin's use of the term Chiraq, 'an insult to the people of Chicago'.

Karen Lewis, President of the Chicago Teachers Union, was also a keynote speaker at the American Federation of Teachers (AFT) Convention. Karen called Roland's call for the National Guard, 'ludicrous' and said she was, 'tired of people offering simplistic solutions'. She further stated, 'this isn't a policing problem, if it was it would be solved. We have places in Chicago that have been economically divested in for decades. How can we pull ourselves up by our bootstraps when we have no boots?'

Jitu Brown, Education Organizer for Kenwood Oakland Community Organization, spoke about how the closing of 50 schools in the Black and Brown neighborhoods of Chicago created a 'powder keg'. He said the violence in Chicago is a result of, 'an open ended lack of regard for a specific group of people; our communities are being set up.'"

Gun violence in Chicago continued to rage as President Obama remained silent on the carnage in his hometown. Forty people were shot during the weekend. Four victims, including 11-year- old Shamiya Adams who was attending a slumber party, were killed. Shamiya was struck in the head by a stray bullet. Mayor Rahm Emanuel repeated his vague call for Congress to provide more resources for education and jobs; he would not support the plea from Jesse Jackson that Obama request federal emergency funding, as he had in response to the Central American child refugee crisis. Emanuel's support of the privatization of
170

Chicago schools, which resulted in the closure of 50 public schools in 2014, was obviously a root cause of the chaos in the city. Chicago had become the poster child for the Democratic Party's total disregard of low-income communities of color.

Yet Obama flew to Newtown right after the heinous spree killing at Sandy Hook, while requesting $ 3.7 billion from Congress to address the influx of Central American child refugees. Obama should be equally proactive in taking on the socioeconomic factors, which fuel gun violence in Chicago and other low-income communities of color across the country.

Malloy's administration refused to take in 2,000 of the Central American immigrant child refugees at the request of the federal government, claiming that the Southbury Training School, the designated site, was too small and not equipped to house the children. Latino advocates expressed disappointment with Malloy's decision and said that another site could be found to house 500 of the children. Obama encouraged governors to house the children while Congress debates his $ 3.7 billion emergency spending bill to address the border crisis. *The New Haven Register* did not accept Malloy's lame excuse, as they responded with a scathing editorial. The Register rightfully pointed out that the real reason why Malloy gave the refugees the boot was because of his fear of offending bigoted swing voters.

"Despite the logistical reasons Malloy cites, there's really only one reason we 'can't' help. Our governor is a Democrat facing a tough re-election fight in November. The bottom line is that too many swing voters fear immigrants, and Malloy doesn't want the 'optics' of hundreds of brown-skinned, Spanish-speaking children being bused into Connecticut as uninformed and misinformed debate over border security and immigration policy meet continued anxiety about the state's economy."

Amen.

Conservatives like to perpetuate the image of undocumented immigrants or "illegals," as they're compassionately labeled by the right, hopping, skipping and jumping across the U.S. border.

171

The reality is different. Undocumented immigrants from Central America face a horrific journey to this country, as they battle oppressive heat. Many do not survive. Bethania Palma Markus of Truth-out.org reported on the death toll.

"According to US Border Patrol statistics, 477 people died crossing in 2012, and 445 died crossing in 2013. The numbers have steadily shot up since 1998, when 263 died, according to the agency's statistics. A total of almost 7,000 people have died between 1998 and 2013. But the true number is likely higher, considering many are never found."

Laura Raymond of Truthout talked about another inconvenient fact that conservatives would rather avoid, which is that undocumented immigrants are often fleeing conditions caused by U.S. foreign policy. "The individual stories of those fleeing Honduras are varied, but most have the rampant violence in their country as a common denominator." As Nelson Arambu, an LGBT community organizer from Honduras recently told me, "The wave of migrants from Honduras are no longer coming here to work, they are coming to save their lives." Since the military coup that ousted President Manuel Zelaya in 2009, violence and repression have continued to increase. Honduras currently has the highest murder rate in the world. The current refugee crisis at the US border is a foreseeable and understandable consequence of this violence.

"Unfortunately, after playing a widely criticized role in legitimating Honduras's post-coup government, the US government is now using this crisis to further entrench its alignment with one of the most corrupt and violent police and military forces in the hemisphere. Couched in language about bolstering 'security' and 'prosperity' in the region, both the White House and the Senate have proposed yet more US 'investment' in the very Honduran security forces that are responsible for the violence, human rights abuses and lawlessness that are contributing to the flight of tens of thousands of Hondurans."

The surge of Central American refugees is a classic case of blowback. This country supports brutal governments around the globe, as long as those governments serve U.S. interests. Then there is the irony of people living on stolen land screaming about "illegals" invading their country. Of course, we're all too familiar with the genocide perpetrated against Native Americans; which is routinely glossed over in the sanitized history of the U.S. The xenophobia, which fuels immigrant bashing by the right, is the height of hypocrisy.

July 16

A Foley campaign ad aired which attacked both Malloy and Foley's primary opponent McKinney as being "insiders" and "career politicians." Foley's ad included a false claim about McKinney supporting Malloy's $1.5 billion tax increase, which the Democratic controlled General Assembly passed in 2011. The ad also used the standard GOP "bigger government" rhetoric. Foley's ad labeled Malloy and McKinney, whose TV ad attacks Malloy and Foley and touts McKinney's commitment to "smaller government", as being in favor of bigger government."

Did you follow all of that? I didn't either.

July 17

Phaneuf of *The Mirror* reported that Assemblyman Juan Candelaria, the chairman of the Connecticut Black and Latino caucus, wrote a letter to Malloy urging him to reconsider his decision not to house Central American child refugees.

"We cannot keep our arms crossed while these detention centers continue to overflow and these children suffer in the direst of conditions through no fault of their own. Let's not make them [the children] suffer for mistakes that others have made. They should not be treated as criminals when they do not represent any threat to our public safety or public health."

The response from the Malloy administration was a kindly worded statement expressing sympathy for the children, while reiterating their position that they could not meet the feds request; in other words, the refugees were Obama's problem.

July 18

WNPR reported that McKinney's ad team lifted audio from an interview with Foley and inserted it into video of Foley speaking on his position regarding budget spending. McKinney spokesperson Jodi Latina claimed that there was nothing shady about the stunt. Foley had said that he would not cut spending, but would instead keep spending flat. McKinney's team chopped up the WNPR audio so that only Foley's comment about not cutting spending was heard over the video of Foley speaking. Politics at its finest. Foley and McKinney quickly broke a gentlemen's agreement not to bash each other during the primary, as Republicans believed the attacks on Foley by former Lt. Gov. Mike Fedele during the 2010 GOP primary weakened Foley when he took on Malloy in the general election. Fedele endorsed Foley in 2014. Both Foley and McKinney were deceiving the public in an effort to win the GOP nomination.

Meanwhile, one thousand people protested the water shutoffs in Detroit. This human rights atrocity remained off the corporate media radar. *Democracy Now!* reported on the protest.

"In Detroit, Michigan, more than 1,000 people from across the United States gathered Friday to protest the city's mass shutoff of water to thousands of residents who are behind on payments. Nine people were arrested for blocking the departure of trucks from a private firm hired to conduct shutoffs. According to the water department, more than 15,000 households saw their taps cut from March through June, with more than 90,000 at risk after falling at least two months behind on their bills. A U.N. panel has called the shutoffs a "violation of the human right to water."

July 21

WFSB *Face the State* host/corporate shill Dennis House aired another infomercial on the Hartford stadium plan. Mayor Pedro Segarra's communications director Maribel La Luz was a guest; she talked about the stadium in terms of the facility being an anchor for high-end stores. La Luz did not mention the proposed North Hartford supermarket once. The focus of the program was how a stadium/retail complex could attract suburban whites into the city. There were no North End residents on the panel. Activist Cornell Lewis led a protest against the stadium plan. Cornell told Fox CT that signatures were being collected to force a referendum on the stadium. Fourteen hundred signatures were needed to place this issue on the ballot.

Kennard Ray was quietly hired as the Deputy Registrar of Voters for the City of Hartford. Last year Segarra hired Ray as his Deputy Chief of Staff. Ray withdrew from the position after sensationalized corporate media reports about his legal history led to Segarra throwing Ray under the bus. Segarra said that Ray messed up because he didn't discuss his legal history during the job interview. The city's Ban the Box ordinance stipulates that an applicant does not have to talk about past legal issues during an interview. Segarra said that Ray had to be held to a "higher standard." A subsequent review by the Hartford Internal Audit Commission found that Segarra had hired several employees in his office who did not undergo a security background check; some had not even filled out a job application.

New Jersey Gov. Chris 'Bridgegate" Christie, the head of the Republican Governor's Association, came to Connecticut to endorse Foley and raise money for the GOP. Christie vowed to come to Connecticut frequently leading up to Election Day on November 4. Christie, who had traded barbs with Malloy in the past, said that he liked Malloy personally but didn't think that he was a good governor. Christie said that his criticism of Malloy was based on policy, as he talked about Connecticut's poor economic numbers during Malloy's first term. Foley

175

aligning himself with Christie was a clear indication that the Republicans believe Christie's scandal had blown over. A few months, earlier emails revealed that Christie's staffers shut down lanes on the George Washington Bridge to screw over Fort Lee mayor Mark Sokolich, a Democrat who did not support Christie's reelection campaign.

July 22

Malloy tried to get on voters' good side by claiming that the state had a $121.3 million surplus. This number was still far short of the $500 million promised at the start of the legislative session. McKinney attacked the smoke and mirrors tactics Malloy and the Democratic Party controlled legislature used to produce this "surplus". Keith Phaneuf of *The Mirror* explained the magic tricks the Malloy administration and Democrat lawmakers used.

"Among the controversial steps taken by Malloy and the legislature's Democratic majority since 2011: Canceling an early $222 million debt payment in June 2012. Instead they used $138 million to close a year-end operating deficit and put $94 million into the Rainy Day Fund. Refinancing debt to push $392 million in total payments owed this year and last until after the election. Borrowing an extra $39 million so that debt payments tied to converting state finances to Generally Accepted Accounting Principles could be deferred until after the election. The last area centers on "bond premiums." These involve bonds sold for an extra sum above their base value. In other words, the state borrows more money than originally planned, but agrees in exchange to pay a higher interest rate. In the 2012 and 2013 fiscal years, the state took $118 million in premiums that had not been anticipated in the budget or planned for use to pay off some other debt. These excess premiums effectively bolstered the operating budget and contributed toward the growing Rainy Day Fund."

Damn, that's a lot of borrowing. McKinney said that the number Malloy released was a "paper surplus," which is an accurate assessment. As CT Voices for Children described in their "Gambler's Budget" report, the rob Peter to pay Paul budget plan by Malloy and the CT Democrats is a reckless approach, which invariably fails if one time revenues fall short of projections. An unexpected boost in federal Medicaid

176

reimbursements and higher than expected revenue from state income tax receipt, coupled with Malloy kicking a nearly $ 400 million debt can down the road until after the election, gave Malloy his fake surplus. Of course economic reality would kick in after the votes are counted on November 4.

In the pot calling the kettle black news, a new ad featured McKinney railing against a Foley ad, which included the false claim that McKinney supported Malloy's tax increases and spending policies. The ad was correct about McKinney supporting Malloy's First Five corporate welfare program and the $400 million in tax credits Malloy gave to United Technologies. It was hard to feel sorry for McKinney, who was busted the week before when WNPR blew the whistle on McKinney's camp doctoring their audio in order to give the false impression that Foley said he would not cut spending. Foley is a proponent of privatizing state services. McKinney continued his smear campaign against public employees. McKinney's ad included a reference to Malloy's "sweetheart deal" with state employee unions. Pazniokas set the record straight in his report on the Foley/McKinney ad war.

"What McKinney calls a 'sweetheart deal' required employees to agree to a two-year wage freeze, a higher contribution for their retirement health care and higher premiums and deductibles for anyone refusing to participate in a wellness program. In return, the employees were given a four-year guarantee against layoffs. McKinney has had his own issues with ethics and advertising. For his first ad, his campaign doctored WNPR audio of Foley to produce a punchy sound bite of Foley saying, 'I'm not going to cut spending.' What Foley actually said was, 'I'm not saying I'm going to cut spending; I'm saying I'm going to hold spending flat' ▪

McKinney, Foley and Malloy are tools of the Wall Street campaign to privatize state and municipal services, which would result in rolling back workers' gains in wages and benefits. Connecticut voters were treated to a smorgasbord of lies, served up by these three buffoons.

Democracy Now! reported that the city of Detroit declared a fifteen-day moratorium on water shutoffs, due to protests and a class action suit by residents who said that the shutoff violated their constitutional rights.

July 23

A coalition of immigration advocates held a protest in New Haven demanding that Malloy reverse his decision not to house Central American child refugees. Malloy was under heavy fire for refusing to take in the refugees because he was afraid of offending right-leaning swing voters. No one was accepting his lame excuse about not having an adequate facility to house the children. Malloy cowering to bigots for the sake of political expediency underscored the hypocrisy of Malloy regarding race issues. He claimed to be a friend to people of color, but proved to be a fair weather friend who was unwilling to take the heat and do the right thing. Since the election season began, Malloy touted his supposed willingness to make "tough decisions." These decisions, such as his refusal to implement a truly progressive income tax on the rich while he soaked the working class with taxes and cut the Earned Income Tax Credit for the poor, usually worked to the benefit of the ruling class. Jordi Gasso of the New Haven Independent reported on the protest.

"'Governor, no more excuses!'

The plea resonated throughout the parking lot of the former Gateway Community College Long Wharf campus. The phrase 'not one more deportation' emblazoned a placard in Spanish.

Another one read, in capital letters, 'We didn't cross the border. The border crossed us.'

Brandishing these posters and banners; over 50 immigration activists and community members convened at 60 Sargent Drive Tuesday afternoon to protest Gov. Dannel P. Malloy's dismissal of a federal request to temporarily house up to 2,000 undocumented children from Central America.

178

The rally stressed the plight of these displaced minors, who have crossed the southern U.S. border often in flight from violence, and called for comprehensive action from Malloy to ensure their well-being in Connecticut. Activists also sought to put a human face on the issue:

Several Guatemalan children, most of whom crossed the border little over a month ago, spoke up during the event to share their stories of hardship and hopes for asylum."

July 24

Johanna Somers of *the New London Day* reported that Foley suggested that McKinney do himself a favor and drop out of the Republican gubernatorial primary. Foley made his comment during an interview with the newspaper's editorial board.

"Gubernatorial candidate and Greenwich businessman Tom Foley said he appreciates the endorsements from former Lt. Gov. Michael Fedele, who ran against him in 2010, and Danbury Mayor Mark Boughton, who has bowed out of the 2014 gubernatorial race, and expects state Sen. John McKinney of Fairfield, a fellow Republican also running for governor, to follow suit. "I think the right thing for John to do is to drop out of the race and endorse me, and I hope he does it," Foley said to The Day's editorial board on Wednesday. "John is a good guy, he has a political future, but I think to run in this primary and to lose, which I think is what will happen, doesn't make sense for him. And to be taking on a Republican candidate who came as close as I did in 2010, is likely to win the primary and also has a very good shot of winning in November, I think is a mistake."

McKinney of course told Foley to take a hike. Foley's strategy of saying as little as possible in response to policy questions was a hot topic with political pundits. Foley was pummeled by McKinney in a debate the previous week.

Although McKinney is full of crap like most major party politicians, his passionate speaking style was a sharp contrast to Foley, who talks as if he's announcing airport boarding times. Foley's poor

179

communication ability was an extension of his sleep inducing personality. The guy was just boring. His prevent defense campaign strategy was working against him. Foley's arrogant request to McKinney underscored his sense of entitlement regarding the GOP nomination.

Paul Ryan's "Opportunity Grant" poverty plan was roasted by the left. Ryan's plan was based on the consolidation of 11 social services programs for the poor, including the Supplemental Nutrition Assistance Program (SNAP) food stamps program. While his proposals to increase the Earned Income Tax Credit and reform the criminal justice system drew praise, the rigid block grant policy was rightfully attacked. Robert Greenstein of the center on Budget and Policy Priorities addressed the flaws of Ryan's budget plan,

"While Chairman Ryan describes the proposal as maintaining the same overall funding as the current system for each participating state; that would be a practical impossibility. His proposal would convert the nation's basic food assistance safety net—the Supplemental Nutrition Assistance Program (SNAP), formerly known as food stamps—from an entitlement that responds automatically to increased need into part of a sweeping block grant that gives each state fixed funding for the year and, thus, cannot respond in the same way. This would be a particularly serious problem when need rises, such as in recessions.

All ten programs other than SNAP that would merge into the block grant serve only small percentages of those eligible, and federal funding for them (other than low-income rental assistance programs) is comparatively modest. As my colleague Donna Pavetti points out, this means that if some people receive more services under the proposal, as Chairman Ryan envisions, those services will likely be paid for by cutting assistance that helps poor families put food on the table or a roof over their head. Some of the service programs to which funds would likely be shifted have higher administrative costs than programs like SNAP and rental vouchers, so less would remain for basic assistance to needy families. And, in some cases, more powerful state and local political forces may seek to corral more of the funding. For example, many state and local officials likely would try to shift part of the former SNAP benefit dollars to CDBG-type "development" proposals that politically powerful local developers (who often make large campaign contributions) often favor."

The block grant is the foundation of the 1996 bipartisan effort to dismantle the cash assistance program. President Bill Clinton, a

Democrat, and GOP Speaker of the House Newt Gingrich signed off on a "reform" bill which requires that individuals work in low paying, dead end jobs in order to maintain eligibility, instead of participating in education and job skills training programs which would make them more marketable and enhance their chances of lifting themselves out of poverty. This resulted in economic conditions which led single mothers in Connecticut to sell their food stamps in order to buy food for their children. Seth Wessler of Colorlines.com spent time with TANF clients in Connecticut. Wessler discussed his observations in a 2010 interview with *Democracy Now!* hosts Amy Goodman and Juan Gonzalez.

"Eva, the woman I spent three months with, talking to, was cut off of cash assistance last March. She's in the state, Connecticut, with the shortest time limit in the country. After welfare reform, states were given vast amount of power to determine how long people could stay on cash assistance, how generous the program would be. And the state set the shortest time limit of any state of the country. She was cut off of cash assistance in the middle of the worst job crisis in a generation and has been searching for work endlessly without any luck. She's a woman who's been working low-wage poverty jobs for the greater part of a decade and now can't even find one of those. She's precipitously close to the edge now of becoming homeless, of not being able to feed her kids. And she's forced to sell her food stamps, like many women who I talked to in Connecticut, in order to get by.

A lot of women I talked to have said that in times when they are out of work, they can't find a job, and there's no income coming in, after being cut off, pushed off of the cash assistance rolls, that they have had to sell their food assistance to get by, to trade it at a bodega, to sell it for cash. And it's become very clear that that trend has increased. It's become a real way of feeding and paying for rent and clothing families at this point. So it's definitely on the increase. I mean, Eva receives $520-something a month in food stamps a month. She's selling—she's buying her food with that money. She's using that money to pay off her debt at the bodega. She has, at the end of every month, about $100 in debt. She's been—and then she trades in the rest for cash, in order to pay for her basics. And about ten other women in Connecticut said that they had to do the same thing.

I mean, we're in a situation in which, almost fifteen years ago, the federal government basically decimated the cash assistance program, after another decade and a half of highly racialized attacks against the program that demonized the program, stigmatized the problem deeply. And at the same time, consecutive administrations,

Republican and Democratic administrations, have de-stigmatized the Food Stamp Program. And we're seeing now that that program is on the rise, that there's more access to that program. So people are leaning more heavily now on that program."

Clinton is a prime example of the power of the propaganda, which has brainwashed Blacks into continued blind support of the Democrats, despite the worsening socioeconomic conditions in their communities under this party's rule. Hartford, New Haven and Bridgeport, three Connecticut cities that have been controlled by the Democrats for decades, are engulfed in poverty and gun violence. The wage and wealth gap between people of color and whites continues to widen; while Black and Latino unemployment is at Depression-era levels. Some delusional Blacks refer to Clinton as the "First Black President." During his two terms in office, Clinton pushed economic and criminal justice "reform" policies such as mandatory minimum jail sentences for certain drug offenses which have fueled poverty and mass incarceration in low-income communities of color. A 2012 CBPP report documented the effect of the TANF program on poverty.

"TANF's record over the last 15 years shows, however, that its role as a safety net has declined sharply over time. In 1996, for every 100 families with children living in poverty, TANF provided cash aid to 68 families. By 2010, it provided cash assistance to only 27 such families for every 100 in poverty. (We refer to this as the TANF-to-poverty ratio.)

Sharply declining TANF caseloads are the main reason for the fall in the TANF-to- poverty ratio. The national TANF caseload declined by 58 percent between 1995 and 2010; from 4.7 million to 2.0 million. TANF caseloads declined by at least 27 percent in every state, and by more than 50 percent in 36 states. Meanwhile, the number of families with children in poverty increased by 17 percent over this period, from 6.2 million to 7.3 million, and the number of poor children climbed by 12 percent, or by 1.7 million children.

The TANF-to-poverty ratio fell in all states but especially sharply in some. In 1994-95, almost half of the states had a ratio higher than 75 (in other words, in these states, more than 75 families with children received cash aid for every 100 living in poverty); in 2009-10, none did.

In 1994-95, no state had a ratio lower than 25; in 2009-10, half of the states did.'

July 27

Foley appeared on *Face the State*. Foley said that he would make Connecticut more "business friendly" (translation: expect an orgy of deregulation). He backpedaled somewhat when asked about his request to McKinney to drop out of the race, claiming that he really meant he hoped for McKinney's endorsement if he won the primary. When pressed he did repeat that he hoped McKinney's endorsement would come before the primary. Foley again attempted to dance around his position on gun control, initially saying only that he thinks the gun bill that the CT legislature passed in 2013 in response to the Newtown spree killing should have placed more emphasis on mental health services. When asked directly if he would repeal the provision in the bill banning high capacity assault weapons, Foley said that he would not. There were no questions about the gun bill's failure to address gun violence in urban neighborhoods.

Foley said that like McKinney he considered highway tolls to be a form of taxation, but that he would support reinstating tolls in Connecticut if they could be used to offset the gas tax. Foley echoed the Republicans' opposition to the New Britain busway, but said that he could not defund the project as the $600 million had already been spent. Foley criticized Malloy's record on unemployment in the state, citing Malloy's tax increase and what he called anti-business economic policies by the incumbent. Foley was asked about how he would keep spending flat with a $345 million increase in debt service coming in 2016 and a $44 billion gap in pension obligations (state workers/teachers). Foley talked about using his business expertise in cutting government waste, which is coded language for privatizing state services. Foley was outspoken about privatization during the 2010 gubernatorial campaign. His track record in Iraq is a clear indication of his plans for Connecticut;

which are in line with the Wall Street agenda of rolling back workers' wages and benefits. Foley again denied that he had a role in closing down Bibb Company textile plant in Macon, Georgia, a business that he acquired and sold after owning it for 11 years. Former Lt. Governor Mike Fedele ran an ad featuring Macon residents blaming Foley for Bibb's demise during the 2010 GOP gubernatorial primary. Predictably, host Dennis House, Chris Keating of the Hartford Courant and Neil Vigdor of Hearst Connecticut Newspapers didn't ask any questions about Foley's urban agenda.

July 28

Foley's strategy to win the 2014 gubernatorial election appeared to be to just stand there and say nothing. His plan was working, according to a poll by the nonpartisan YouGov research group. Poll results showed Foley leading Malloy by nine points, 42-33. The most significant stat was Foley leading Malloy 50-15 among unaffiliated voters, the largest group of voters in Connecticut. The poll numbers sent a negative message: the gubernatorial candidate who was running the most opaque campaign was experiencing success with that approach.

Foley said that his plan to erase the projected $1.4 billion deficit was to maintain the current $19 billion spending level for the next two years. Foley was on the record as saying that he would not ask for more concessions from state employees. When CT Mirror reporter Keith Phaneuf asked Foley if he would instead ask state workers to accept a wage freeze or if he would order layoffs, Foley ducked the question: he just touted his prowess as a business negotiator. Foley told Phaneuf that he didn't want to see state colleges and universities jack up tuition fees, while at the same time he talked about funding cuts, which usually resulted in tuition hikes by these institutions. Foley told Phaneuf that he planned to lean on insurance companies and health care providers to give the state a better deal on health care benefits for current and retired state workers. Foley's strategy drew belly laughs from both the Democrats and his primary opponent. State Comptroller Kevin Lembo told Phaneuf that his work on health care purchasing for state employees was going very well, thank you: the yearly hike in costs had been lowered to 2 percent, compared to 9 percent in 2013. McKinney told Phaneuf that Foley was not giving voters specifics on where he would implement cuts.

Phaneuf reported that a state health care advocate believed Foley's strategy wouldn't help to lower Medicaid costs, another major state budget cost driver. "Ellen Andrews, Director of the New Haven-based Connecticut Health Policy Project, said she doesn't believe Foley could cut Medicaid costs much in the short-term by trying to negotiate better deals with hospitals and doctors. "To be honest, we are already underpaying our providers," she said, adding that lower provider rates means fewer will treat poor patients, limiting health care access for many. A better solution, Andrews said, would be for Foley to spend more money in the short term, increasing rates and providing grants to help providers develop better electronic patient records." The bipartisan criticism of Foley's health care plan was telling. His overall platform was shrouded in mystery; what was he actually going to do if elected? According to the YouGov poll, Connecticut voters weren't really concerned about that.

July 29

It seemed like a good idea at the time... Foley traveled to the town of Sprague to hold a press conference in front of Fusion Paperboard, a paper mill that was being closed in September by OpenGate Capital, a private investment firm. Foley's plan was to use Fusion as a prop while he bashed Malloy's economic policies. Foley ended up being embarrassed by Fusion employees and Democratic Party Sen. Cathy Osten, who was also the town's first selectwoman. Foley was berated by

Osten and the Fusion employees for exploiting the paper mill's closure and being clueless about the factors which actually led to the company's demise. The "highlight" was this exchange between Foley, who made a fortune as a serial company killer, and a Fusion employee. Pazniokas of *The Mirror* reported.

"'You're a businessman,' said Rich Harrelle, a 29-year employee of the mill and president of United Steel Workers Local 1840, which represents the Fusion employees. 'That's right,' Foley said. 'You close mills down,' Harrelle said. 'Yeah,' Foley said. 'Have you ever made a decision?' Foley interrupted to correct himself and Harrelle. 'I have never closed a mill down, sir. I didn't close the Bibb mill. A subsequent owner closed it. So, please get your facts right,' Foley said. 'I want you to get your facts right,' Harrelle replied. 'Because when you come here, I can tell you about 140 lives that just went down the tubes.' 'That's a shame, and it's policy driven,' Foley told him. 'It's a result of the policies of this governor and maybe the first selectwoman.' (Mike) D'Auria told him market forces were responsible, not Malloy. Fusion specializes in food packaging, and the industry is using more plastic and less paperboard. 'If you understood the paper industry, plastic is overtaking cardboard. Day by day by day, the industry changes,' D'Auria said. 'I'm just telling you that.'"

The reality was that the Malloy administration loaned Fusion $2 million in 2013 and was going to loan the company another $1 million. If the mill increased its employee roster and stayed open another 10 years, part of the loan would have been forgiven. Foley wanted to use Fusion to spread his gospel of deregulation. His attempt flopped miserably. As Fusion workers read him the riot act, Foley looked like an out of touch rich guy, which is exactly what he is. Foley never set foot in Sprague prior to July 29: this was a calculated ploy by a politician to use the plight of the working class for his own personal gain. To the delight of the Malloy and McKinney camps, Foley's slimy move blew up in his face.

The Working Families Party did nothing to shake their image as a satellite of the Democratic Party, cross endorsing Malloy and Wyman despite Malloy's bullying of state workers and teachers. When state workers rejected the concessions deal between SEBAC and Malloy, he responded by issuing thousands of layoff notices. Malloy smacked teachers in the face with an anti-teacher bill that was mostly dismantled by the legislature. Malloy knew that he could count on Working Families to avoid holding him accountable, no matter what he did.

July 30

 McKinney and his running mate David Walker appeared in a new ad touting tax cuts for the middle class as part of their budget plan. The reality of course, was much different. The actual McKinney/Walker plan would consist of gradually phasing out the income tax during each year of McKinney's first term. You have to read that fine print...

July 31

Obama's $3.6 billion emergency spending bill aimed at addressing the border crisis stalled in the Senate. Observers believed that there would be no more action on the bill prior to Congress' summer vacation. Aren't you supposed to do some actual work before you take time off?

Fundraising doesn't count.

Part 4

August 1

In *The 14 Defining Principles of Fascism*, Dr. Lawrence Britt wrote,

10. Power of labor suppressed or eliminated.

> Since organized labor was seen as the one power center that could challenge the political hegemony of the ruling elite and its corporate allies, it was inevitably crushed or made powerless. The poor formed an underclass, viewed with suspicion or outright contempt.

Under some regimes, being poor was considered akin to a vice.

David G. Mills' Information Clearing House article, "It's the Corporate State, Stupid," is a must read. Mills discusses the definition of corporatism by Italian dictator Benito Mussolini, who said, "Fascism should more properly be called corporatism because it is the merger of state and corporate power." One of the objectives of the corporate state in this country is to roll back workers' gains in wages and benefits. Unlike his GOP primary opponent Foley, McKinney made no attempt to downplay the fact that he's a corporatist. Mirror health reporter Arielle Levin Becker interviewed the gubernatorial candidates about their health care policy positions. McKinney laid out his plan of attack against state workers, who had agreed to concessions twice since 2009. That wasn't enough for McKinney, who made scapegoating state employees the focal point of his campaign. McKinney described the state workers health care package as a "platinum plan"; he wanted the SEBAC unions to return to the negotiating table yet again to surrender more of their wages and benefits. McKinney threatened to lay off state employees if they did not agree to his demands.

McKinney of course had no interest in changing Connecticut's regressive tax system, where the people who make the most pay the least. Matthew Santacroce of Connecticut Voices for Children broke down the inequity of the state tax structure in his report, *Reality Check: Who pays Taxes in Connecticut?*

"This brief finds that Connecticut's wealthiest residents pay a smaller share of their income in state and local taxes than middle-income and low-income residents. The report, which is based on analysis of federal, state, and local tax data by the Institute for Economic and Tax Policy, finds:

While the federal tax system is progressive, meaning that higher-income people pay a greater share of their income in taxes, Connecticut system is the opposite, asking the most of those with the least. In Connecticut's regressive system, the wealthiest 1% of taxpayers pay about half the share of their income on state and local taxes (5.5%) that middle-income (10.5%) and lower-income (11%) residents pay."

Foley and Malloy were also uninterested in a progressive tax code. Pelto was the only candidate who made taxing the rich a part of his platform. Santacroce listed recommendations that would level the tax playing field and generate much need income for the state.

"Raise marginal income tax rates on our state's wealthiest residents to align with those in New York State. Raising Connecticut's rates just on income over $1 million could generate over $400 million annually.

• Close corporate tax loopholes that reward companies that ship profits and jobs out of state. Instituting mandatory combined reporting and the throwback rule would increase state revenues by over $100 million next year, while leveling the playing field for the small businesses that are vital to Connecticut's economy.

• Report regularly on how much people at different income levels and businesses of different sizes pay in state and local taxes (tax incidence analysis), which will provide policymakers with a clear picture of taxes in Connecticut, and will help to inform complicated tax policy debates in an objective, data-driven fashion."

McKinney's budget plan included privatizing state services, which would also result in lower pay and benefits for workers. McKinney's BS meter was off the charts. His populist rhetoric about standing up for the middle class was directly contradicted by his
190

ideological opposition to the recommendations in the CT Voices for Children report.

Part 5

As the August 12, GOP primary approached and the 2014 election moved closer to coming into focus, the similarities between the major party candidates were clear. Malloy, Foley and McKinney were all liars. Foley lied about McKinney's voting record, McKinney lied about Foley's fiscal policy regarding spending cuts, and Malloy lied about his first term in office. Malloy's Ronald Reagan "Morning in America" style (more like mourning) campaign ad touted his so-called balanced budget, which was achieved through borrowing, postponing the payment of debts, raids of the transportation, tobacco health trust, school bus seat belt and other funds by the Democrat controlled legislature and other assorted gimmicks.

Malloy ad pumped up the gun control bill as a response to gun violence: this legislation did not contain any provisions, which would address the socioeconomic causes of urban gun violence. The legislative gun violence task force that was created following the Sandy Hook mass shooting excluded urban lawmakers. The task force held public hearings in suburban Connecticut towns including Newtown, while avoiding Hartford, New Haven, and Bridgeport, cities with annually high gun homicide rates. Hartford, the capital city where lawmakers met every day, was the site of over 200 gun deaths in the previous 10 years. Other than Foley's disingenuous CNN editorial on urban policy, none of the candidates talked about the plight of low-income communities of color engulfed in poverty, Depression-era levels of unemployment, gun violence and gaping disparities in wages and wealth. Connecticut Justice Party state coordinator Carlos Camacho posted a blog commentary about the Democrats' total disregard for Blacks and Latinos.

"When it comes to diversity, the Democratic Party has always been at the forefront in our political system. However, it is becoming clear that Democrats are failing immigrants and minorities. They have failed to aggressively push for and achieve immigration reform, they have failed to implement educational policies that will achieve equality in educational opportunities and are responsible for more deportations under President Obama than any other administration. Perhaps that is why he has been called by one Latino organization as the "Deporter-in-Chief."

While Connecticut's richest have grown richer, many of their fellow residents are barely treading water. Disproportionately, those on the losing end belong to already disadvantaged groups; the median incomes of Connecticut's Hispanics and Blacks are barely half that of Whites. There are reasons to be concerned about the prevalence of income inequality in Connecticut. The situation is worse still for Black and Hispanic wage earners, and the hardship for workers without college is more pronounced in Connecticut than elsewhere. Forty percent of Connecticut's whites have a bachelor's degree, compared to only 18 percent of blacks and 14 percent of Hispanics.

Across the country, Democrats are waving carrots in front of Latinos; assuming their support in the face of anti-immigrant hysteria that has gripped the GOP. However, Latinos and other minorities should demand more, they should demand justice."

August 7

Both Pelto and Visconti announced that they had collected petition signatures in excess of the 7500 required for them both to appear on the election ballot. Verification of the signatures was expected to be complete by the end of the month. The possibility of a four-way gubernatorial race appeared likely, albeit with four candidates who did not represent the interests of communities of color. McKinney's team released an ad about Foley's Fusion Paperboard debacle. The ad purported to show Foley telling Fusion workers that they were responsible for the company's closure. Foley's 2010 blood feud primary against former Lt. Gov. Michael Fedele was cited by political observers as a factor in Foley's loss to Malloy, as Foley was viewed as having been weakened by Fedele's attacks. The gentlemen's agreement between Foley and McKinney to play nice dissolved quickly under the heat of political ambition.

The Hartford Courant's duplicitous editorial endorsing Shawn Wooden for State Senate underscored the need for a third party organization that truly serves the people. Wooden and incumbent Sen. Eric Coleman as usual had avoided discussion about poverty, racial wage/wealth disparity, Black/Latino unemployment, and police containment of communities of color. The Courant made the preposterous claim that Coleman had "ended racial profiling." Coleman actually helped to water down the Alvin W. *Penn Act*, supporting amendments by the so-called Racial Profiling Prohibition Project that protect the police. The establishment butt kissing didn't end there, as the Courant explained away Wooden's flip-flop on the Rock Cats stadium issue as Wooden "correcting" himself. Yeah, Wooden's "correction" came after protests erupted over the deal. The BS meter at the corporate controlled Courant was off the hook, as usual.

August 8

BRIDGEPORT POLICE OFFICER CLIVE HIGGINS INDICTED FOR CIVIL RIGHTS VIOLATION

REPORT FROM NEWS 12 CONNECTICUT

A third Bridgeport police officer has been indicted for his role in a case where the officers beat a man in custody.

Prosecutors charged Clive Higgins with violating the civil rights of Orlando Lopez-Soto. The two other officers involved have already pleaded guilty in the case.

Elson Morales and Joe Lawlor will be sentenced in September. They face up to a year in prison and could be forced to resign.

The 2013 conviction of East Haven police officers Dennis Spaulding and David Cari on federal charges of racially profiling Latinos is irrefutable evidence that biased policing is happening in Connecticut. Malloy's administration had gone to great lengths to protect the police, who wield considerable political influence at the State Capitol. Office of

Policy and Management Undersecretary Mike Lawlor and the so-called Racial Profiling Prohibition Project focused on an esoteric data collection process, while ignoring the conviction of the EHPD officers. It remained to be seen if they would also try to sweep the Bridgeport case under the rug. Contrary to Lawlor's assertion that biased policing is a "perceived problem," police containment of Black and Latino neighborhoods by racial profiling, intimidation and violence is a real issue. Right next door in New York, a medical examiner ruled that the death of Eric Garner at the hands of the NYPD was a homicide. I reported on the CRP3 attempt to bury the East Haven case in an October 2013 *Hartford News* column.

"The members of the Connecticut Racial Profiling Prohibition Project, the puppet Alvin W. *Penn Act* advisory board of Gov. Dannel Malloy, have not mentioned the Department of Justice investigation of racial profiling by the East Haven Police Department during any of their meetings which were televised on the Connecticut Network, nor have they mentioned the 2012 DOJ indictment of EHPD officers David Cari, Dennis Spaulding, Jason Zullo and Sgt. John Miller or the trial of Cari and Spaulding on their website. Last week I left messages with advisory board members Ken Barone, American Civil Liberties Union legal director Sandra Staub and Redding Police Chief Douglas Fuchs asking for an explanation. Predictably, Staub did not return my call. Fuchs told me that informing the public about the East Haven case or studying the DOJ investigative report on the EHPD isn't something that the advisory board, which is supposedly working to stop racial profiling in this state, needs to do. "That's not our charge," Fuchs said. "Our job isn't to look backward. Our job is to collect traffic stop data in the best manner possible." I then asked about the disparity in the reactions to the Newtown school shooting and the East Haven case.

Following the spree killing at Sandy Hook, a legislative task force on gun violence was created. The task force visited suburban towns, including Newtown (while excluding gun violence plagued cities Hartford, New Haven and Bridgeport) to discuss possible solutions. The gun laws in Connecticut were subsequently strengthened. Police officers were assigned to selected schools. I pointed out to Fuchs that clearly the state "looked backward" at the Newtown shooting and implemented measures designed to prevent that tragedy from happening again. The reaction by the state, reflected by Fuchs' comments, to the East Haven case has been the exact opposite. After a lengthy pause, Fuchs reiterated his position that the East Haven case is not the advisory board's concern. After questioning my "professionalism," Fuchs would not respond when I asked him if he had anything to say to the Latino East Haven residents who have testified at the trial about being harassed and brutalized by Spaulding and Zullo. Testimony by EHPD Sgt. Anthony Rybaruk supports residents' testimony against Zullo.

The advisory board's stated purpose of data collection is to determine if racial profiling is happening in Connecticut (duh). The East Haven case is irrefutable evidence of biased policing which the board has chosen to ignore.

Barone, who has been the public face of the advisory board and is listed as the contact person on their website, would not answer my questions and ever so politely referred me to Bill Dyson, the advisory board chair/figurehead (and the Black guy). Dyson started off by totally contradicting Fuchs, as he said that the East Haven case was the impetus for the formation of the board, and that the board is formulating policies in direct response to the case. Dyson then said that he has not read the DOJ investigative report of the EHPD! Like Fuchs, Dyson had no answer for why the advisory board hasn't discussed the case during their televised meetings and community forums or during any legislative hearings and why there is no mention of the case on the advisory board's website. Dyson had a problem with my contention that he could not effectively develop policies to respond to the case if he didn't know squat about what actually happened. I submit that the board has not mentioned the DOJ investigation of the EHPD or the trial of Cari and Spaulding because their true assignment is to protect the police. My conversations with Fuchs, Barone and Dyson and Staub's display of cowardice have strengthened my belief. In an astonishing display of arrogance, Dyson repeatedly asked me why the advisory board should study and discuss the DOJ report. I challenge Dyson to ask the Latino East Haven residents who have suffered at the hands of Cari, Spaulding, Zullo and Miller that question, if he has the guts."

August 12

Malloy vs. Foley II became an official sequel, as Foley easily defeated McKinney in the GOP gubernatorial primary. McKinney, who spent the past several weeks explaining in vivid detail why Foley sucked, immediately vowed to do anything that Foley asked of him to make Malloy a one-term governor. Foley said, "Change is on the way!" Yeah, right... Within the next couple of weeks, we would find out if third-party candidates Pelto and Visconti would get an opportunity to steal the show.

August 21

Activists responding to the police shooting of unarmed Black teen Michael Brown in Ferguson, Missouri circulated a petition calling on President Obama to introduce federal legislation, which would require all state, county and local police to wear cameras. This law would end the he said she said crap and cable news bickering that surround cases like this with no video evidence. CP added the camera provision to our *Trayvon Martin Act*. The corporate media predictably fixated on a video, which purportedly showed Michael stealing cigars from a local store. The legal fact is it doesn't matter if Michael stole cigars or assaulted Officer Darren Wilson. If Wilson shot Michael after he surrendered as community residents claim, Wilson was supposed to go to jail. How could we consider this street execution to have been an isolated incident when a Black person is killed by police, security guards and vigilantes every 28 hours? These street executions are not isolated incidents.

The unrest in Ferguson resulted in militarization of the police becoming a hot topic. Brian Dowling of the Courant reported that state and local police in Connecticut have acquired $12.9 million in military weapons from the Pentagon through their 1033 program. Dowling noted that the Hartford Police received $850,000 in weapons over the past few years, including a grenade launcher and a mine resistant tank. The HPD lied to Dowling about having this arsenal. *Black Agenda Report* commentator Glen Ford talked about the bipartisan effort to militarize the police in an effort to contain low-income communities of color.

"If the mission of police forces in the United States is to contain, suppress, hyper-surveil and incarcerate huge numbers of Black people as a matter of policy, then police departments require all the tools the federal government has been giving them since President Lyndon Johnson signed the Omnibus Crime Control and Safe Streets Act of 1968—a cornerstone in the construction of a truly national, integrated gendarmerie, which is defined as 'a military force charged with police duties among civilian populations.' SWAT teams, first formed in Philadelphia in 1964 and Los Angeles in 1967 as unabashed counter-Black insurgency units, have proliferated to the far corners

198

of the land, and are now standard drill for warrant-serving cops. The domestic counterinsurgency army has been methodically expanded by each successive administration, first through the Law Enforcement Assistance Administration, and ultimately drawing on the stocks of, not only the Pentagon, but virtually every armed agency of the federal government.

President Obama, to whom idiots appeal to scale back police militarization, is as hawkish as any of his predecessors in about keeping America safe from Black inner city insurgency. The lead sentence in an item in today's *New York Times*, blandly titled 'Data on Transfer of Military Gear to Police Departments', tells the tale, succinctly: 'Since President Obama took office, the Pentagon has transferred to police departments tens of thousands of machine guns; nearly 200,000 ammunition magazines; thousands of pieces of camouflage and night-vision equipment; and hundreds of silencers, armored cars and aircraft.' Clearly, the U.S. is at war with Black America."

Christine Stuart of CT News Junkie and Daniela Altimari of *the Hartford Courant* both wrote articles on how the so-called Connecticut Racial Profiling Prohibition Project have used the East Haven police scandal, which resulted in the conviction of EHPD officers Dennis Spaulding and David Cari on federal charges of racially profiling Latinos, as the foundation of their work. As I mentioned earlier, CRP3 gave me a different story last October: Bill Dyson and Redding Police Chief Douglas Fuchs told me that they had not studied the East Haven case at all. Fuchs claimed that they didn't have to. He said, "That's not our charge." CRP3 members Sandra Staub (executive director of CT ACLU) and Ken Barone, the public face of CRP3, never responded to my requests to question them about the advisory board ignoring the EHPD case.

August 25

Reports surfaced about the Democrats setting up voter registration booths at rallies for Michael Brown. In 2012 and 2013, I wrote columns about the Democrats exploiting the lynching of Trayvon Martin. Author Kevin Powell et al. turned CNN's coverage of Michael Brown's funeral into a Democratic Party infomercial, with the November elections weeks away. What we need is body cameras for cops. Memo to Powell: voting for Democrats won't stop police murder. Urban areas occupied by police have been controlled by the Democrats for decades. Community residents must organize to address this issue. An inconvenient fact for Powell is that the Democrats partner with the police in the containment of Black and Latino neighborhoods. Hillary Clinton added to the Democrats' embarrassing handling of the Michael Brown case. Clinton ignored a reporter's question about the shooting after a Westhampton, New York press conference promoting her memoir, *Hard Choices*.

August 29

Luis Anglero, Jr. faced a September 3 court date after being charged with interfering and breach of peace. The barbaric Taser attack on August 20 by Hartford Police Det. Shawn Ware on Luis, which was captured on video, is an example of the brutal tactics police use to contain urban neighborhoods and underscores the need for state, county and local police to wear cameras. Criminal justice professor Charles Katz told MSNBC commentator Lawrence O'Donnell that there is a 40-60% reduction in misconduct when police officers wear cameras. Brutality complaints against police departments, which use body cameras also dropped. We cannot pray our way out of this problem. "Community leaders" must stop shucking and jiving and push elected officials to support public policies, which will provide low-income communities of color with a layer of protection against police violence. Remember,every 28 hours—if not today then tomorrow—a Black person is killed by police, security guards and vigilantes. Body cameras would also protect the police against frivolous complaints. The CP will add a provision to our 2015 *Trayvon Martin Act* requiring state, county and local police to wear cameras.

200

Corporatism on parade... Mayor Pedro Segarra cut funding for Marshall House and obliterated a proposed North Hartford supermarket, which would have anchored a desperately needed health and nutrition complex, while rabidly pursuing a baseball stadium. Last week, Segarra bowed to public pressure and restored funding to Marshall House, one of just two shelters in the city that houses women and children (South Park Inn is the other). The demise of the revolutionary Downtown North plan had been eclipsed during the debate over the proposed stadium. Coupled with the attempt by Segarra to euthanize Marshall House, it's clear that health and human services are a nuisance to the Segarra administration, whose priorities are so far out of whack, it isn't even funny.

Secretary of State Denise Merrill announced that independent gubernatorial candidate Jonathan Pelto failed to obtain the 7500 signatures necessary to appear on the ballot in November. Pelto turned in about 4,000 signatures. The announcement marked the end of an ill-fated campaign. Pelto totally ignored communities of color, as he excluded an urban agenda from his platform. Pelto infuriated liberals and progressives when he gave a petition to former Republican state chairman Chris Healy, and then made the preposterous claim that he did not expect Healy to circulate the petition among his fellow GOP members. Healy said that he told Pelto he would circulate the petition; Healy's publicly stated goal was to use Pelto to help challenger Tom Foley by bleeding votes from incumbent Gov. Dannel Malloy. When Pelto colluded with Healy, he officially crossed the line from third party candidate to being an agent of the Republicans. Pelto's confession that his organization had only obtained 4,000 signatures explained his alliance with the GOP, which was a sleazy attempt to gain ballot access. That stunt made it obvious that Pelto's objective all along had been to settle his personal grudge with Malloy, who rejected Pelto's application for employment with his administration.

Congratulations, Pelto. You blew a once in a lifetime opportunity to force a seismic shift in Connecticut politics toward social justice.

Malloy vs. Foley II now includes Tea Party member Joe Visconti (certified for the ballot the previous week), repeating the scenario in 2010 when conservative Tom Marsh made the ballot as an independent candidate. Marsh received 18,000 votes, which Foley blamed for his narrow loss to Malloy. Visconti made it clear that he would aggressively challenge Foley on his evasive stance regarding the gun violence bill, which was passed by the General Assembly in 2013 as a response to the mass shooting in Newtown. The divisive gun issue now looms as the possible deciding factor in the race for governor.

Here's a recap of the highly anticipated first Malloy/Foley debate. Malloy: "You're lying about Bibb Company." Foley: "You're lying about crime stats!" Very inspiring!

Segarra communications director Maribel La Luz's tweet during the debate about crime being down in Hartford was pure BS. The classic HBO television series *The Wire* addressed the institutional practice known as "juking the stats." Law enforcement and education officials routinely cook the books to give the illusion of progress. Incumbents running for re-election will always tell you that things are getting better. Don't believe the hype.

Part 6

September 4

Working Families Party councilwoman Cynthia Jennings introduced a proposal for all Hartford Police officers to wear body cameras... Police brutality victim Luis Anglero, Jr. appeared in court on trumped up charges of interfering and breach of peace. Luis was the victim of an unprovoked Taser attack by Hartford Police Det. Shawn Ware last month. The assault was caught on surveillance and cellphone video. Luis' case was continued until October 15th. Ware had not been charged.

A public hearing was scheduled for mid-September at City Hall on the Downtown North development proposals the city received as Mayor Segarra and city council president Wooden continued to pursue their Rock Cats stadium vanity project, at the expense of a proposed North Hartford supermarket and health/nutrition complex. The proposal Segarra sent to the city council would cram a supermarket into a mixed-use complex anchored by the stadium. Martha Page, executive director of Hartford Food System and Rex Fowler, executive director of Hartford Community Loan Fund, the two organizations working to bring a full-service supermarket to Hartford, wrote an op-ed to *the Courant* warning the city not to go this route. They stated that traffic congestion on days that the stadium is in use would make the supermarket inaccessible to shoppers.

"Following the announcement of the city's new vision for Downtown North, no longer to be anchored by a supermarket but instead by a baseball stadium/entertainment venue, our operator and investors indicated the proposed development's change in orientation increased the risk of our project too much. Many if not most of the supermarket's projected shoppers would still be driving to a Downtown North store and might understandably opt to buy food in the suburbs on game days to avoid stadium traffic.

That doesn't mean supermarkets and stadiums can't co-exist. The risk is mitigated in cities such as Boston and San Francisco, where good public transportation systems allow stadium patrons to take a subway to a game rather than drive, or where supermarket customers are more likely to walk to the store rather than take their cars. Hartford isn't there yet.

Other experienced operators and investors concur—if we want a sustainable, successful supermarket that will serve city residents for the long term, Downtown North may no longer be a wise location... In 2011, with growing demand for a downtown grocer, the city provided financial backing to open the Market at Hartford 21. Private investors with industry expertise had passed on that project for a variety of reasons. Six months after it opened, the Market at Hartford 21 closed. More recently, a highly publicized market in downtown Bridgeport closed after less than a year. We should listen to those who know more about this than any of us...

Why not bring in a reputable supermarket consultant and let them offer guidance on the best location for a supermarket, one we all agree the city desperately needs?"

The demise of the revolutionary plan supported by Page and Fowler is equally as important as the funding issue, which triggered protests against the stadium.

The race for governor kicked into full gear following the Labor Day holiday. A new Tom Foley ad touted Foley's tenure in Iraq during the U.S. occupation. Foley was the Occupation Authority's representative for private sector development. The ad stated that Foley "created jobs" in Iraq. Um, not quite. Foley actually put many Iraqis out of work as the point man for the U.S. privatization campaign. Foley promised not to lay off state employees as part of his plan to close a projected $1.4 billion budget deficit. Foley made the comments on his budget plan in interviews with *The Connecticut Mirror* and WDRC-AM 1360. Most state employee unions were due for wage negotiations in 2015. The current contract covering health care, retirement and other benefits does not expire until 2022. Both Foley and incumbent Gov. Dan Malloy promised not to attempt to renegotiate the benefits contract.

Malloy, who did not mention Black and Latino unemployment or poverty once during any of his State of the State addresses, talked about urban employment in a shameless attempt to get votes. Malloy's "urban initiative" was the equivalent of a playboy putting the moves on female customers during happy hour at the local bar. Malloy told people of color that he really loved them and would hook them up after he was re-elected; just forget about that minor ignoring you during my first term thing. Following the mass shooting in Newtown, a legislative gun violence task force was created. Urban legislators were excluded. The task force visited suburban towns, including Newtown, while avoiding gun violence plagued cities Hartford, New Haven and Bridgeport. There have been over 200 homicides in Hartford during the past decade. During the debate over the gun bill that was passed in 2013, Rep. Douglas McCrory spoke passionately on the House floor about the bill lacking any provisions regarding urban gun violence. Now that he wanted the Black/Latino vote, Malloy promised the urban community that he would make everything better. The Democrats have controlled communities of color for decades. That hasn't worked out for areas like North Hartford, where the poverty rate is annually among the highest in the country. Malloy's announcement was election year BS. The Malcolm X Grassroots Movement Jackson Plan is a real blueprint for economic justice.

Fast food workers in 150 cities, including Hartford, staged a strike for a $15.00 minimum wage and the right to unionize. Thirteen strikers were arrested for acts of civil disobedience during a peaceful protest on Washington Street. Seven hundred were arrested nationwide. The Socialist Equality Party made a persuasive argument for why all low-wage workers should make a living wage as high as $21.00.

"In a statement May 29, Socialist Alternative hailed the impending passage of the (Seattle) minimum wage increase, declaring, 'One hundred thousand workers will be lifted out of poverty.' This is a lie. Even with a full-time job, which many low-wage workers are denied, at $15-an-hour a family of four cannot sustain a decent standard of living and still qualifies for food stamps. Speaking on MSNBC's 'Morning Joe' program, Seattle's Democratic mayor, Ed Murray, admitted, 'The minimum wage would be about $21 an hour here in the city of Seattle, which is a very expensive city, if we actually wanted to get a real livable wage. Fifteen dollars would still be very hard for someone making that wage.' "

September 10

A Qunnipiac University poll found Foley ahead in the race for governor, 46 percent to 40, while a YouGov internet poll had Malloy leading, 42 percent to 41 percent. YouGov's targeted market based polling method uses online surveys, which is controversial within the political arena. The Quinnipiac poll uses the accepted method of randomly calling individuals. Visconti had a 7 percent total in the Quinnipiac poll, 3 percent in the YouGov poll, where he was not listed by name, but instead referred to as "other." QU poll director Doug Schwartz noted that Visconti had taken away the same amount of votes from Malloy and Foley: the expectation was that Visconti would hurt Foley the most. Schwartz said that Foley would still have a 6-point lead if Visconti was not in the race.

September 11

The so-called Connecticut Racial Profiling Prohibition Project released a report, which showed that (surprise) there is a disparity in the rate of traffic stops between people of color and whites in Connecticut. However, the CRP3 report is not telling the whole story. Under the current *Alvin W. Penn Act* state law, patrol officers must provide all drivers who they stop with an information card, which provides instructions on how they can file a complaint if they believe they have been racially profiled. However, there is no way to track whether or not officers are actually giving these cards to motorists. We have received complaints from individuals who were not given a card, and thus were not informed about their rights under the current law. This gaping

206

loophole destroys the credibility of data on the number of racial profiling complaints that have been filed since the current law went into effect. The CP's traffic stop receipt provision was one of three *Penn Act* amendments that were passed by the Connecticut General Assembly in 2012 and scheduled to go into effect July 1, 2013. Last year the receipt provision was repealed due to political pressure by the police. Under the current law, community residents are frozen out of the data collection process: they don't know if their race has been misrepresented by the patrol officer who stopped them.

The Department of Justice investigation of racial profiling by the East Haven Police Department found that Officers Dennis Spaulding and David Cari, who were sentenced to five years and 30 months respectively in prison for violating the civil rights of Latinos, either filed false traffic stop reports, or did not enter ethnicity data at all. "Our own review of the data showed that a large number of entries reflecting traffic stops were devoid of ethnicity data or appeared to misreport ethnicity data."

The New Haven Independent reported on a study by Yale law school students, who provided statistics on how EHPD officers, including Spaulding, were blatantly lying on the traffic stop reports.

"They (Yale students) found that police 'failed to correctly identify the race of vast majority of individuals to whom they issued traffic tickets. Police reported giving tickets mostly to white people. Police recorded Hispanic drivers for only 4.8 percent of tickets, according to the report. An accompanying graph shows that one officer in particular, Dennis Spaulding, is responsible for 97 tickets issued to people with Hispanic names. Another graph shows that Spaulding reported issuing 120 tickets to white people, four to black people, and none to Hispanic drivers in the same period. Spaulding has been accused by name of racial harassment by Latino business owners."

CP's traffic stop receipt would act as a deterrent against officers falsifying data and provide community residents with access to essential information they would need to guide their decision about filing a complaint.

CP has been pushing racial profiling legislation at the State Capitol since 2010. Each year, the Connecticut Police Chiefs Association has a different reason for opposing our receipt provision. In 2010, they said printers would have to be installed in cruisers, which is false. Officers already have to fill out a traffic stop report every time they stop a driver. We proposed that a carbon copy of the report be given to the driver. In 2011, Office of Policy and Management Undersecretary Mike Lawlor said that there was no money to fund the receipt provision. The most recent explanation is that the receipt would "compromise officers' safety," because they would have to spend extra time on the side of the road in order to provide drivers with a copy of the traffic stop report. This assertion is nonsensical, because officers would be creating the carbon copy while they filled out the original form. Nonetheless we responded to that argument by proposing that drivers could receive instructions on how to pick up the receipt in person at the police department, through the mail or online. This proposal has been met with resistance by CRP3.

Mary Sanders, who wrote CP's bill language, shared her thoughts.

"I have spoken with various people who have been stopped and have NOT received the card informing them of their options. I also believe that the same way federal Department of Justice money was secured to implement this electronic data system, funding could be requested to cover the cost of producing traffic stop report copies for motorists. Funding secured was intended to ensure fair and unbiased policing and the motorists' copies could make all the difference as far as data integrity. The full CRP3 report shows that profiling is indeed happening.

We still believe it's underexposed and thus the need for the motorists' copies of the stop reports."

We are currently trying to find out if we can obtain information from the Office of Legislative Research on the current cost of producing the traffic stop report forms, and what the cost would be if the forms included carbon copies.

Meanwhile, George Zimmerman made the news for threatening to shoot a Black man during a road rage incident. The shooting of unarmed teen Black teen Michael Brown by Officer Darren Wilson in Ferguson, Missouri has led to a grassroots movement in that city that is exposing the link between biased policing and economic justice. Black unemployment, the racial wage/wealth gap, a racist, profit driven criminal justice system and the Democratic Party's complicity in these conditions are issues which are finally being discussed in the mainstream media, thanks to fed up Ferguson residents who personify the Democrats' biggest fear: they are making the connection between the street execution of Michael Brown and the socioeconomic problems in their community. *Democracy Now!* host Amy Goodman reported on the money cities are making from biased policing.

"As the police killing of Michael Brown has focused global attention on the racial divide in the counties in and surrounding St. Louis, Missouri, a new report may explain why residents' mistrust of the police runs so deep. It shows how a large part of the revenue for these counties comes from fines paid by African-American residents who are disproportionately targeted for traffic stops and other low-level offenses. In Ferguson, the fines and fees are actually the city's second-largest source of income, which is expected to generate $2.7 million in fiscal year 2014. We speak with Thomas Harvey, executive director of ArchCity Defenders and co-author of their new report, which has been widely cited—including in a stunning chart in Monday's *New York Times* that shows how Ferguson issued on average nearly three warrants per household last year— the highest number of warrants in the state, relative to its size. 'What my clients have told me since the first day I've ever represented anybody is, this is not about public safety, it's about the money,' Harvey says.

So, in Ferguson and the surrounding municipalities, there is a substantial amount of income that's derived from these low-level ordinance violations. These are the least significant, lowest- level contact with the justice system. They are typically traffic tickets, moving violations. And as a system, as a structural problem, these— revenue from these municipal courts can represent either the second- or third-highest source of income for the municipality. Ferguson is $2.7 million a year. In neighboring Florissant, the adjacent municipality, it's $3 million a year. It's a line item on a budget, and enforcement of the laws and ticketing and fine amounts are in keeping with the expectation that that income is going to come in to fund the city.

And our clients believe that they are targeted initially because they're black, and then they are harassed, and they are exploited because they are poor. And it has led to a level of distrust between the community and law enforcement that you saw manifested in some of the protests in the last two weeks. I'm not trying to say that traffic tickets are the reason people are on the streets of Ferguson, but it's certainly a contributing factor when you've got the tragedy with Michael Brown and the very same people that my clients believe are targeting them because they're members of community of color and then exploiting them because they're poor, are now asking them for patience and trust and promising to get to the right answer involving the shooting. And our clients are skeptical."

Racial profiling is big business. Were Gov. Dannel Malloy and the Democrat controlled General Assembly, who faced a projected $1.4 billion budget deficit (if Malloy was re-elected), resisting true reform of *the Alvin W. Penn Act* because they were afraid of the effect this would have on the revenue stream currently flowing into Hartford, New Haven and Bridgeport? The revelation from Ferguson definitely supported that theory.

September 14

WFSB *Face the State* host Dennis House continued his repugnant display of racism and classism when Gov. Dannel Malloy appeared on *Face the State* last month to talk about his election battle against Republican challenger Tom Foley. House, Connecticut Mirror reporter Mark Pazniokas and Connecticut Magazine group editor Matt DeRienzo did not ask Malloy any questions about core urban issues (e.g. poverty, Black/Latino unemployment, racial wage/wealth gap, mass incarceration) during the program, despite the fact that Malloy held a press conference a few days earlier to promote an initiative, which he promised would address the jobless rate in communities of color. House's refusal to acknowledge the plight of urban neighborhoods was underscored by the recent release of U.S. Census data, which reveals that child poverty, the poverty rate among families, the amount of people whose income is below the federal poverty level and the number of residents without health insurance in Connecticut has increased since 2003.

House uses *Face the State* to promote an elitist, corporatist agenda, a prime example being his role as a shill for the Hartford stadium plan. I have seen one *Face the State* program which included opponents of the stadium; the rest have been infomercials for the proposal. House recently made an assertion about unnamed, unseen North End residents who think that the stadium is a great idea, by golly. House obviously hasn't talked to Jamil Ragland, a resident of North Hartford who eloquently explained his opposition to the stadium when he was interviewed by *New York Times* reporter Benjamin Mueller in July. The fact is that House doesn't want Jamil or any other uppity Black or Latino North End residents who oppose the stadium on his show. Of course, House is just being a company man. WFSB promotes three images of North Hartford residents: 1) chalk outlines in the street 2) mugshots 3) shiftless spooks who don't vote. House's role as Hartford Stadium Plan Minister of Information was sickening to watch.

September 21

As the Hartford stadium plan championed by Mayor Pedro Segarra and City Council President Shawn Wooden cleared legal hurdles at City Hall, the question that loomed was whether the supermarket and health / nutrition complex that was originally planned for the site of the stadium would be a part of the equation. Wooden spoke enthusiastically about the "vision" for a full service supermarket during a city council meeting on the stadium plan, a big change from the past couple of months when the supermarket was not mentioned at all by Segarra or his communications director Maribel La Luz and glossed over by Wooden. Shop Rite emerged as a possible tenant: the supermarket chain requested an increase of the original 25,000 square feet allotted for a grocery store. Up to 50,000 square feet was now the plan. A source told me that Shop

Rite was open to the idea of housing a "healthy hub" in the Downtown North location. However the issue of access remains. How would North Hartford residents get to the supermarket on days that the stadium is in use? Traffic congestion and lack of parking would be a major issue. This problem had to be resolved if the supermarket plan was to be considered viable in terms of serving the North End, the current site of a food desert.

October 2

Moody's Investor's Service downgraded the city's bond rating. City council member David MacDonald urged his colleagues to reject the proposed stadium complex because of the rating, while Mayor Pedro Segarra argued that the rating justified moving ahead with the plan. City council president Shawn Wooden was noncommittal, as he spoke in vague terms about the city needing economic development. A source told me that the bond rating would not impact the progress of the stadium deal. "You can argue it both ways. Some say this shows we need to grow the grand list, some say that the city is broke. It's a chicken or the egg thing."

October 4

Gov. Dannel Malloy, who trails Republican challenger Tom Foley by six points according to a Quinnipiac University poll, joined with his Democratic Party colleagues in slamming Foley's urban policy paper. Malloy was throwing stones from a glass house, as his urban agenda consists of just a few paragraphs. Contrast that with the United for a Fair Economy plan for low-income communities of color that I refer to in this book: the report is 32 pages long. The complex plight of Black/Brown communities is obviously a mere afterthought for the incumbent. Malloy's plan does not come close to adequately addressing

212

poverty or Black / Latino unemployment, doesn't mention racial wage/wealth disparity, racial inequities in the state criminal justice system or police containment of low-income communities of color. Malloy's ConnectiCorps proposal is modeled after a federal program (AmeriCorps) that has done NOTHING to reduce Black / Latino unemployment in this country, currently at Depression-era levels.

The plagiarism issue regarding Foley's plan is well documented. The reality is that neither the Malloy nor the Foley urban policy plans effectively addressed the plight of Black/Latino neighborhoods. Malloy ignored core urban issues during his first term: he did not mention the word poverty once during any of his State of the State addresses. This neglect is evident in the data that was recently released by the U.S. Census. Child poverty, the poverty rate among families, the amount of people whose income is below the federal poverty level and the number of residents without health insurance in Connecticut have all increased since 2003.

The bickering between Malloy and Foley over urban policy was all about their battle for the Black/Latino vote, which was a huge factor in Malloy's razor thin margin of victory over Foley in the 2010 election. The plight of low-income communities of color has been a nonissue at the State Capitol for years.

While Foley's urban policy plan was much more detailed than Malloy's, it was basically a business deregulation and privatization scheme disguised as an urban agenda. Privatization of education targets public school teachers, and perpetuates segregation. Foley's CNN op-ed on his urban agenda avoids specifics, while hinting at criminal justice policies that would contribute to continued disproportionate incarceration of Blacks and Latinos.

Foley's urban job initiative included a provision where his administration would request that every large employer in Connecticut "fairly distribute their jobs among varied communities." This was not a realistic plan at all. I could go to work tomorrow and request that my employer reduce my work schedule to Tuesdays and Thursdays and triple my salary. That doesn't mean they're going to do it.

Racial Wage/Wealth Disparity

Rocky Anderson, the Justice Party's 2012 candidate for president, included in his platform a job creation initiative modeled after Franklin D. Roosevelt's New Deal Work Progress Administration program. Anderson described his plan during the *Democracy Now!* "Expanding the Debate" special; which aired in conjunction with the October 3, 2012 presidential debate between President Barack Obama and Republican challenger Mitt Romney.

"During the last 43 months we have had more than 8% unemployment. It is the only time in this nation's history that we have had a president that has presided even over three years of over 8% unemployment. There are things that have been proven in our history to work. We could have put in place, and it needs to be put in immediately, a WPA Works Progress Administration kind of program where we are investing in the future by building up our nation's rapidly deteriorating infrastructure, putting people to work. In the WPA project they put 8.5 million people to work. We could be putting 20 million to 25 million people to work and making that kind of investment in our nation's future."

The UFE *State of the Dream* report found that funding from Obama's 2009 job stimulus initiative did not reach urban areas and focused on industries that mostly employed white people.

"Most of the job-creation projects in the American Recovery and Reinvestment Act (ARRA) and other federal initiatives are investments in infrastructure and transportation, 'green' building retrofits, and pass-through funds that help states maintain schools and other important programs. All are worthy, but there is no evidence that the jobs these initiatives create are going to the communities most in need. In some cases, the opposite is true.

• The Associated Press found that, across the U.S., stimulus money for transportation was directed away from where the economic conditions are most dire. More money went to areas with higher rates of employment.

• The New York University report *Race, Gender and The Recession* reported that federal recovery money is creating more jobs in construction and retail than any other industries. These are industries that traditionally have not been major job sources for African American communities.

If the rain falls on relatively well-watered areas of economic opportunity, it does little to revive the driest economic landscapes in our country. Targeted approaches are much more likely to be effective. Prioritizing our nation's highest-unemployment communities is precisely the way to end the downward economic spiral in those places and start a real, broad-based recovery for the entire nation.

Congress must identify communities with the highest unemployment rates and target job- creation initiatives toward those communities, whether by census tract, zip code, or other method. This policy direction will lift up working-class white communities while narrowing the racial income gap. Congress should also ensure that as many of those jobs as possible pay a living wage. This report shows that broad-spectrum, universal solutions to the economic crisis will neither solve the pervasive racial wealth divide nor end gaping racial differences in income. We need job-creation and foreclosure-prevention programs that are targeted to communities most in need, including those with the highest unemployment and foreclosure rates. Such focused strategies will not only help close the racial wealth divide, but will lift up working-class families of all races."

A federally funded state WPA style program monitored through equity assessments would ensure that program dollars would reach low-income communities of color. UFE explained how equity assessments would function.

"To ensure that stimulus funds reach working class and disenfranchised communities, equity assessments should be required for all federal spending. A proper equity assessment will track where funds go, what jobs are created and in what communities. Demographic data on race, ethnicity, gender, class, and geography will be required for an equity assessment. This information will help future government programs reach the disenfranchised and the working class, the communities who must be at the center of an economic recovery."

Blacks and Latinos currently earn about 60 cents for every dollar whites make, and possess about 10 cents of net wealth for every dollar whites have. Houses are the primary wealth asset for Blacks and Latinos. The toxic mortgage scam that contributed to the 2008 economic collapse disproportionately targeted people of color, who subsequently have lost their homes at a higher rate than whites. UFE recommends a plan to build wealth in low-income communities of color.

Foreclosures—Draining the Wealth Reservoir:

Foreclosures continue to rise alarmingly. There were an estimated 3.4 million foreclosures in 2009 'Due to the rise in homeowner walk-a-ways, lack of forced bank modifications, growing unemployment figures... Housing Predictor forecasts foreclosures will now top 17-million homes through 2014.'

In addition to rampant unemployment, communities of color experience higher foreclosure rates due to racially targeted predatory lending, in which virtually every sector of the mortgage industry participated. A 2006 study that controlled for income and credit worthiness found that non-whites were significantly more likely than whites to receive high cost loans.

Revisiting the State of the Dream 2008: Foreclosed

The wealth-stripping effects of the recession and foreclosure crisis were documented in UFE's 2008 *State of the Dream: Foreclosed,* which showed that predatory lending practices were stripping wealth from communities of color.

216

• People of color were more than three times more likely to have subprime loans than whites.

• Commonly, lenders gave people of color loans with less advantageous payment rates, even when they qualified for better ones.

• Lenders failed to provide those applying for a home loan with information on the strenuous repayment schedule.

• Lenders inserted stiff fines for people to pay to get out of a subprime loan if they discovered it was too expensive. Since homes are the main form of wealth for working-class families and especially for communities of color, these practices drained their wealth reservoirs to dangerously low levels.

Source: RealtyTrac reports, with NCRC projecting foreclosures for December 2009 (see Endnotes in report for full citation).

In the three years, 2007, 2008, and 2009, there were respectively 1.3 million, 2.3 million, and 3.4 million foreclosures, totaling over 7 million foreclosures.

Over half of the mortgages to African-Americans in recent years were high-cost subprime loans. This predatory lending formed the epicenter of the first stage of the foreclosure crisis. Significantly, more than 60 percent of those subprime loans went to borrowers whose credit ratings qualified them for lower-cost prime loans, according to a 2008 *Wall Street Journal* study.

The disproportionate damage from foreclosures compounds the economic challenges that communities of color face and makes their economic recovery more difficult. A recent study shows that workers laid off in an economic downturn can take up to 20 years to replace their lost earnings. Replacing the wealth stripped from communities by predatory lending and foreclosure could take even longer. And while some economic indicators are improving, unemployment and the foreclosure crisis continue to do long-lasting damage to the nation's economy.

Are we narrowing or widening the racial wealth divide? Arresting the foreclosure crisis is a critical first step toward restoring health to the national economy. The housing industry employs millions of workers and provides the property tax base of cities across the country. Housing is also a main pillar of the nation's credit markets; while that pillar remains shaky, credit cannot fully recover.

The irresponsible and predatory lending practices of our nation's financial institutions directly led to the current foreclosure crisis that is stripping wealth from communities of color at alarming rates. The Obama Administration and Congress missed opportunities in 2009 to stop foreclosures, stabilize the economy, and start rebuilding wealth in the communities that the predatory mortgage industry targeted. Our government has an important role in protecting communities from the destructive actions of any party, be it the breaking and entering of a common burglar or the deceptive actions of the mortgage industry. On this front, the government has failed.

While the Administration and Congress set up several programs to stem the tide of foreclosures, these efforts have been largely ineffective in getting the mortgage industry to renegotiate most mortgages.

Actions that could have been taken include:

• Declare an immediate moratorium on foreclosures. This would have stabilized housing markets, stopped the vicious spiral of wealth stripping in communities of color, and given the financial industry an incentive to renegotiate predatory loans.

• Give bankruptcy judges the power to lower mortgages for insolvent homeowners. This would have kept millions of families in their homes.

• Make mortgages more affordable by requiring cooperation from financial institutions with the affordability programs, including loan modifications, set up by the Administration.

• Strongly regulate financial markets and protect consumers. This would prevent future financial market failures that strip wealth and jobs from all communities and take down the nation's economy.

A key component of the Jackson Plan is the creation of worker owned cooperatives. MXGM described the objectives of the Jackson Plan in their policy paper.

"The Jackson Plan is an initiative to apply many of the best practices in the promotion of participatory democracy, solidarity economy, and sustainable development and combine them with progressive community organizing and electoral politics. The objectives of the Jackson Plan are to deepen democracy in Mississippi and to build a vibrant, people centered solidarity economy in Jackson and throughout the state of Mississippi that empowers Black and other oppressed peoples in the state.

The Jackson Plan has many local, national and international antecedents, but it is fundamentally the brainchild of the Jackson People's Assembly. The Jackson People's Assembly is the product of the Mississippi Disaster Relief Coalition (MSDRC) that was spearheaded by MXGM in 2005 in the wake of Hurricane Katrina's devastation of Gulf Coast communities in Mississippi, Louisiana, Alabama and Texas. Between 2006 and 2008, this coalition expanded and transformed itself into the Jackson People's Assembly. In 2009, MXGM and the People's Assembly were able to elect human rights lawyer and MXGM co-founder Chokwe Lumumba to the Jackson City Council representing Ward 2."

My colleague Mary Sanders wrote the following policy recommendations for addressing poverty and the need for reform of the federal Temporary Assistance for Needy Families (TANF) program.

POVERTY AND THE NEED FOR TANF REFORM IN CONNECTICUT

The candidates running for office this year are all avoiding the "P" word! Poverty is a hot potato that causes candidates to cringe when questioned about their agenda to improve the lives of those most in need. For many single parents who are unemployed or underemployed, public assistance, also known as 'welfare', makes the difference in meeting their basic survival needs. It used to be that people could get help as long as they needed it, there were also programs available to prepare people to become self-sufficient. What we have now does not meet the needs of families and individuals living in poverty. The candidates for public office, all the way up to the governor's seat, do not seem to understand or care enough to change things.

When President Bill Clinton's administration announced the overhaul of the welfare system, what resulted was a federal maximum of 5 years of assistance throughout a person's life. The message was, grab any job and don't use up all your time in case you need it down the road!

Even in those states with the maximum of 5 years, this is problematic. Imagine CT where you are only allowed 21 months and if you qualify a couple six-month extensions. The goal is to get as many people off assistance as possible during the year and look good to the feds. I know that someone analyzing the data may say, "CT has lowered the number of AFDC cases—Aid to Families with Dependent Children (now TANF, Temporary Assistance for Needy Families) households by 10%." But because important information is not attached to those closed cases, they neglect to say—or may not even know—that 3% of the clients are gainfully employed and 7% got kicked off the program for a variety of reasons. After years of President Reagan's demonization of "welfare queens," CT's welfare reform created an illogical timeline of activity that Department of Social Services caseworkers and the subcontractors are expected to enforce. The program used to be Job Connection and is now Jobs First. In the old program, recipients were assessed for potential return to school and/or vocational training. They were asked what they were good at and what career they would like to pursue and, if reasonable, their DSS social worker, the employment counselor and the school would work as a team to make sure nothing interfered with their training and job placement. This was changed to recipients spending a year looking for work before education or training is considered. It used to be that individuals needed a high school diploma to get a decent job; now that is not enough.

The last 2 decades have seen the largest growth of income for the elite few and the worst decline and climbing poverty rates for too many. And it's not just that there are more poor people, it's that more people are experiencing a deeper kind of poverty. As "cash assistance" has ended for many, and people only have their food stamps, studies have shown that families exchange food benefits to buy their kids' shoes and other household necessities.

http://www.democracynow.org/2010/2/19/welfare_recipients_forced_to_sell_food

Unscrupulous storeowners are complicit in this deprivation of food for the kids. They pay pennies on the dollar for whatever is left on the Supplemental Nutrition

Assistance Program (SNAP) card. Parents do whatever they need to do when cash benefits end. This system is cruel and punitive; there is no way to get out of the vicious cycle of poverty. For adults with no dependent children it's even worse, as city welfare departments were all closed in favor of the new State Administered General Assistance program. SAGA is a misnomer as little assistance is actually given. Recipients used to receive about $300 cash monthly in addition to their food stamps & Medicaid. At least recipients could rent a room from someone. Now there is no cash assistance, resulting in extremely harsh circumstances for anyone who loses their job who has no unemployment benefits coming in. Lack of housing assistance is a huge problem and many new homeless are seeking some type of relief. The new 211-shelter line has at least 3 or 4 weeks of wait time for even an assessment and possible placement in shelters. This is not a good system for those seeking employment and stability. This is especially true for the able-bodied but long-term unemployed. That's another story for another day but housing vouchers are what's needed, so people can pay a portion of their income and have the stability they need to work towards self-sufficiency.

Back to TANF; in spite of all the spending that goes to meet the DSS goals, pending cases sit on piled-high desks waiting for review, clients have no way to pay rent, buy food, get medical care, get childcare assistance, etc. Applications are frequently lost, and it's almost impossible to reach workers by phone. Caseworkers are overloaded and cannot provide the services they would like to for their clients. Restrictions on what type of supports, training opportunities, and other services can be provided tie the hands of workers. On top of all the restrictions and the time limits, due to former Gov. Rowland's privatization of the Jobs First program, state workers are no longer doing the case management they used to. Now it's up to private nonprofits, who are charged with getting X number of participants off the rolls each year. Get out there and prove you went to see 25 potential employers, filled out applications and got the names of the people you saw. Recipients must attend the workshops on how to fill out applications, how to interview, how to dress, etc., whether you've never worked or have an extensive work history and just need a decent job. The benefit of 1 or 2 years of schooling would raise recipients' potential earnings. If people could get the proper supports and enter training paid by the Department of Labor or DSS, they might have a decent chance to become self-sufficient but those opportunities are few and far between. It's no wonder so many low-income people are lured into student debt trying to attend 'private educational institutions' that offer high cost trainings to anyone that will sign the loan notes. Unfortunately, many people are falsely led to believe their training will be subsidized then all of a sudden, they are signing off on loan applications. Many of them are unprepared and not able to complete successfully; they still owe thousands of dollars. Someone needs to do something about these for-profit schools and those that have changed their status to non-profit are no better. Lives are ruined and children are even more deprived when these predators take

221

advantage of low-income folks seeking training opportunities that they'll be repaying for the next decade or so.

For those TANF clients who have found employment; how about not terminating people's benefits as soon as they become employed and letting them put a little something away for a rainy day? Clients are afraid to accept any job that will cause them to lose their benefits because these days jobs are temporary, do not provide benefits, and most do not pay livable wages. Don't say, "Well they can get back on assistance if they need to." It's not that easy! If an individual sends their application in by mail, it's frequently misplaced and needs to be done again. Forget about getting through to DSS workers by phone; clients can be on hold 30 minutes to 2 hours and may get to speak to the right person. Most low-income people have free government phones with very limited monthly minutes. Those could be used up in a couple calls to DSS. I know the department is overwhelmed by all the new cases being opened, but there has to be a way to process people's redetermination forms so that they do not constantly have their benefits cut off. Many of them end up at our food pantry asking for groceries and the toilet paper we purchase for distribution. It's a damn shame that in our wealthy state, we cannot properly administer mandated entitlement programs that provide for the basic needs of our residents. Apparently, the computer system in place is programmed to automatically terminate people's benefits on certain dates, if a worker does not physically enter data to stop that from happening. That means that if the worker is behind, and has 100 redetermination forms piled up on a desk, whose due dates have past, all those cases will automatically be closed. People who were expecting to receive their cash or food benefits are then in a crisis situation, and when told they did not send in their redetermination forms, will just send them over again, creating an even bigger pile. More people comply than do not; therefore, it would make sense to de- program that automatic cutoff feature and have workers physically enter data to close any cases that warrant termination, either for noncompliance or eligibility reasons.

CT was already cited by the feds for their inability to get SNAP applications processed quickly enough and for disqualifying too many who actually qualified. People should not be going hungry, especially the kids. Their parents should have decent employment but if they do need assistance, their food stamps also shouldn't run out mid-month. In another case, the young mother with a 4-year-old shouldn't have been cut off her cash benefits after 21 months when she hadn't finished preparing for her HS exam. Now she sleeps on the couch at her mom's house with her son on a cot near her. Someone should give her a housing voucher, daycare, a good educational/vocational program and help her, not punish her for missing an appointment and denying her extension. I opted our agency out of participating in the Jobs First model; I didn't want to be part of that, because I knew that most people

222

needed more time. We run a food pantry and have a social worker, but we also have English and GED classes and help people go to college. I don't want to send people out to look for work if they have education and training needs. Some of the regulations have eased up a little, allowing people minimal training & education opportunities, but the majority of recipients of public assistance are still denied real vocational training or college, which would truly help towards self-sufficiency.

Tell our public officials that money needs to be allocated for the hiring of additional caseworkers to handle the backlog; we need timely processing of applications for assistance. We also need to be able to speak with caseworkers directly and not be relegated to a phone system that routes calls to full voice mailboxes. Tell them that more time needs to be allowed on public assistance while folks are going through adult education and vocational training or higher education so they can reach self-sufficiency (New York City recently implemented reforms, see our Resources section below). SNAP benefits also need to be increased, as food prices continue to climb and more housing vouchers need to be issued for all municipalities, not just urban areas. Those becoming homeless or jobless are flocking to the cities in search of services that are already stretched thin. Additionally, a committee of diverse stakeholders should meet regularly to assess the progress the department is making towards the goal of true client self-sufficiency. The department should not take credit for reducing welfare rolls when half of those exited simply were deemed non-compliant and were therefore removed. There are hungry children out there whom the department has forgotten about.

At the federal level, we already know that poor people are not a priority, and military and corrections systems are more fully funded than education, health and social services. Government officials believe it is more important to avoid taxing the rich and corporations, than to make sure kids have their needs met. It is time we rethink our priorities and come up with ways to protect our most vulnerable. There have been a few active grassroots community groups and non-profits trying to improve the lives of families living in poverty, a couple of them in Hartford have been around for years, organizing and meeting with legislators.

The Community Party is also part of the discussion and we have some ideas on how to come up with the money needed. Plans to address hunger, affordable housing, healthcare, and education for low-income CT residents are the topics I want to see on the candidates' platforms. Why aren't they discussing these critical issues? Why are they afraid of the "P" word?

October 7

Foley spoke to the Metro Hartford Alliance, a local business group. He said that healthcare providers should adopt the model of "great businesses" like Walmart. Damn. Foley also talked about his plan to cut spending by having social service providers outsource to private entities. Unfortunately, this is why the Democrats take their voter base for granted, because the Republicans say shit like this that rightfully scares the hell out of people. The reality is that the Democrats and Republicans are two wings of the same corporate controlled party. Both are awash in cash, money received from corporations, wealthy individuals, outside spending groups and PACS. 2014 passed 2012 as the top outside spending cycle for congressional elections. 2014 passed half a billion in non-party outside spending.

October 21

Mayor Pedro Segarra's absence from city council meetings on the Downtown North stadium plan (approved with six votes and three abstentions) is proof that this has always been a "done deal," as Segarra described it. The question remains as to how North Hartford residents will gain access to the Downtown North supermarket on days that the stadium is in use.

October 22

Quinnipiac poll: Malloy 43% Foley 42 % Visconti 9%

With Election Day less than two weeks away, Foley stumbled badly. Foley's performance at a housing policy forum was a joke. Advocates were stunned at Foley's total lack of knowledge on policy issues such as public and supportive housing.

224

October 23

The series of debates between Malloy and Foley were carbon copies. Malloy repeatedly brought up Foley's tenure as owner of the Bibb Company, his arrests for road rage, lying to the FBI about the arrests when he was vetted for the ambassador to Ireland position, and his income tax dodging (Foley had not paid taxes for three straight years). Foley hammered away at Malloy's unprecedented tax increases, portrayed Malloy as being 'anti-business' and his administration as engaging in out of control spending. The NBC CT debate was different:

Foley didn't show. There had been murky reports for weeks about Foley and NBC CT being unable to come to an agreement on parameters for the debate, with much of the speculation centering on Visconti's inclusion in the event. Visconti pressed Malloy on the gun control bill that the general assembly passed in 2013, the projected $1.3 billion budget deficit and a subsequent need for tax increases. Malloy said there would be no deficit and no tax increases.

October 29

Latest Quinnipiac poll: Gov. Dan Malloy & GOP challenger Tom Foley tied @ 43%. Joe Visconti trailed with 7%.

November 3

Visconti, who days earlier had vowed to stay in the race for governor to the end, suddenly announced that he was suspending his campaign and endorsing Foley.

The move turned out to be mostly symbolic, as Secretary of State Denise Merrill said that Visconti's name would remain on the ballot and people could still vote for him.

Visconti had drawn votes equally from Malloy and Foley, so he really had no impact on the race. The final Quinnipiac poll had Malloy ahead, 47% to 44%. Doug Schwartz, director of the Quinnipiac poll, said that the race was too close to call. A study by the Wesleyan Media Project found that the Connecticut gubernatorial election was the most negative in the country. The attack ads reflected the absurdity of the current electoral process. Malloy and Foley were being compared as products, like cable and satellite television. The corporate power brokers behind each candidate were fighting to get consumers (voters) to buy their brand. There was really no difference between the two candidates. Neither Malloy nor Foley talked about closing corporate tax loopholes or implementing a progressive tax code as a means of generating much needed revenue for the state. Both were privatizers, endorsing the lucrative charter school industry. These candidates had much more in common than they had differences.

November 4/Election Day

The much anticipated rematch between Malloy and Foley was quickly thrown into chaos, due to issues at polling locations in Hartford. Several locations did not have the required list of registered voters when polls opened at 6:00 am. Some locations did not receive the list until almost 2 hours after opening. Lawyers for Malloy filed a motion in Hartford Superior Court, requesting that voting hours in the city be extended one hour due to the debacle. Foley's legal team of course objected. President Obama called into WNPR to urge voters to go to the polls, despite any anger they may be feeling over the situation.

As state political observers experienced flashbacks to 2010 when issues arose at polling locations in Bridgeport, Judge Carl Schuman ruled that two Hartford polls would be allowed to stay open an extra 30 minutes. The Connecticut GOP stated that they were satisfied with the decision.

Now all there was left to do was wait for the results. The outcome was anticlimactic. Media reports throughout the evening had Malloy ahead. At 12:30 am, Malloy appeared onstage at the Society Room in Hartford and declared victory. Malloy campaign spokesperson Mark Bergman told reporters that Malloy led Foley by 12,000 votes; Democratic Party strongholds Hartford and New Haven were the only precincts yet to report. Foley appeared in front of his supporters at the Hyatt Regency in Greenwich and said that it appeared he had lost, but he would not officially admit to defeat. Wednesday afternoon Malloy called a press conference to announce that Foley had called him at 12:30 pm to concede.

Malloy's victory over Tom Foley was not the cliffhanger pundits anticipated, which really is more an indicator of voters rejecting Tom Foley's opaque campaign than it is a vote of confidence for Malloy. Foley's strategy was to say as little as possible, hope that voters didn't notice, and count on the state's poor economy and Malloy's personality issues to sweep him into office. Foley never explained how he was going to wipe out a projected budget deficit of over $1 billion, while delivering on his promise to cut taxes. The math simply didn't add up. Malloy's bullying of state employees and public school teachers without a doubt resulted in the poll numbers which made the 2014 gubernatorial election too close to call. Apparently, voters were pissed off at Malloy, but not enough to take the plunge and elect a billionaire who was going to do God knows what if he won. The reality is that both Malloy and Foley are corporatists who have more in common than they have differences.

When Foley made the ridiculous assertion that the insurance company friendly Affordable Care Act was a step toward a single payer system, Malloy's lieutenant governor Nancy Wyman actually boasted about how the ACA catered to the health insurance industry. Not a good look when a new study found that the United States ranks last among other industrialized nations in affordability and access to health care. Neither Foley nor Malloy talked about implementing a progressive tax code or closing corporate tax loopholes as a means of generating much needed revenue for the state. Instead, we heard about the likelihood of tolls returning to Connecticut, which would be yet another tax on the working class and the poor. The urban policy plans of Malloy and Foley were both laughable, as neither addressed poverty, Black/Latino unemployment, racial wage/wealth disparity, mass incarceration or police containment of low-income communities of color.

While Malloy took his victory lap, state residents faced 'four more years' of the corporatist policies which keep this country's economy in the toilet. The only hope for change is that the left grows a spine and pushes Malloy and the Democrats to implement egalitarian policies that will address the growing class and racial disparities in Connecticut. Don't hold your breath waiting for that to happen.

Meanwhile on the national level, voters continued their futile strategy of switching their support back and forth between the Democrats and Republicans, hoping for positive change in Congress. Putting the Republicans in charge of the Senate is the equivalent of rearranging the deck chairs on the Titanic. While liberals and conservatives scream at each other, the Dems and the GOP are counting their money. The Center for Responsive Politics projects that $3.67 billion (that's BILLION, with a B) was spent on the 2014 election cycle. The two parties are swimming in corporate cash.

Do you really think that corporations are donating all of this money so elected officials will look out for you?

We need a third party movement that will represent the interests of the working class and the poor.

Links:

ABC News: Obama to Bypass Congress on Immigration Reform

http://abcnews.go.com/Politics/video/obama-bypass-congress-immigration-reform-24371699

Alternet: Massachusetts House Votes to Curb Union Rights

http://www.alternet.org/newsandviews/article/572861/massachusetts_house_votes_to_curb_union_rights/

BBC: Iraq crisis: Key oil refinery 'seized by rebels'

http://www.bbc.com/news/world-middle-east-27990478

BBC: Iraq army 'routs Isis rebels' in offensive on Tikrit

http://www.bbc.com/news/world-middle-east-28069800

Black Agenda Report: Freedom Rider: Detroit and Iraq

http://blackagendareport.com/content/freedom-rider-detroit-and-iraq

The Buie Knife: 50 Examples of White Privilege in Daily Life

http://jimbuie.blogs.com/journal/2007/11/50-examples-of-.html

California Budget & Policy Center: For Local Labor Markets, the Public Sector Is Still a Drag

http://californiabudgetbites.org/2014/06/23/for-local-labor-markets-the-public-sector-is-still-a-drag/

Care 2 Petition: Undocumented Immigrants Pay More In Taxes Than Wealthy

http://www.care2.com/causes/undocumented-immigrants-pay-more-in-taxes-than-wealthy.html

CBS Chicago: Rev. Jackson: Obama, Feds Need To Do More To Combat Chicago Violence

http://chicago.cbslocal.com/2014/07/09/rev-jackson-obama-feds-need-to-do-more-to-combat-chicago-violence/

Center on Budget & Policy Priorities: Lessons for Other States from Kansas' Massive Tax Cuts

http://www.cbpp.org/cms/index.cfm?fa=view&id=4110

Center on Budget & Policy Priorities: TANF Weakening as a Safety Net For Poor Families

http://www.cbpp.org/cms/index.cfm?fa=view&id=3700

CBPP: Studies show that Tom Foley/GOP propaganda about rich people leaving the state idf their taxes go up is a myth.

http://www.cbpp.org/cms/index.cfm?fa=view&id=3556

Citizens United:

http://www.amazon.com/Citizens-United-Karl-Rogers-ebook/dp/B00B3DNLOU

CNN: Seattle mayor: $15 minimum wage for city workers

http://money.CNN.com/2014/01/05/news/seattle-minimum-wage/index.html

CNN: How to fix our cities

http://www.CNN.com/2014/07/10/opinion/foley-zimmer-fix-cities/index.html

CNN: Michael Brown Shooting Aftermath

http://ac360.blogs.CNN.com/2014/09/11/new-information-on-aftermath-video-of-the-michael-brown-shooting/

ColorLines Race & Economic Recovery

https://www.youtube.com/watch?v=LaM6iI-eCdk

Connecticut gubernatorial election, 2010:

http://en.wikipedia.org/wiki/Connecticut_gubernatorial_election,_201
0

CT Mirror: Pelto commits to third-party run, promises 'profound impact'

http://ctmirror.org/pelto-commits-to-3rd-party-run-promises-profound-impact/

CT Mirror: CT AFL-CIO mocks Foley: 'Did I say something funny?'

http://ctmirror.org/afl-cio-mocks-foley-did-i-say-something-funny/?hvid=1gpQ1Z

CT Mirror: Tom Foley: A very, very careful GOP frontrunner

http://ctmirror.org/tom-foley-a-very-very-careful-gop-frontrunner/?hvid=4RMjkm

CT Mirror: AFT looks past tenure flap, endorses Malloy

http://ctmirror.org/aft-looks-past-tenure-flap-endorses-malloy/

CT Mirror: Reporting live from Church Street ... Tom Foley?

http://ctmirror.org/reporting-live-from-church-street-tom-foley/

CT Mirror: Boughton quits race, calls for GOP to unite behind Foley

http://ctmirror.org/boughton-ends-campaign-calls-for-gop-united/

CT Mirror: SEEC grants Malloy campaign funds, rejects complaint

http://ctmirror.org/seec-grants-malloy-campaign-funds-rejects-complaint/

CT Mirror: Malloy and Pelto finally at same microphone, if hours apart

http://ctmirror.org/malloy-and-pelto-finally-at-same-microphone-if-hours-apart/

CT Mirror: Not quite the nominee, Tom Foley puts stamp on GOP

http://ctmirror.org/not-quite-the-nominee-tom-foley-puts-stamp-on-gop/

CT Mirror: Foley, McKinney find plenty of common ground at first GOP forum

http://ctmirror.org/foley-mckinney-find-plenty-of-common-ground-at-first-gop-forum/

CT Mirror: Campaign enters new phase as Foley buys TV time

http://ctmirror.org/campaign-enters-new-phase-as-foley-buys-tv-time/

CT Mirror: McKinney: Initial SEEC review questions just $4,600

http://ctmirror.org/mckinney-initial-seec-review-questions-just-4600/

CT Mirror: Tom Foley a 'regular guy' and 'great dad' in first TV ad

http://ctmirror.org/foley-a-regular-guy-and-great-dad-in-first-tv-ad/

CT Mirror: Common Core? Try common ground for Pelto, Visconti

http://ctmirror.org/common-core-try-common-ground-for-left-right/

CT Mirror: Money assured, McKinney-Walker tape first TV ad

http://ctmirror.org/mckinney-walker-to-begin-tv-ads/

CT Mirror: Deficit 2015: McKinney's solution lies with 'ignored' ideas

http://ctmirror.org/mckinneys-solution-to-connecticuts-budget-woes-lies-with-ignored-ideas/

CT Mirror: Latino advocates knock Malloy on Central American immigrant children decision

http://ctmirror.org/latino-advocates-knock-malloy-on-central-american-immigrant-children-decision/

CT Mirror: Foley ad takes liberties with McKinney record

http://ctmirror.org/foley-ad-takes-liberties-with-mckinney-record/

CT Mirror: WNPR says McKinney edited its audio for attack on Foley

http://ctmirror.org/WNPR-says-mckinney-edited-its-audio-for-attack-on-foley/

CT Mirror: RGA's Christie endorses Foley, promises: 'We'll be here a lot.'

http://ctmirror.org/christie-endorses-foley-promises-well-be-here-a-lot/

CT Mirror: CT minority caucus chairman urges Malloy to reconsider housing migrant children

http://ctmirror.org/minority-caucus-chairman-urges-malloy-to-reconsider-housing-migrant-children-in-ct/

CT Mirror: Final CT surplus report renews partisan budget debate

http://ctmirror.org/final-ct-surplus-report-renews-partisan-budget-debate/

CT Mirror: Ad wars escalate as McKinney accuses Foley of lying

http://ctmirror.org/ad-wars-escalate-as-mckinney-accuses-foley-of-lying/

CT Mirror: Internet poll shows Foley up 9 points over Malloy

http://ctmirror.org/internet-poll-shows-foley-up-9-points-over-malloy/

CT Mirror: Foley has lots of confidence, few details, on plans to fix CT budget

http://ctmirror.org/foley-has-lots-of-confidence-few-details-on-plans-to-fix-ct-budget/

CT Mirror: A Tom Foley press conference goes awry in Sprague

http://ctmirror.org/a-tom-foley-press-conference-goes-awry-in-sprague/

CT Mirror: McKinney-Walker promise income tax cut in new commercials

http://ctmirror.org/mckinney-walker-promise-income-tax-cut-in-new-commercials/

CT Mirror: Pelto concedes his petition effort will fall short

http://ctmirror.org/pelto-concedes-his-petition-effort-will-fall-short/

CT Mirror: As Pelto fades, Visconti ramps up with pitch to gun owners http://ctmirror.org/as-pelto-fades-visconti-ramps-up-with-pitch-to-gun-owners/

CT Mirror: After all the campaign promises, a lot of tough choices loom

http://ctmirror.org/after-all-the-campaign-promises-a-lot-of-tough-choices-loom/

CT Mirror: Judge orders two Hartford polls to stay open an extra half hour

http://ctmirror.org/democrats-likely-to-ask-judge-to-extend-hartford-voting-hours/

CT Mirror: Foley struggles on a deep dive into housing policy

http://ctmirror.org/foley-struggles-on-a-deep-dive-into-housing-policy/

CT Mirror: General election coverage

http://ctmirror.org/live-blog-keep-up-with-todays-election/#blogItem51

CT Mirror: GOP gains, but Democrats control CT General Assembly

http://ctmirror.org/democrats-hold-control-of-state-legislature/

CT Mirror: Connecticut 4th Congressional District issues comparison: Himes vs. Obsitnik

http://ctmirror.org/outside-spending-on-governors-race-topped-18-million/connecticut

CT Mirror: Connecticut takes a deep look at racial profiling in traffic stops

http://ctmirror.org/connecticut-takes-a-deep-look-at-racial-profiling-in-traffic-stops/

CT News: Malloy gets "Pelto-ed" from the left?

http://blog.ctnews.com/politics/2014/04/18/malloy-gets-pelto-ed-from-the-left/

CT News 12:

http://connecticut.news12.com/

CT Post: Malloy sends out layoff notices to more than 4,500 state employees

http://www.ctpost.com/news/article/Malloy-sends-out-layoff-notices-to-more-than-1373286.php

CTRP3:

http://www.ctrp3.org/

CT Voices: Reality Check: Who Pays Taxes in Connecticut?

http://www.ctvoices.org/publications/reality-check-who-pays-taxes-connecticut

The Crime Report: 3 Strikes Reform in CA: "Victory for Common Sense"

http://www.thecrimereport.org/news/cjn/2012-12-three-strikes-reform-in-california-a-victory-for-hum

Daily Beast: Send the National Guard to Chicago

http://www.thedailybeast.com/articles/2014/07/09/send-the-national-guard-to-chiraq.html

The Day: Legislature gives Malloy more budget-cutting authority; 1,000 more state workers could face layoffs

http://www.theday.com/article/20110701/NWS12/307019845/0/Search

Democracy Now!: "Baghdad is a Frightened City": As ISIS Gains Ground, Iraqi Capital Gripped by Fear & Uncertainty

http://www.democracynow.org/2014/6/23/baghdad_is_a_frightened_city_as

Democracy Now!: Water is a Human Right: Detroit Residents Seek U.N. Intervention as City Shuts Off Taps to Thousands

http://www.democracynow.org/2014/6/24/water_is_a_human_right_Detroit

Democracy Now!: Iraqis Denied Worker Rights Under U.S. Occupation

http://www.democracynow.org/2003/10/30/iraqis_denied_worker_rights_under_u

Democracy Now!: UNHCR Asks U.S. to Consider Refugee Status for Central American Migrants

http://www.democracynow.org/2014/7/9/headlines#797

Democracy Now! HEADLINES JULY 08, 2014

http://www.democracynow.org/2014/7/8/headlines

Democracy Now!: HEADLINES JULY 22, 2014

http://www.democracynow.org/2014/7/22/headlines/detroit_temporarily_halts_water_shutoffs_after_protests#.U8

7ZF2h_Jf8.twitter

Democracy Now!: Welfare Recipients Forced to Sell Food Stamps to Buy Basic Necessities

http://www.democracynow.org/2010/2/19/welfare_recipients_forced_to_sell_food

Democracy Now! New York Police Killing of Eric Garner Spurs Debate on Chokeholds & Filming Officer Misconduct

http://www.democracynow.org/2014/8/5/new_york_police_killing_of_eric

Democracy Now! How to Buy a City: Chevron Spends $3 Million on Local California Election to Oust Refinery Critics

http://www.democracynow.org/2014/10/31/how_to_buy_a_city_chevron

Democracy Now! Sen. Bernie Sanders: The United States is on the Verge of Becoming an Oligarchy

http://www.democracynow.org/2014/11/5/sen_bernie_sanders_the_united_states

Democracy Now! The Citizens United Senator: After GOP's Midterm Rout, Mitch McConnell Likely Next Majority Leader

http://www.democracynow.org/2014/11/5/the_citizens_united_senator_after_gops

Democracy Now!

http://www.democracynow.org/2014/8/27/is_ferguson_feeding_on_
the_poor

Democracy Now!

http://www.democracynow.org/2010/2/11/charter_study

Democracy Now!

http://www.democracynow.org/2012/10/4/expanding_the_debate_e
xclusive_third_party

Department of Justice: Findings Letter

http://www.justice.gov/crt/about/spl/easthavenpd.php

EPI: 'Small business' and top marginal rates

http://www.epi.org/publication/ib349-small-business-top-marginal-
rates-filers/

ecsu-aaup: Revised SEBAC Agreement July 2011

http://www.ecsuaaup.org/?page_id=574 SEBAC agreement

Fight For 15

https://twitter.com/fightfor15

Food Empowerment Project: Food Deserts

http://www.foodispower.org/food-deserts/

Hartford Courant: Hartford Withdraws $60 Million Bond Plan For New Stadium; Wants Private Funding

http://www.courant.com/news/connecticut/hc-hartford-stadium-funding-0712-20140711,0,6704064.story

Hartford Courant: State Board Finalizing Report On Racial Profiling By Police

http://www.courant.com/news/connecticut/hc-racial-profiling-connecticut-0815-20140814,0,618383.story

Hartford Courant: Homeless shelter

http://www.courant.com/news/connecticut/hc-hartford-homeless-shelter-0830-20140829,0,2172893.story

Hartford Courant: Hartford's Bond Rating Downgraded

http://www.courant.com/news/connecticut/hc-hartford-bond-rating-1003-20141002-story.html

Hartford Courant: Wesleyan Media Project study which found the Malloy vs. Foley race had the most negative ads of any election in the nation:

http://www.courant.com/politics/capitol-watch/hc-study-finds-ct-gov-race-has-most-negative-ads-20141014-story.html

Hip Hop Wired: Hillary Clinton Pretends Not To Hear Journalist's Question About Mike Brown

http://hiphopwired.com/2014/08/25/hillary-clinton-mike-brown-question-video/

Information Clearing House: It's the Corporate State, Stupid

http://www.informationclearinghouse.info/article7260.htm

Journal Inquirer: McKinney would seek talks on state benefits

http://www.journalinquirer.com/page_one/mckinney-would-seek-talks-on-state-benefits/article_920f566a-078d-

11e4-ad09-0019bb2963f4.html

Malcolm X Grassroots Movement Jackson Plan:

http://mxgm.org/the-jackson-plan-a-struggle-for-self-determination-participatory-democracy-and-economic-justice/

McClatchy: Iraq Watch: Maliki denounces calls for unity government as 'coup,' Syria reportedly bombs ISIS targets in Iraq

http://www.mcclatchydc.com/2014/06/25/231472/iraq-watch-maliki-denounces-calls.html

McCutcheon v. FEC

http://en.wikipedia.org/wiki/McCutcheon_v._FEC

http://www.fec.gov/law/litigation/McCutcheon.shtml

Medicine Net: U.S. Ranks Last Among Wealthy Nations in Access to Health Care

http://www.medicinenet.com/script/main/art.asp?articlekey=184795

Mother Jones: Did Citigroup Get Off Easy With $7 Billion Penalty?

http://www.motherjones.com/politics/2014/07/7-billion-citigroup-settlement-department-justice

MSNBC segment on police body cameras

https://www.youtube.com/watch?v=P_CwpgUvDic&feature=youtu.be

The Nation: Access of Evil

http://www.thenation.com/article/access-evil

NBC CT: Malloy Says 7,500 Layoffs are Imminent

http://www.nbcconnecticut.com/news/politics/Unions-Reject-Labor-Deal-124490634.html

NBER: Quantifying the Lasting Harm to the U.S. Economy from the Financial Crisis

http://www.nber.org/papers/w20183

New Haven Independent: Immigration Rally to Spur Malloy

http://www.newhavenindependent.org/index.php/archives/entry/immigration_rally_seeks_to_spur_malloy_into_a

ction/#.U9AxUiNhWoQ.twitter

New Haven Independent: East Haven Police Target Latinos

http://www.newhavenindependent.org/index.php/archives/entry/report_tickets_show_east_haven_targets_latinos/

New Republic: The Post Office Should Just Become a Bank

http://www.newrepublic.com/article/116374/postal-service-banking-how-usps-can-save-itself-and-help-poor

NY Times: Connecticut Governor, Tackling Budget, Criticizes Christie's Approach
http://www.nytimes.com/2011/02/16/nyregion/16malloy.html?pagewanted=all

No Sellout: Democrats Are Failing Immigrants and Minorities

http://hendu39.wordpress.com/2014/08/06/democrats-are-failing-immigrants-and-minorities/

No Sellout: Election 2014: Urban Agenda Analysis/CT Polling Locations/Media Coverage

http://hendu39.wordpress.com/2014/11/02/election-2014-urban-agenda-analysisct-polling-locations/

No Sellout: Community Party Trayvon Martin Act Bill Language

http://hendu39.wordpress.com/2014/07/21/community-party-trayvon-martin-act-bill-language/

Open Secrets:

http://www.opensecrets.org/outsidespending/fes_summ.php

http://www.opensecrets.org/news/2014/10/straw-into-gold-candidates-trading-leadership-pac-dollars-for-

campaign-cash/

Operation Ghetto Storm report:

http://www.operationghettostorm.org/

OTG: US Military Equipping Local Police With War-Zone Armored Vehicles

http://www.offthegridnews.com/2013/12/03/us-military-equipping-local-police-with-war-zone-armored-vehicles/

Postal Reporter: NAPUS: Obama FY 2015 Budget includes several USPS related proposals

http://www.postal-reporter.com/blog/napus-obama-fy-2015-budget-includes-several-usps-related-proposals/

Real News: Will $10 Minimum Wage Get All Working Americans Out of Poverty?

http://therealnews.com/t2/index.php?option=com_content&task=view&id=31&Itemid=74&jumival=11510#.UwodJ

G6AfxE.twitter

RT: 40 shot, 4 dead from gun violence in Chicago over weekend

http://rt.com/usa/174424-chicago-violence-slumber-party/

September 2014 Connecticut Racial Profiling Report

http://s429795233.onlinehome.us/september-2014-report/

TANF reform implemented by New York City Mayor Bill de Blasio:

http://www.wnyc.org/story/welfare-overhaul-departure-bloomberg-and-giuliani/

Think Progress: Walmart Penalized For Closing Store Just After It Unionized

http://thinkprogress.org/economy/2014/06/30/3454511/walmart-canada-union/

Truth Out: Borderland Deaths of Migrants Quietly Reach Crisis Numbers

http://truth-out.org/news/item/25116-borderland-deaths-of-migrants-quietly-reach-crisis-numbers

Truth Out: To Address Honduran Refugee Crisis at the Border, US Should Stop Financing Repression in Honduras

http://truth-out.org/opinion/item/25178-to-address-honduran-refugee-crisis-at-the-border-us-should-stop-financing-repression-in-honduras

UFE: STATE OF THE DREAM 2010: DRAINED

http://www.faireconomy.org/news/state_of_the_dream_2010_draine
d

UFE: REPORT FACT SHEET

http://www.faireconomy.org/state_of_the_dream_2010_fact_sheet

United for a Fair Economy report on racial economic disparity:

http://www.faireconomy.org/state_of_the_dream_2010_fact_sheet

Video of Bridgeport police beating:
https://www.youtube.com/watch?v=0AO_7YGma-I

Voices for Children summary of U.S. Census data on poverty, median
income and health insurance in the state:

http://www.ctvoices.org/publications/poverty-median-income-and-
health-insurance-connecticutsummary-2013-american-community-s

The Wire: Juking the Stats:

https://www.youtube.com/watch?v=_ogxZxu6cjM

WNPR: Stadium Deal Not Approved Yet, But Hartford Goes Out to
Bid

http://WNPR.org/post/stadium-deal-not-approved-yet-hartford-goes-out-bid#.U6igsTj8C10.twitter

Worker Cooperative:

http://en.wikipedia.org/wiki/Worker_cooperative

YES!: How State Banks Bring the Money Home

http://www.yesmagazine.org/issues/new-livelihoods/how-state-banks-bring-the-money-home

www.ingramcontent.com/pod-product-compliance
Lightning Source LLC
Chambersburg PA
CBHW060011050426
42448CB00012B/2695